CW01390978

202204156

THE RAF'S CROSS-CHANNEL OFFENSIVE

THE RAF'S CROSS-CHANNEL OFFENSIVE

Circuses, Ramrods, Rhubarbs and Rodeos 1941–1942

John Starkey

AIR WORLD

AIR WORLD

THE RAF'S CROSS-CHANNEL OFFENSIVE
Circuses, Ramrods, Rhubarbs and Rodeos 1941–1942

First published in Great Britain in 2022 by
Air World
An imprint of
Pen & Sword Books Ltd
Yorkshire – Philadelphia

ISBN 978 1 39908 892 3

Typeset by SJmagic DESIGN SERVICES, India.

Printed and bound in the UK by CPI Group (UK) Ltd.

Pen & Sword Books Limited incorporates the imprints of Atlas, Archaeology, Aviation, Discovery, Family History, Fiction, History, Maritime, Military, Military Classics, Politics, Select, Transport, True Crime, Air World, Frontline Publishing, Leo Cooper, Remember When, Seaforth Publishing, The Praetorian Press, Wharncliffe Local History, Wharncliffe Transport, Wharncliffe True Crime and White Owl.

For a complete list of Pen & Sword titles please contact

PEN & SWORD BOOKS LIMITED
47 Church Street, Barnsley, South Yorkshire, S70 2AS, England
E-mail: enquiries@pen-and-sword.co.uk
Website: www.pen-and-sword.co.uk

Or
PEN AND SWORD BOOKS
1950 Lawrence Rd, Havertown, PA 19083, USA
E-mail: Uspen-and-sword@casematepublishers.com
Website: www.penandswordbooks.com

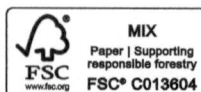

MIX
Paper | Supporting
responsible forestry
FSC
www.fsc.org   FSC® C013604

Contents

Acknowledgements

I could not have written this book without substantial factual help. I thank all the authors listed in the bibliography, who contributed their acquired knowledge to discovering what took place in RAF Fighter Command in the Second World War, as well as in the earlier struggle of the First World War.

I was fortunate to be born late on in the Second World War, and thus have always had an abiding interest in warfare and, in particular, air warfare. To gain extra knowledge of what the fighters of the period were like to fly and fight in, I also had the good fortune to have known Tony Bianchi, of Personal Plane Services, at Booker aerodrome in England. He and his company have restored many Spitfires, among other wartime aircraft. Tony was a fount of knowledge about these aircraft.

On the American side, Rob Collings was unstinting in his comments about the handling of such aircraft as the P-38 Lightning, the P-51 Mustang, the B-17 Flying Fortress, and the Bf 109. After all, he owns and flies examples of all of them.

Rob Collings recommended I speak with Joe Schell, who has an encyclopedic knowledge of Rolls-Royce, in particular of the Merlin and Griffon engines. He was good enough to impart a lot of his observations about the operation of these engines.

I have to thank also David Kenyon, who imparted some of his great knowledge about the history of the British codebreakers at Bletchley Park. Without ULTRA and 'Enigma' intercepts, the heads of RAF Fighter and Bomber Commands, to say nothing of all the

ACKNOWLEDGEMENTS

other services, would have been even more in the dark about the movements of the German forces in Occupied Europe.

I must also thank John Grehan, my commissioning editor, for his tireless patience, and Martin Mace for helping so much with the finding of the photographs for this book.

And finally, I must thank my editor (I've always wanted to type those words!), Karyn Burnham. Her encyclopedic knowledge of the subject matter, not to mention her expertise in written English, impressed me greatly.

Preface

This book tells the story of what happened to the Royal Air Force's (RAF) Fighter Command in 1941 and 1942, when they tried to take the war in the air to the Luftwaffe, over Northern France.

The history of events concerning Fighter Command in 1941 and 1942, and what led up to them, has, until very recently in this writer's opinion, been kept 'under the covers'. Some excellent historians of air warfare, such as Norman Franks, Donald Caldwell, Tony Holmes, and others, have written accounts of this period, but I fear that few writers have taken a detailed look at what led up to this defeat, which, in this writer's opinion, dates back to the decisions taken by commanding officers in the First World War.

Although this book is principally concerned with these events, particularly in relation to Fighter Command, I also consider what happened in the air war over Europe between 1943 and 1945, to explain how much the pilots, and to a lesser extent their commanders, had learned.

One other thing I have tried to do is to explain the workings of the aircraft that flew and fought in the wars. Although interested in flying, I'm not a pilot and I've always noticed, in the myriad of books written by wartime fighter pilots, that they (naturally) assume the reader knows just how an aircraft operates. I suppose that we all know about the actual flying controls, the joystick which one pulls back to climb, pushes forward to dive, and the rudder pedals which, in conjunction with moving the joystick sideways, enables the aircraft to turn and bank.

But there's more to it than that. For instance, the throttle, which was usually on the left-hand side of the cockpit. How much was applied when dogfighting the enemy. Full? Three-quarters? A half? Then there's the constant speed airscrews. They act as the gearbox/ transmission of a car does and that system also needs explanation.

Then there's tactics. Basically, climb as high as you can as fast as you can, shadow the enemy below, hopefully without him seeing you, dive on him, fire, try and follow him until he's mortally wounded but don't follow him down, or you may finish up surprised from behind, as he was by you. Dogfighting, trying to out-turn the enemy was only if strictly necessary. The real killers, the 'aces' or 'experten', didn't go in for that. Too much wasted effort, and dangerous too.

One of my favourite books about the design and construction of the piston aero engine is *The Power to Fly* by the late L.J.K. Setright. Written in 1971, this highly erudite engineer and wordsmith told the story of the piston aero engine from the birth of flight, up to 1970.

In Chapter 5 (Si Vic Pacem, Para Bellum) he wrote:

> By the time the Napier Sabre [the engine of the Hawker Typhoon – October 1941, with 56 Squadron] came into service, all too many of the really good pilots of fighter command had gone, and those who had taken their places were generally of poorer quality and were given only the most hasty and superficial of training before being sent out to do battle.

The line 'really good pilots of fighter command had gone' stuck with me for a long time until quite recently, when I bought a book on the subject of the battles over the Channel and Northern France, entitled *The JG26 War Diary, Volume 1: 1939–42*, by Donald Caldwell. In this excellent book, the author gives a day-by-day account of the fighting that this German Jagdgeschwader (fighter group) had done from 1939, in particular when it was stationed on the Channel coast in France, from 1941 to the end of 1942. The book included the group's claims, and actual, well-researched victories and losses of the group and its opponents – Britain's Fighter

Command, with its Spitfires and Hurricanes, and Bomber Command's Blenheims, Hampdens and Stirlings in the Battles of France and Britain in 1940, and the regular sweeps of Fighter Command over Northern France during 1941 and 1942.

Used as I was to the legends of our gallant RAF fighter pilots, in their Battle of Britain Spitfires and Hurricanes, fighting the dastardly 'Hun' in their inferior Bf 109Es and Fs, then later on in the formidable radial-engine Fw 190s, it came as something of a shock to find that, in 1941 and 1942, the British had lost aircraft and pilots in the ratio of up to 4 to 1 in favour of the Germans. No wonder that Setright had been so correct in his earlier quotation.

An observation from another friend, many years ago, who had been brought up as a small boy during the Second World War, in a working-class household on the border between England and Wales, also came back to me recently:

> When I watched the newsreels of the day in the local cinema every week, I listened to the fighter pilots talking among themselves while standing by their Spitfires and Hurricanes. From their plummy, public school accents, I believed that they actually owned their own airplanes.

This, in particular, shows just how isolated the officer class in the 1940s was from the 'man in the street', as well as the men who were their ground crew and who carried out all the necessary maintenance work upon 'their' fighters.

Then there were the sergeant pilots. As they were not 'proper' officers, simply Non-Commissioned Officers (NCOs) they could not share the officers' mess but were expected to drink and dine in their own mess. Yet they were expected to fight alongside the officers in the same struggle for Britain. Class distinction was in full force in Britain in the 1940s, as it is today, though in a subtly different form.

Introduction

It is eighty-two years since the beginning of the Second World War as I write this in 2021. I was born in 1944 and, as I grew up, I was surrounded by people of my parents' generation who were all proud of the fact that 'England [Britain] had won the war.' Of course, over the years we've discovered that that's not strictly true and that actually, the Russians won the war in Eastern Europe, with some help from America, particularly with trucks and lend-lease aircraft. It may be more accurate to state that 'England [Britain] was on the winning side(s).'

In the West of Europe the Americans, with some help from the British, won that part of the war, particularly from D-Day onwards. In the Pacific and Indochina, the Americans, with a little help from the British, won that one too. Britain ended the war bereft of empire and with a debt to the Americans that was not paid off until 2006. That's why their air force has had so many air bases in England since 1945. Forget the 'Special Relationship', it's all about money.

I find myself referring to the two world wars, both in 1914–18 and from 1939–45, as 'The Great European Civil War, Parts One and Two.' Certainly it was a time when Europe tore itself apart, and the effects are still with us today. In particular an apparent refusal to understand the lessons that those two wars taught us. I refer, of course, to Brexit and the ramifications of what that will bring to Britain and Europe, particularly where the interests of the two intersect, and they are many.

Over the years since the end of the Second World War, it seems to me that a myth has been carefully cultivated among the powers that be, which successive British governments in particular, mainly Conservative, have cultivated. Namely that Britain, standing alone in 1940, with Winston Churchill speaking his immortal lines, such as: 'Never in the field of human conflict has so much been owed by so many to so few.' And... 'We shall fight them on the beaches' etc, won the war that followed on afterwards. Serious scholars of the war and anyone who wants to make a cursory examination of history knows now that this is not the real truth but still, there remains this common belief in Britain that 'We beat the Jerries!'

Well, 'we' may have done in 1940 but in the two years immediately following the end of the Battle of Britain in October 1940, things did not go at all well for the British, particularly among the civilian population during the Blitz in 1940/41. Also, some dreadful mistakes were made by Britain's military leaders, and some of these people, in positions of power, were busy settling private feuds within their commands, instead of thinking clearly about how to beat the Germans and win the war.

This book sets out to examine the conduct of the leaders of the Royal Air Force, primarily its Fighter Command, in the Second World War, particularly the period from 1941 to 1942. To place the situation in context I have given a preamble, in this case what happened with air power in the First World War, principally from 1916, when this new force began to be used in a truly serious fashion. Then the book takes us past the inter-war years, when so many hard-learned lessons, particularly where fighting in the air itself was concerned, were forgotten and discarded, through the years of 1941/42 and on to the end of the war in 1945. A last chapter investigates exactly why these mistakes were made and who was responsible.

Here, then, is the story of what happened to the RAF when led, in this author's opinion, by the wrong people in the wrong jobs, at the wrong time.

Chapter 1

1914–1918

*The art of war is of vital importance to the State. It is
a matter of life and death, a road either to safety or to
ruin. Hence under no circumstances can it be neglected.*
Sun Tzu, *The Art of War*

'War is Hell', said William Tecumseh Sherman, a general who had
fought in the American Civil War, during his address of 1879 to the
Michigan Military Academy's graduation class and in war, both sides
suffer casualties. It is the bounden duty of commanding officers and
generals alike to keep their casualties to a minimum. After all, if you
suffer too many casualties, there will be no one left to fight the enemy.

In looking for the answer as to just why the British incurred such
terrible losses of men and machines in the air in both the First, and
Second World War, I came across what I believe to be the main reason.
Put very simply, it was all down to the strategy and tactics planned
out by the men in command of the Royal Flying Corps (RFC) and
then the Royal Air Force (RAF, founded in April 1918) and again in
1941 and 1942, blindly following on the principles set down by the
commander of the RFC, starting in 1915/16.

When looking at what happened in those two world wars, it is hard
to escape the conclusion that the British men in command during
those times frittered away the lives of valuable pilots, observers and
aircraft in the same way that British, French and, to a lesser extent,
the German soldiers were massacred in the First World War by the
decisions of the generals of their armies.

1

Most of the high-ranking officers in the RAF in the Second World War had themselves flown as pilots in that first dreadful struggle and, going into the Second World War, with the exception of Air Chief Marshal Hugh Caswall Tremenheere Dowding, the son of a teacher, and New Zealander Group Captain Keith Park, the son of a geologist, they appear to have learned very little from it.

These two men, respectively, had been the head of RAF Fighter Command and the commanding officer of 11 Group, based in the South East of Britain and tasked with the air defence of that part of Britain against the Luftwaffe during the Battle of Britain in 1940.

Hugh Dowding had married Clarice Vancourt in 1918, a widow with a young daughter. His new wife died suddenly in 1920 leaving a son, Derek (who became a wing commander in the RAF and survived the Second World War, after having scored several victories in 1940 and becoming a test pilot in the Middle East). Hugh Dowding's sister, Hilda, helped with looking after his children, and he remained single until marrying again after the war.

Air Vice-Marshal Dowding and Group Captain Park were elbowed unceremoniously out of their commands in late 1940, after the Battle of Britain. Dowding, after he had successfully led Fighter Command during the daylight struggle, and Park for his refusal to fight the Luftwaffe in the way that Trafford Leigh-Mallory, Commander of 12 Group (guarding the Midlands) wanted.

Dowding's successors in office, Deputy Chief of the Air Staff William Sholto Douglas, the son of Robert Langton Douglas, who was related to the Marquis of Queensbury, became the commanding officer of Fighter Command. Air Vice-Marshal Trafford Leigh-Mallory, the son of a Rector from Mobberly, Cheshire, took over the command of 11 Group, the sector which covered the South East of England, up to and including London, and led Fighter Command over the years of 1941 and 1942 with almost no regard to the casualties it suffered, and for no discernible strategic purpose, that would help Britain in her conduct of the war.

It may be true that every army starts the present war by using the methods of the last one, but surely the man in command of the day-to-day operations of Fighter Command of the RAF in 1941/42, William Sholto Douglas, must have realised the extent of the disaster that he and Trafford Leigh-Mallory were helping to inflict upon the pilots of their own command, though they never seem to have understood this.

William Sholto Douglas wrote a book after the Second World War called *Combat and Command*, which covered his experiences in combat in the First World War, and then when he was in command of Fighter Command from late 1940 in the Second World War, covering 1941 and 1942, until his retirement after the war ended; although admitting to 'hard times' in 1941, he doesn't seem to have given much attention to the reason for the losses that he was helping to cause.[1]

The heart of the problem lay in the fact that Sholto Douglas was a great admirer of the commander of the Royal Flying Corps in the First World War, Brigadier-General Hugh (later Viscount) 'Boom' Trenchard. Trenchard was the son of a former captain in the Kings Own Yorkshire Light Infantry, who was in the legal profession by the time his son was born.[2]

Trenchard was not good at learning while at school and only just scraped together enough marks to be commissioned as an officer in the British Army in 1893; analytical thinking does not appear to have been his forte – this is not to say that he lacked bravery. He fought in the Boer war, was wounded and lost a lung. After recovery, he then went to Nigeria and served there until 1912, when he returned to Britain and learned to fly. After gaining his licence, Trenchard transferred to the Royal Flying Corps (RFC) and served as the second in command at the Central Flying School. He acted as an observer during Annual Army Manoeuvres of 1912, thwarting a certain general's proposed offensive ... thus did he come to the notice of General, later Field-Marshal, Douglas Haig.

With the outbreak of the First World War in August 1914, Trenchard was made commander of the RFC home garrison. He soon found his way out to France and took command of the First Wing, which supported General Douglas Haig's First Army in December 1914. During August 1915, Trenchard was made a brigadier-general and given command of the RFC in France.

Air fighting itself was just beginning in 1915. During the early months of the war, a few pilots or observers had taken a pistol, carbine or rifle with them in the cockpit of their aircraft and, if they encountered an enemy aircraft, which was rare, would try their luck with a few shots, hardly any of which were effective.[3]

By 1915, a few experiments had been tried with a machine-gun mounted ahead of the pilot on a single-engine, single-seat 'scout' type of airplane, firing through the propeller, with steel wedges bolted to the rear of the propeller blades to deflect any shots that hit the propeller. Frenchman Roland Garros, a former pioneer of aviation, tried this and found that, though crude, it worked. Garros shot down at least three German aircraft before his Morane aeroplane suffered a broken fuel line and he came down behind enemy lines, where he and his Morane were soon captured.[4]

Anthony Fokker, a Dutchman with his own aircraft company in Schwerin, was invited by the German High Command to examine the mechanism mounted on Garros' Morane. Seeing how crude it was, Fokker suggested and developed an 'Interrupter' device, which did not allow the gun to fire when the propeller blade was directly in the line of fire. It's probable that Fokker copied an interrupter gear that had been previously invented by a Swiss, Franz Schneider, which had been described in a magazine about flight before the outbreak of war. Thus equipped with this device mounted in his Fokker EI, II and IIIs (E – Eindecker – monoplane) the 'Fokker Scourge' began.[5]

Pilots such as Oswald Boelcke, Max Immelman, Kurt Wintgens and Hans-Joachim Buddeke all became 'aces' with this airplane, having shot down five or more Allied aircraft. The 'Fokker Scourge' did not end until 1916, when a new breed of aircraft with 'pusher' engines, such as the de Havilland 2 and the F.E. 2B ('Fighting Experimental') were developed, mainly by the British, whose performance was better than the Fokker Eindecker which, truth to tell, was not a very good flying machine.[6]

It took until late 1916 for Germany to regain the performance initiative, with their then new Mercedes engined Albatros DI and IIs and Halberstadt DV biplanes. (D – Doppeldecker – biplane).[7]

It was at this time that Trenchard resumed his friendship and cooperation with Douglas Haig, who had been promoted to field-marshal by this time[8] and had been given command of the British Expeditionary Force in France. Haig was in command of the British Army at the Battle of the Somme in 1916, Passchendaele, Arras, Cambrai and other bloodbaths in 1917–18. It would appear that Haig and Trenchard had a lot in common, as they both firmly believed in the power of the offensive, at all costs, while the German army stood on the defensive in the west.

In March 1916, Trenchard was promoted to the rank of Major General. When the idea of combining the Royal Flying Corps (the army's flying service) and the Royal Naval Air Service (the Navy's flying arm) was mooted in 1917, Trenchard was initially opposed to the idea of the two services being amalgamated to become the Royal Air Force, but acquiesced when he saw the inevitability of this occurring.[9]

Major General John Salmond became the general officer commanding the RFC in January 1918 and then became the commander of the RAF, when that was formed in April 1918. He was an avid disciple of Trenchard's methods.

Trenchard's view was that it was up to the RFC/RAF to constantly send aircraft out over the German lines 'on the offensive', doing Offensive Patrols (OPs, as they were known among the squadrons) and spotting for the artillery (Art Obs) and reconnaissance, in order to try and see what the enemy was doing on the ground. On these missions, if they were intercepted by German aircraft, as they many times were, it was up to the British pilots to fight them and then, if they were still intact, to make their way back over the trenches to friendly territory, often against the stiff prevailing headwind, in aircraft which – even by 1918 – could fly at little more than 120 mph at best.[10]

Trenchard believed that it was 'good for morale' that the British soldiers in the front line would only see Allied aircraft above them, but there is no evidence either way to prove or disprove this theory. It did not deter the great German advance of March 1918, although ground-attacking aircraft of the RFC certainly hindered the German army's *Michael* Offensive of 1918. Trenchard was also a firm believer in Field Marshal Haig's ideas of carrying out successive offensives on the Western Front by the British Army, and very few of those succeeded, all of them having little to show at the end of each offensive except for a horrendous list of casualties. Except for the Battle of Verdun in 1915–16, and *Michael* Offensive of 1918, the German army stood very much on the defensive in the First World War, while the Allies carried out many offensives to try and break through their defences, few of which succeeded.

The Recording Officer of No.1 Squadron, Lieutenant Thomas Hughes, RFC, wrote in 1916 about Trenchard that he:

> follows the good military principle of repeating any tactics that have not been actually disastrous – and often those that have – again and again, regardless of the fact that the enemy will probably think out some very good reply, until they really are so disastrous that they have to be abandoned.

Hugh Dowding had been a squadron leader in France in the Royal Flying Corps and had opposed Major General Hugh Trenchard over rest periods for the pilots; the pair had fallen out, with Trenchard writing to Dowding to tell him that he was a 'dismal Jimmy', and that he intended to remove him from his command. Trenchard was as good as his word and had Dowding removed from commanding a squadron in France and sent back to England to command a training squadron, as a punishment. Dowding later refused to lower the hours flown in pilot training as Trenchard wanted, as he was always demanding more pilots to replace those who had been shot down and were either killed or had become prisoners of war during the offensive patrols over the German lines that he championed.[11]

Flying training time in 1916 was a mere fifteen hours before going solo. Because of the demand for new pilots at the front to replace those who had been killed or captured, many pilots arrived at the squadrons insufficiently trained to fly and fight well enough to defend themselves. In late 1916 and into 1917, life expectancy of a pilot at the front was a mere two weeks. Major William Read, who commanded 45 Squadron RFC, reported in his diary entry of 24 October 1916:

A day of rain and no flying – Except in the afternoon when some of my pilots flew around the airdrome. That shocking pilot, flight sergeant Webb crashed another machine and Gones broke a propeller getting off the ground. Some of my pilots are cruel bad. Have put in application today to get rid of them. They also lack ginger.[12]

British RFC/RAF casualties in the First World War, among their airmen, numbered some 9,000 killed or missing and 7,000 wounded. The equivalent German Air Force casualties were less than 7,000 killed or missing and just over 5,000 wounded.

By 1917, the High Command of the German air force (Luftstreitkraft) had their fighter squadrons (staffeln) gathered together into squadrons and groups (Jagdgeschwaders) and these were termed 'Circuses' by the Allies. Gathered just behind the front lines, the German squadrons' ground observers, located on their airfields, were able to give the order to take off and intercept the marauding British flights and squadrons when they were spotted approaching the trench lines. This allowed the German staffeln to take off, gain height and a favourable position from which to attack the oncoming enemy, meaning the Germans nearly always fought their enemy over, or just behind, their own front lines. It also meant that if a German pilot survived a crash landing, he would shortly be available to fight again, whereas a British or Allied airman, if he was lucky enough to survive having been forced down and the ensuing crash landing, became a prisoner. The Germans made their 'Circuses' highly mobile, so that they could quickly be moved along the line to wherever the fighting was heaviest and their skills could best be used.

The two high scoring German aces and leaders of the First World War were Oswald Boelcke (before being killed in October 1916) with forty victories, and Rittmeister Freiherr Manfred von Richthofen, who replaced him as the leader of Jasta II; both led their men in defence on their side of the lines. Neither felt it necessary to mount offensive patrols over the Allied lines.

To keep up the image of the Allies causing the Germans many more casualties than they received, Allied pilots often inflated their claims for aircraft shot down. Post-war analysis showed that the Allied pilots in both the First and Second World War over-claimed by a factor of 2 or 3 to 1. This was not intentional on the part of Allied pilots, merely a result of the confusion that occurred during fighting in the air. Having said that, there were some, such as the Canadian 'Billy' Bishop, who submitted almost outrageous claims for aircraft shot down in the First World War. He once claimed to have attacked an enemy airfield single handed, for which action he was awarded a Victoria Cross. Later investigations have shown that this probably did not happen, as there is no mention of such a raid in German records.[13]

Try to imagine what it must have been like, encumbered with heavy leather clothing in order to keep warm in the cold at altitude, goggles pulled down over your eyes and in a 100 mph slipstream, inside a small cockpit, looking around fearfully for any sign of an enemy aircraft about to attack you. The engine roars, drowning out any other sign. If you have an observer aboard, it's probably very difficult to hear anything that he shouts at you over the slipstream. You're at 12,000ft over enemy territory and trying to make sense of everything, especially if this is your first flight over 'Hunland'. Oh sure, your fellow squadron mates have tried to help you, given you tips on what to do in any given situation, but suddenly, there's a terrible 'rat-tat-tat' of enemy machine-gun fire. You look around, terrified, and see that your observer is dead, shot through from the first rounds of a black-crossed enemy aircraft, now lining up on you again. Flames are licking at your tailplane. What do you do? You have seconds to live. No one told you it would end like this but during the First World War, for many raw recruits, it did.

As the British were usually flying over enemy-held territory when they fought, a German aircraft seen spinning down 'out of control', or OOC, would often be credited to the pilot's score, whereas the fact was that many of these spinning aircraft were trying to throw their enemies off attacking them again – and frequently succeeded. The Germans, as they flew and fought over their own lines, were able to confirm their victories by the fact that the claimed aircraft usually fell behind (although not always) their own trench system.

In the First World War, as we have seen, the aircraft's primary role was to act as an observation platform for the artillery. To a certain extent, and mainly later on in the war, daylight and night-time bombing by the Allies was carried out by two-seater aircraft, but it was to aid the artillery by spotting the gun's fall of shot that they were usually employed. All other operations were subordinate to that task.[14]

For the British and their allies, this meant that the men flying these two-seater observation aircraft were the air force's true heroes; day after day flying over the lines, usually at low altitude, not more than 6,000ft in slow, cumbersome aircraft and observing the fall of artillery shells onto chosen targets, tapping out in Morse code to the gunners where their shells were falling while trying, at the same time, to keep a look out for enemy fighters and avoiding the ever present 'Archie' (anti-aircraft gunfire) and machine-gun fire from the ground. It wasn't easy. If the two-seaters weren't flying on 'Art-Obs' missions, they were often employed on photographing the trench lines or some specific target over the lines, such as marshalling yards where arriving troop trains could be counted.

The same could be said of the Germans, but it does appear that their two-seater aircraft often had a substantial height advantage over the British aircraft when on reconnaissance, some of them crossing over the lines at over 20,000ft. For instance, the German Rumpler C.IV could climb to 21,000ft by the end of 1916, with its crew already equipped with oxygen at this early stage of the war, and an LVG C.VI of 1918 could reach 21,500ft, while the Hannover CL.IIIA could reach 24,600ft, its rate of climb being eighteen minutes to 10,000ft, making it very difficult for Allied fighters to climb up and intercept these aircraft.[15] To help them in the crippling cold of high altitude, the German crews wore heated flying suits as well as using oxygen.

One of the experts at shooting down German two-seaters, flying high on reconnaissance missions, was James Thomas Byford McCudden, who had started the war as a mechanic with the RFC, joining in 1912. He progressed, becoming an observer by 1915 and then becoming a pilot, first of all with de Havilland DH2s, the single-seat 'pusher' biplane 'scout' (fighter) of 1915/16. It was in one of these that he was lucky to survive an encounter with Manfred von Richthofen, the 'Red Baron' himself, flying a much superior Albatros DII, fitted with two forward-firing Spandau machine-guns, which were themselves copies of the original Maxim invented machine-gun. Of that encounter, McCudden later wrote the following account in his book *Flying Fury*, which was given to his publisher in 1918 when the events described were still fresh in his memory:

On December 27, 1916, I was one of six DH 2s, which left the ground at about 2 pm and crossed the lines at 10,000ft near Arras, and patrolled about a mile East of the lines. About 3pm I saw several Huns coming up off their aerodrome at Croisilles. They very soon got our height and then flew parallel to us, gradually coming nearer.

By this time the Huns had got so close to us, that we could see their crosses, and there were only three DH 2s left, Captain Payn, lieut. Jennings and myself, and very soon one of the Huns came near enough to our leader to be fired on by us. As soon as Captain Payn chased this Hun, another dived onto his tail, so Mr Jennings dived at this one, and then two went after Jennings and made him throw his machine about like anything to avoid their fire. Indeed, Jennings looked like he was having a bad time.

I now fired at the nearest Hun who was after Jennings, and this Hun immediately came for me nose on, and we both fired simultaneously but after firing about twenty shots my gun got a bad double feed, which I could not rectify at the time as I was now in the middle of five Albatrosses, so I half rolled. When coming out I kept the machine past the vertical for a few hundred feet and had started to level out again when, 'cack, cack, cack, cack,' came from just behind me, and on looking round, I saw my old friend with the black and white streamers again. I immediately half rolled again, but still the Hun stayed there, and so while half rolling I kept on making headway for our lines, for the fights had started east of Adinfer wood, with which we were so familiar.

I continued to do half rolls and got over the trenches at about 2000ft, with the Hun still in pursuit, and the rascal drove me down to 800ft a mile west of the lines, when he turned off east, and was shelled by our anti-aircraft guns. I soon rectified the jam but by this time the Hun was much higher, and very soon joined his patrol who were waiting for him at about 5000ft over Ransart.

Soon after landing I met Captain Hill, who looked at me as at a ghost. 'What?' He said. 'You here? Why Payn has just said that you went down out of control over Hunland, with a fat Hun in attendance.' 'Yes.' I said. 'So I did. That is why I am here.'[16]

McCudden's squadron was re-equipped with the Royal Aircraft Factory produced SE5A in 1917, a fast and sturdy fighter, although early examples suffered from engine problems, which took some time to correct. This Hispano-Suiza 90 degree V8 engine, designed by the Swiss, Marc Birkigt, was a clever design, the 90-degree angle of the aluminium blocks of the 'V' giving a more rigid engine than would have been possible with the more normal 60-degree configuration.

As a result, the crankcase itself was lighter than would have otherwise have been possible. The engine was equipped with a single overhead camshaft per bank of four cylinders, driving the two upright valves per cylinder via mushroom headed cam followers, which were screwed into the valves and were adjustable, to give the correct clearance. The valve gear was totally enclosed, and lubricated by oil from the crankcase, which was pumped around by its own oil pump. Power for the first engines was given as 150bhp from just 11.775 litres capacity, for a dry weight of just 445 pounds. Some later, higher powered versions of this engine used reduction gearing to make the propeller more efficient, but these engines suffered gear failures because the science behind choosing the right strength of steel for the gear wheels was still not completely understood at the time.[17]

With his knowledge of all things mechanical, McCudden tuned the Hispano-Suiza V8 engine in his own SE5A, rebuilding it with higher compression pistons, so that he had the fastest 'scout' in his squadron. He also looked after his own guns, practising frequently on the ground and making sure the sighting was correct for his requirements of not opening fire until close to the enemy that he was stalking. McCudden would also go through his ammunition carefully, in order to try and weed out rounds which might jam in his single fuselage-mounted Vickers and also in his Lewis machine-gun, which was mounted to fire over the propeller, on the centre section of his top wing

McCudden became extremely skilled at stalking his prey until he got into the right position to attack, once shooting down four German two-seaters in the space of a few minutes, but even he admitted in his book that if he lost the element of surprise and had to fight a German two-seater for more than just a few minutes, he would break off the combat and go and look for other prey, as an alerted and experienced German two-seater crew could be a formidable opponent.[18] On 28 December 1917, he shot down three German two-seaters within thirty minutes. He was a truly professional air fighter with fifty-four victories to his credit before dying in a flying accident in July 1918.

For the British two-seater crews life was very different in that, after the BE2C, they flew mostly the RE8 type (RE – Reconnaissance Experimental) from November 1916, when the type was introduced. The RE8 could only climb to a service ceiling of 13,500ft, making it vulnerable to attack from above by German fighters.[19]

The Armstrong Whitworth FK8 (FK – Frederick Koolhooven, the designer) was similar in performance (or lack of) to the RE8, having a ceiling of just 13,000ft and a top speed of 95 mph. However, most artillery observation operations were usually carried out at a height of up to 6,000ft, so it was only in the reconnaissance role that altitude and speed really mattered. At one time, six RE8s were sent out on a 'long distance reconnaissance' behind enemy lines. Unfortunately, they ran into the crack fighter pilots of JG II, Manfred von Richthofen's squadron, and all six were shot down.

The RE8 had, in its turn, replaced the previous two-seater reconnaissance/observation machine in the RFC, the BE2 (Bleriot Experimental, second type) in 1916. This aircraft was one that was already in use in August 1914, when war broke out and had suffered severely at the hands of the German Luftstreitskraft, particularly during the 'Fokker scourge' of 1915–16, when the then new machine-gun equipped Fokker 'Eindecker' was introduced. In a nutshell, the BE2 was too stable and too slow to fight an enemy single-seater Eindecker.

The BE2 had the added disadvantage of having the pilot seated behind the observer, whose job as a defensive gunner was made even more difficult than the later practice of seating the gunner behind the pilot, in trying to avoid the various struts and wires, which held the centre section of the top wing in place, while attempting to fire back at his opponent. Sadly, many of them were still in service in 1917 and many were shot down during 'Bloody April', a month when the RFC suffered very heavy losses, many at the hands of von Richthofen's Jasta II.

Sholto Douglas had flown a BE2 in 1915–16 and in one of his combat reports, described being attacked by both of the top German aces of the day, Oswald Boelcke and Max Immelman, in their synchronised machine-gun equipped Eindeckers, on 29 December 1915. Somehow, he survived. His combat report read:

Observer Lieut. Child. 2 Hours 45 minutes. Height 6,500ft. Reconnaissance to Cambrai and St. Quentin. Archie very good near Cambrai. [Anti-aircraft fire] Then met six Huns. Glen, my escort was shot down, followed by two of the Huns. I was then set upon by the remainder. Child, my observer, downed one Hun. We fought the remaining three for half an hour. Petrol began to get low and engine sump was hit. So, relying on the stability near the ground, of our BE2c, as against Fokker, came down in a steep spiral to 10ft above the ground. Came back from Cambrai to Arras just over the trees. Huns shot like mad. Child turned Lewis gun onto one lot of

Huns by a farmhouse. Saw several small convoys and a Staff Officer on horseback. Fokkers left us a mile from the lines. Climbed to 800ft and dived over the trenches. Engine failed and landed among French heavy batteries just south of Arras. About a hundred holes in machine. Engine sump pierced about 1½ inches from bottom.[20]

By 1917, there were other two-seaters in the RFC, as well as the RE8. For instance, the RFC by then also had the excellent Bristol F2B two seat fighter fitted with the Rolls-Royce Eagle engine, which could climb as high as 18,500ft. The Bristol Fighter 'Brisfit' F2B was a very good aircraft; strong, manoeuvrable and relatively fast for such a big aeroplane, it could be flown as a single-seat fighter, but with a gunner to guard its tail. Some F2B crews racked up remarkable scores of enemy aircraft shot down. Canadian Andrew McKeever shot down thirty enemy aircraft, together with his 'usual' rear gunner, Englishman Leslie Powell, who claimed nineteen enemy aircraft destroyed. Maximum speed was given as 125 mph and time to 10,000ft was 11.5 minutes.[21]

From the latter part of 1916 through to November 1918 British bombers, first FE2Bs but then mainly de Havilland DH4s and 9s, of the Independent Force raided targets behind the lines, usually going unescorted and suffering heavy casualties as a result. On 31 July 1918, ten out of twelve de Havilland bombers were shot down on one raid against Saarbrucken in Germany.

The de Havilland DH4 was a day bomber, also fitted with the Rolls-Royce Eagle engine, which entered production in 1917 and was used to bomb targets in Germany in retaliation to the raids by the multi-engine Gotha bombers on Britain, principally on London, in 1917. Its basic specification gave it a maximum ceiling of 22,000ft and a top speed of over 140 mph. It could climb to 10,000ft in nine minutes from ground level. Its only problem was the distance between the pilot and the observer/gunner, that space between them being filled up in the fuselage by the fuel tank, which made communication difficult. Its successor, and ordered in large numbers, was the DH9, which turned out to be a disastrous choice, having the troublesome BHP/Galloway Adriatic, or the Siddeley Puma engine installed, both of which were deficient in power output.

With these unreliable engines, the service ceiling was limited to 15,500ft at best and maximum speed was 113 mph, making it fly slower and lower than its predecessor. Compared to the preceding DH4, its climb rate was also inferior, from the ground to 10,000ft in 18½ minutes. Also, the engines were so unreliable that frequently a third of the attacking force would have to turn back before their target was reached. Nevertheless, the British commanders kept sending their pilots and observers out on long range bombing raids over Germany in these aircraft from March 1918, where they suffered severe casualties if they came under German fighter attack.[22] So bad was the DH9 that it was rapidly re-fitted with either the Rolls-Royce Eagle V8 of 375 HP, or the American Liberty V12, which gave 400 HP. Sadly for their crews, these aircraft, now called the de Havilland DH9a, did not come into service until September 1918.

Going on the strategic bombing offensive over Germany with their later multi-engine Handley-Page 0/400s and 0/1500s became the Mantra of the new RAF Independent Air Force, commanded by Trenchard, but the war finished just as these large multi-engine bombers started coming into service.

As discussed, during the First World War the British and their Allies would send out artillery observation aircraft over the trench lines in order for them to spot targets for the artillery, who supported the infantry. These aircraft sometimes had the protection of single-seater fighters, which would patrol over the lines daily and their job was to help any Allied aircraft which they saw being attacked. On the British side, these fighters by 1917–18 were usually either SE5As, or Sopwith Camels, although various other types, such as Sopwith Dolphins, Pups, Triplanes or French built Spads were also in use.

The SE5A, the mount of the top scoring British aces, such as McCudden, Mannock, Ball, Beauchamp Procter and Rhys-Davids was, as we have seen, a Hispano Suiza V8-powered biplane that was strong and relatively simple to fly. The engine itself gave trouble early on in the aircraft's career in 1917, particularly in the higher output geared versions, but these problems were largely solved by 1918. It could achieve 138 mph in level flight and, although the service ceiling was given as 18,000ft, McCudden recounts in his book of being able to get up to over 20,000ft, no doubt due to his tuning of the engine, particularly with its high compression pistons.[23]

The Sopwith Camel, powered by a Clerget or Bentley rotary engine (with its cylinders arranged in a radial fashion, and which rotated around the stationary crankshaft, which was bolted to the front bulkhead to aid cooling), was not as fast, nor could it climb as high as the SE5A, speed being given as 113 mph and service ceiling as 19,000ft, although most Camel pilots recounted that performance fell off drastically above 12,500ft; the Camel could climb to 10,000ft in twelve minutes, but the SE5As could climb faster and higher. However, the Camel was extremely manoeuvrable and a good pilot could use its ability to turn tightly to the right to advantage, particularly in a dogfight. Reputedly, it was actually quicker to turn 270 degrees to the left, to turn right, than to turn right through 90 degrees against the torque of the spinning engine. Its main drawback was that it was tail-heavy and so sensitive on the controls that it killed almost as many pupil pilots as it did the enemy.[24]

As a schoolboy, and mad about aircraft even then, I once met a man who told me that he had flown a Camel in the First World War. Intrigued, I asked him what it had been like to fly. 'Tricky!' he replied. 'But as lots of us were flying them then, we simply accepted them for what they were – very manoeuvrable dogfighters. I'll never forget their turn to the right.' I asked him if he'd shot down any Germans. He thought for a moment before replying. 'Only four in eighteen months,' he told me. 'Shot at quite a few others though.'

The French, far and away the leading innovators of powered flight when the war started in 1914, came out with several very good fighters during the war, several types being made by the Nieuport factory and several by the SPAD (Société Pour L'Aviation et ses Dérivé) factory. Of the French reconnaissance and bomber aircraft little good can be said; certainly the French never built any two-seaters as good as those of the Germans or the British.

The Nieuport fighters came in many versions, from the II, and later in 1916, the 17, to the 27 of 1918. In each case it was a small, light and manoeuvrable 'sesquiplane'. That is, it had a much narrower lower wing, usually with only one main spar, whereas the upper wing was larger and had two longitudinal spars for more strength. Like the German Albatros DIII-V, which copied this layout, it used 'V' struts between the outer wings to brace them together. Where the early Nieuports scored was in the fact that the early ones, by 1916, carried a machine-gun, usually a comparatively lightweight Lewis, on a mounting above the top wing. The British ace, Albert Ball, and the Canadian ace, 'Billy' Bishop, flew Nieuports in 1916/17. This upper wing-mounted gun enabled the little fighter (it was nicknamed the 'Bebe') like the Fokker Eindeckers that it met in combat, to be aimed in the same way, i.e. the pilot could shoot straight ahead of his aircraft without destroying the propeller.

By the time that the Nieuport 27 arrived in 1917 and equipped most of the fledgling American air service in France, it had two Vickers machine-guns, mounted in the fuselage and firing, via an interrupter gear, through the propeller. One drawback that this aeroplane did possess was a distressing tendency to shed the fabric off its top wing in stressful situations, such as a high speed dive.[25]

Designed by Louis Becherau, both the SPAD VII and later the XIII, were single-bay, wire-braced biplane designs. The SPADs possessed another pair of interplanetary struts, much like a two-bay biplane, but these were installed to quell vibration rather than as bracing struts. The earlier SPAD VII was smaller than the XIII and featured only one Vickers machine-gun, whereas the larger XIII had two guns. Both aircraft were powered by the ubiquitous Hispano-Suiza V8 and both were fast and strong, though perhaps not as nimble as such as the Sopwith Pups and Camels and the Fokker DR1 Triplane. Nevertheless, they were the mounts of the top scoring French and American aces. Indeed, the prototype SPAD XIII was timed at 140 mph during its flight trials, although those in service trim were rated at 131.2 mph.[26]

By 1918 the Germans still had many Albatros fighters in service, which basic design dated from 1916. When first introduced, with their 160hp liquid-cooled, inline six-cylinder Mercedes engines and twin Spandau machine-guns, they had proved formidable, but by 1918, despite having been developed, they had been overtaken in performance by the Camel and the SE5A. Also, the Albatros DIII-DV variants (which were most of them) being of sesquiplane format, suffered from a weakness in the construction of the lower wings, which meant that one could tear away, when diving or carrying out tight manouvres.[27]

The Fokker DR1 Triplane, probably the most famous aircraft of the First World War, succeeded the Albatros DIII in 1917 and this was the aircraft flown by Manfred von Richthofen, the German ace of aces, after his usual Albatros scout, from 1917–18. It was powered by a 110hp Oberursel rotary engine, a copy of the French 110hp Le Rhone. German pilots thought the Le Rhone original was a more reliable engine than the Oberursel copy and several had captured engines installed in their triplanes, including Werner Voss, another of the German high scorers. One of the problems suffered by the German rotary engines in 1918 was an inferior brand of castor oil, 'Rizinus', being used, due to the naval blockade inflicted on Germany by the British Grand Fleet.[28]

In total, von Richthofen shot down some eighty-one Allied aircraft. (He has frequently been credited with eighty victories on the Western Front, but McCudden was listed among his claims and although fought down to 800ft by von Richthofen in 1916, McCudden managed to make his way back to his airfield safely.) Von Richthofen also shot down two more aircraft, for which his claims were not allowed, early on in his career in 1916 when acting as an observer/ gunner in a two-seater on the Russian front, but he was not credited with them, as there was not a separate witness, apart from his pilot.

A mention should be made here about the ability of the aces to shoot accurately. It does appear that in all air combat the ability to get close and shoot accurately were the top priorities required, so the need to be a good shot, particularly when allowing for the speed of the opposing aircraft (deflection) ranked high on the list of the desirable qualities of an ace. Von Richthofen, for instance, came from the landed gentry in Prussia and his father's estates were huge. From an early age, Manfred had been taught to shoot accurately when out hunting on these estates and so not waste ammunition. His flying ability was only rated as 'Moderate', and he certainly never indulged himself in unnecessary aerobatics.[29]

Although the Fokker DR1 had a formidable reputation as a fast climber and was very manoeuvrable, only 300-plus of them entered service, the maximum at the front line being just 171 in April 1918. By the beginning of 1918 they were outclassed in performance, particularly speed, by the newer British types. They had also gained a reputation of being fragile, with a tendency to shed the fabric from their upper wing in a dive, which did not endear them to their pilots in some cases. The Fokker factory had to stop production of several models, including the DR1, during its lifetime due to shoddy workmanship which resulted in several fatal crashes.

Germany's most formidable fighter of the First World War was undoubtedly the Fokker DVII, introduced in 1918. First of all using the six-cylinder Mercedes IIIau 180hp engine, or the 'high compression' BMW IIIa engine of 185hp, also of six cylinders, the DVII was highly sought after by the German fighter pilots, particularly the BMW variant. When going to collect a new DVII from a supply depot, most pilots 'in the know' tried to get a BMW, rather than a Mercedes-powered aeroplane, due to its superior power, particularly at higher altitude. A Mercedes-powered DVII, took twenty-four minutes to climb to 16,400ft, while a BMW-powered DVII took just seventeen minutes. Furthermore, the service ceiling of the Mercedes DVII was given as 20,000ft, while the BMW DVII could climb to 24,200ft. No wonder German pilots wanted a BMW!

With its cantilever wings needing no flying or landing bracing wires, and with a welded steel tube fuselage, the DVII was fast, strong and light and was the only aircraft specifically demanded by the Allies to be handed over to them in quantity at the close of the war. Indeed, those German pilots 'in the know' preferred to fly an Albatros-built DVII in 1918, as they thought it a better built aeroplane than a Fokker-built example. Fokker DVIIs replaced most DR1 equipped staffeln in summer 1918.[30]

Towards the end of 1918, Fokker brought out another Eindecker – the EV/DVIII, this one being very different to his earlier effort, and being of parasol construction. That is, with the single wing located above the fuselage. It looked similar to a DR1, but with just the one wing. It was fast and manoeuvrable and its pilots liked it; unfortunately it had the Oberursel rotary engine and, with supplies of the correct oil drying up, not many could be used in action.[31]

By the time of the Fokker DVII's introduction in April 1918, its pilots were going into combat wearing a Heinecke parachute harness, designed by a ground crewman, Otto Heinecke. At least they now stood a chance of survival should their aircraft be damaged beyond redemption in a dogfight. Nearly a third of the first fifty pilots leaping from their doomed aircraft died when the lines to the parachute became entangled, or the thigh straps tore through when the parachute opened. This last was cured with the introduction of stronger thigh straps. Several of the German aces, including Ernst Udet, Germany's second highest scorer with seventy-two victories, saved their lives in a desperate situation with the parachute.[32]

No such luck for the British pilots. The desk-bound officers at the Air Ministry in London concluded that issuing parachutes to pilots might encourage them to abandon their aircraft, which otherwise might have been nursed to the ground. The indifference of the 'higher ups' for the welfare of their men was apparent. It would not change in the Second World War.

In May 1918, Trenchard was appointed as the General Officer Commanding of the Independent Air Force. This had been created with the purpose of bombing industrial centres, railways and airfields, and eventually became RAF Bomber Command.

Also in 1918, the Junkers Company of Germany produced an all-metal monoplane, using corrugated duraluminium, much in the same way as their later Ju 52/3m Trimotor of the Second World War did. The CLI, also known as the J8/J10, was intended mainly for the ground attack role and despite only fifty-one being built, was a harbinger of things to come in the Second World War, with German aircraft in this role primarily supporting their troops on the ground.[33]

Incidentally, performance figures for all these aircraft appear to vary widely, depending on whose figures one accepts today. It must be remembered that most figures are for aircraft when new, and just leaving their factories. By the time these aircraft were in regular squadron use, they probably suffered from worn engines, tended by too few mechanics, who were having to work extremely hard just to keep them serviceable at all.

For the purposes of this book, I have used performance figures that are quoted in *Janes Fighting aircraft of WW1 and WW2*. They do not quote service ceilings and here, where available, I have used the figures quoted in the various 'Osprey' publications on these subjects.

Hugh Trenchard's offensive policy was deeply ingrained into the British RFC/RAF officers who flew in the First World War, and it was mainly these officers who would go on to command the RAF in the Second World War.

Chapter 2

1919–1939

The accumulation of power before warfare is
the most important preparation.

Anon

The war was won. The dead were buried. The wounded and maimed were looked after as well as could be expected at the time. The world tried to move on after 1918.

No one seems to have questioned the strategy and tactics employed by the generals on either side until very much later, and usually then the huge blunders and losses – particularly of the men, both on the ground and in the air – were glossed over. They would not rise to be discussed in any meaningful fashion until many years after the Second World War.

So Trenchard's policy of always being on the offensive in the air war was never the subject of any official discussion or inquiry at the Air Ministry to any degree after the First World War, that is in the twenty-one years before the next war erupted. No inquiry into the effectiveness, or otherwise, of the bombing of Germany in 1917/18 was ever carried out.[1]

The newly formed RAF's high command, the staff officers at the Air Ministry, carried on blithely and unquestionably believing this to have been the correct course of action. The defeated Germans thought that they knew better.

After the First World War, the RAF was quickly and drastically reduced in size, both in the numbers of aircraft and men being employed, from 280 squadrons down to twenty-eight. After the enormous cost of four years of warfare, the British Government was keen to cut down on costs wherever possible. The RAF was used in the early 1920s as a deterrent force to the tribesmen of Somaliland and Iraq, with bombers being used to put down insurrections, instead of the army. From Trenchard (appointed Chief of the Air Staff on 31 March 1919) downwards in the RAF's command structure at the newly created Air Ministry, the belief in the offensive was absolute. Future wars could, and would, be won by bombers alone.

In 1921, Italian General Giulio Douhet wrote *The Command of the Air*.[2] In this book (subsequently revised in 1927) Douhet promoted the idea of a large, well-armed and armoured bomber, which would bomb the enemy's industry, cities and population. Furthermore, as it would be capable of protecting itself from intercepting fighters, escort fighters would not be needed.

The thinking ran that these bombers would fight their way to the target and carry enough defensive armament to deter any interceptor that might be able to find them. The RAF High Command adopted this policy. Once the aircraft had bombed the towns and cities of the enemy, striking terror into the civilian population, in a democratic society that population would then force their government to sue for peace; so ran the thinking among Britain's air force commanders.

Because most of the British High Command in the Air Ministry had become wedded to the idea of an independent bomber force being used on the offensive, many staff officers simply did not believe in the necessity for modern defensive interceptor fighters. The last of the British biplane fighters, the Gloster Gladiator, was still in service with the RAF at the start of the Second World War.

In the early 1920s, Trenchard, fearing the break-up of the RAF, also oversaw the beginning of the RAF (Cadet) College at Cranwell and of the Aircraft Apprentice system, which managed the training of ground crew. Trenchard retired as Chief of the Air Staff on 1 January 1930, but continued to meet with current and future officers of the

RAF, both within the Air Ministry and outside it, influencing them still with his beliefs. Even as late as 1943, Trenchard was to be seen, in full RAF uniform, inspecting men of the RAF Regiment.

By the early 1930s the British Government seems to have become convinced that massed bomber raids would always get through to their target. On 10 November 1932, Stanley Baldwin, the then Prime Minister of Britain, gave a speech in which he said:

> I think it is well for the man in the street to realise that there is no power on Earth that can protect him from being bombed, whatever people tell him; *the bomber will always get through* ... the only defence is offence, which means that you have to kill more women and children more quickly than the enemy, if you want to save yourself.[3] [Author's italics]

And so, without any actual proof of the theory that bombing alone could break any enemy's will to resist, without examining the effect that Allied bombing had had on German cities during the First World War (very little), the staff at the Air Ministry continued to believe in the offensive, always carried out by bombers, to be an obvious fact.

Later, right through the Second World War and afterwards, the chiefs of the Air Ministry appear to have accepted hook, line and sinker, the primacy of the bomber in any struggle that the RAF was involved in. Without any great thought or inquiry, they accepted the offensive policy of Trenchard and the theory of Douhet. In their world, the bomber would bring any enemy to its knees. Not for them a world where the army and navy were necessary adjuncts to the winning of a war. No, their wonderful bombers would smash the enemy's will to resist. It didn't quite work out that way.

Where aircraft and their engines for the RAF were concerned, Rolls-Royce designed and built their Kestrel engine, starting the design in July 1925 and calling it the Falcon X. The Air Ministry had taken an American 400hp Curtis V12 engine, which had been very successful in racing, particularly in the Schneider Trophy, to Rolls-Royce and asked for something better. The Kestrel was also in the V12 format (two banks of six cylinders, arranged in a 'V' shape) displacing 21.25 litres.

The ex-Napier designer A.J. Rowledge was responsible for the design of the Kestrel, he having previously designed the excellent W-formation 12-cylinder engine the Napier Lion, which was built in quantity over many years. This engine powered many aircraft of the inter-war period and some, such as the Supermarine Sea Walrus, that served during the Second World War as well. That aircraft saw considerable use as an air/ sea rescue aircraft in the English Channel in 1940–45.[4]

The Napier Lion had been a 4-valve per cylinder engine, with twin overhead camshafts per bank of three blocks four cylinders each, spaced in a 'W' configuration, and having a capacity of almost 24 litres. At 2,000rpm it gave, depending on which model was being tested, between 450 to 550hp. When used to power the Supermarine S4 Monoplane, R.J. Mitchell's first Schneider Trophy design of 1925, the Napier Lion VII was developed to give 680hp. The S4 was, incidentally, the first of a line of racing aircraft designed by R.J. Mitchell for the Supermarine company based in Portsmouth which, indirectly, led on to the design of the Spitfire. The S5 of 1927 was powered by a shorter stroke version of the Lion, giving 898hp at 3,300rpm and, according to L.J.K. Setright, the engine could be revved to 3,900rpm, where some 1,400hp was realised.[5]

The centrifugal supercharger of the Kestrel was designed by J.E. Ellor, who the Air Ministry had recommended to Rolls-Royce. He had been responsible for all the early work done on superchargers at the RAE (Royal Aircraft Establishment at Farnborough) and by May 1928, the Kestrel was delivering 580hp at 2,000ft altitude in RAF service, while another version was giving 520hp at 13,000ft.[6]

During the 1920s, the Schneider Trophy, a race for seaplanes first run at Monaco just before the First World War and afterwards every year, later every two years, became a hot favourite with the air-minded public in many countries.[7] This contest, by the late 1920s, had evolved into who could put the most powerful engine into the smallest, lightest, most aerodynamic floatplane design.[8]

Many countries tried for that elusive three wins in a row, which would gain for them the trophy in perpetuity, but it was the British High Speed Flight, composed of service personnel, who finally took that third win in 1931.[9]

It had been a hard struggle. America had shone in the early 1920s; in 1923 with a very streamlined biplane (for the time), the Curtis CR-3, powered by the aforementioned Curtis D-12, a V12 direct-drive engine design of some 400bhp. They won again with the same design in 1925, at Baltimore, now with their engines producing over 500bhp. For them, all hinged on 1927.[10]

Air Marshal Sir Hugh Trenchard, at that time the head of the RAF, declined to spend public money on competing for the trophy in 1923, although Parliament did promise £3,000 to buy the winning aircraft, provided that it was of British design and had not won the trophy before. Things changed under a Socialist government for 1925, with money being given to aircraft manufacturers for 'experimental aircraft', and RAF personnel being employed in servicing and flying them.[11]

Supermarine's designer, Reginald Mitchell, produced a beautiful monoplane floatplane design, the S.4, powered by an uprated Napier Sea Lion engine. Before setting out for Baltimore, in 1925, the S.4 gained the world seaplane record for Britain at 226.742 mph. Ironically, because they favoured the biplane configuration for RAF fighters, the British Government gave a contract to Gloster to produce two racing biplanes, which they did, but left Supermarine and Napier to finance the superior S.4 monoplane design themselves. Sadly, the S.4 crashed during qualifying but the pilot, the very experienced Henri Biard, survived, almost uninjured.

Britain did not compete in the 1926 race. The Air Ministry reasoning, via a report prepared by Air Vice-Marshal Sir Geoffrey

Salmond, being that British high-speed technology was incapable of producing a winning aircraft/engine combination for 1926, but could in 1927. The Air Ministry took heed, and no entry was forthcoming for the 1926 event. The French felt the same and so the contest came down to a duel between the Americans and the Italians.

Italy came to the fore in 1926, with their Macchi M.39 monoplane floatplanes with engines by Fiat. The V12 AS.2 installed in the M.39 gave 800bhp, and De Bernardi, the winner, averaged 246.5 mph for the almost fifty-three minutes that he was racing. Previously, the engines used in the Italian entries had been designed and built by Curtis and Hispano-Suiza. America fielded their tried and tested Curtis R3C biplane racers, with uprated engines, more V12s but this time built by Packard. They were reputed to be developing over 700bhp but, being down on power compared to the Fiat engines, and having the added drag of the biplane configuration, they were simply not fast enough to win.[12]

The country to hold the next race was always the one that had won the previous competition. So, it was to Venice in 1927 that the competitors went for that year's race. This time it was to be between Italy, the current champions, and Britain. America had decided that the cost of developing and running a team, some half-a-million dollars, was too much for the public purse and declined to enter, but New York Sportsmen put up $100,000 for a machine built by Kirkham and powered by a projected X-24 Packard engine to enter.[13]

The British entries were by Gloster, Short-Bristow and Supermarine; that by Gloster being a continuation of their biplane experience, called the Gloster IV and powered by a Napier Lion VIIA W-12 engine, giving some 900bhp. It was fast but the biplane configuration, which included a cranked, low-set top wing faired into the fuselage had limited visibility and, in the race proper, part of the spinner failed, and the biplane was forced to abandon the race, which was a shame at it had been running fast – around 275 mph. The Short-Bristow monoplane featured an air-cooled radial engine, the Bristol Mercury, which claimed to develop over 800bhp. Sadly, at some point it appears as if a mechanic crossed the aileron control wires over and the resulting accident in practice at Venice virtually destroyed the machine. Luckily, the pilot survived.

The Supermarine entry, designed as usual by Reginald Mitchell, was the S.5. This built upon Mitchell's previous S.4 but now had wire-braced, as against cantilever, wing construction. It handily won the race, and its sister S.5 was placed second. The Italians had the misfortune to have a fast monoplane floatplane, the Macchi M.52, again fitted with the Fiat AS.2 V12 engine, which had been developed from the previous year to produce a claimed over 900hp. Sadly, the engine developers went too far in their planning, fitting pistons made of magnesium and this lightweight metal did not take kindly to the heat and pressures that it was subjected to and both Italian entries were forced to retire in the race with melted pistons. The Kirkham entry failed to materialise, as troubles with the bearings of the Packard X-24 were too great at the time to be overcome.

Now that the next race in 1929 was to be held at Calshot, in Britain, near to Southend, the advantage would appear to have been passed to Britain, but where the finances were concerned, it was a different matter. Trenchard was now against having RAF personnel take part in the competition, his argument seemingly built around the 'star' treatment that the pilots of the RAF High Speed Flight were receiving in the press. Winston Churchill was now Chancellor of the Exchequer and despite having previously been against public money being used to pay for the British entries, he now saw the technological value of the competition and instructed Trenchard to keep the High Speed Flight intact.[14]

Mitchell, of Supermarine, had recognised that the Napier Lion 'Broad Arrow' W-12 engine was at the end of its development and that a new, more powerful engine was needed for his next design, the S.6.

In June 1927, Rolls-Royce started working on a larger version of the Kestrel, called the Buzzard, to be fitted into Supermarine's S.6.

This large V12 engine had a capacity of 36.7 litres and was intended to power large passenger and freight-carrying aircraft. Only fifty were built and sold but in 1928, Rolls-Royce started to develop the Buzzard, now called the 'R', as a racing engine of 35 litres capacity for Supermarine's current Schneider Trophy racing aircraft, the S.5 floatplane.

With Ellor designing the double-sided compressor of this redesigned engine, a power output of 1,900hp at 2,900rpm was achieved by May 1929. By September, the R could manage this power output for an hour, when fuelled with a mixture of 22 per cent Romanian petrol/gasoline, 78 per cent benzol and a small quantity of Tetraethyl lead. Weight of the 'R' was given as 1,530 pounds. With this engine in the Supermarine S.6 floatplane, Britain won the Schneider Trophy in 1929. The Napier Lion powered S.5, now giving 875bhp, was third, behind the second-placed Italian entry, a Macchi M.52R (still using a Fiat AS engine, now the AS.3) which gave a claimed 1,000bhp.

After the race concluded, George Stainforth, one of the RAF High Speed Flight's pilots made an attempt at the world speed record for aircraft and won it with the Gloster Mk VI, posting an average speed over four runs of 336.3 mph. Sadly for him, one of his companions, Squadron Leader A.H. Orlebar, then took the Supermarine S.6 out for an attempt at the record and handily beat Stainforth's speed, posting an average of 355.8 mph.

The French also prepared entries in 1929, the Bernard company proposing the HV.47, to be powered by a Hispano-Suiza W18, called the R18 and giving 1,500hp. It was completed too late, the engines arriving at the Bernard factory months after the 1929 race took place.

The Italians prepared new aircraft and engines for the race. They hedged their bets, producing the Macchi M.67, with an Isotta-Fraschini W-18 engine and the Fiat C.29, which although appearing at the race, did not take part. An M.52R did fly though, in the race itself.

Gloster produced their first monoplane floatplane, the Mk VI, which was a beautiful looking Napier Lion-powered aircraft. It did not start the race, having failed to qualify through problems with the carburettors and being classified as a 'reserve'.

The Rolls-Royce R engine was used again in 1931, at the last Schneider Trophy race, in the Supermarine S.6B.

Once again, Trenchard showed that he simply did not understand the public mood, the Schneider Trophy races now being the single 'must see' event of the sporting year in Britain. He refused to allow the RAF to take part and no money would be forthcoming for the event from the Chancellor of the Exchequer, as the British Government, so soon after the Wall Street Crash of 1929, refused to give taxpayers' money to the project. However, the Labour Prime Minister, Ramsey McDonald, did say that if £100,000 could be found from the private purse, he would instruct the RAF to operate the High Speed Flight at the race. It was left to Lady Houston, a fervent supporter of Britain and of flying in general. Houston had started her professional career as a dancer and had then 'married well' and become the publisher of a right-wing newspaper, as well as becoming a suffragette and philanthropist. She donated the £100,000 needed, thus wiping out a debt owed by her late husband to the British taxpayers.

For Italy, Mario Castoldi designed, and had Macchi build, the MC.72, which was fitted with a revolutionary V-24 engine, which was effectively two Fiat AS.5 V-12 engines, linked together and developing some 2,500hp driving contra-rotating propellers, to cancel out the dreaded swing on take-off that such torque, driving a normal propeller, would create. Although a good idea, the prototype was plagued with backfires caused by pulses in the long inlet manifold and despite all their best efforts, the Italians were forced to pull out of the race. They did, however, later set a world speed record of some 440 mph, the highest recorded speed for a propeller-driven floatplane before the war. The French also withdrew from the contest, citing a lack of time to prepare their machines. And so it was left to the three British machines entered,

Supermarine S.6 number N.248 and two S.6Bs, N.1595 and N.1596, to complete virtually a demonstration run and for Britain to retain the Trophy in perpetuity.[15]

Developed still further than its 1929 specification, the Rolls-Royce 'R' engine gave 2,350hp for an hour on a slightly different fuel specification and the trophy was won by Britain outright at 340.1 mph. A little later in the day, its sister S.6B set a world speed record of 379.1 mph. Of course, all the time that the 'R' had increased in power, it was continuously being developed parts-wise to take the enormous pressures that were being exerted within its crankcase. It was later used as a basis for the Rolls-Royce Griffon V12 engine, which powered the Spitfire Mk XIV when that fighter was introduced into RAF squadron service in 1943.[16]

By 1930, Hugh Dowding had become the member for supply and research on the RAF's Air Staff. It was he who investigated the need for more advanced monoplane fighter aircraft in the interceptor role than the biplanes then in current use in Britain. After all, if the bomber was always supposed to get through, as the High Command at the Air Ministry believed, a faster fighter than those already in service with the RAF was going to be a necessity…

In 1937 and 1938, as AOC Fighter Command, Hugh Dowding oversaw the introduction of the Hawker Hurricane and the Supermarine Spitfire, into RAF service and which were the RAF's first monoplane fighters of the 1930s. Dowding was a practical man, not given to vague theories. He believed in technology above all else and wrote about the then prevalent 'fear of the bomber':

> The best defence for the country is fear of the fighter. If we are strong in fighters, we should probably be attacked and in force. If we are moderately strong, we shall probably never be attacked, or we shall probably be attacked and the attack will be brought to a standstill. If we are weak in fighter strength the attacks will not be

brought to a standstill, and the productive capacity of the country will be virtually destroyed.

The first Spitfires' and Hurricanes' performance, when introduced into service in the late 1930s, and for quite a long time thereafter was greater than any of the bombers of the period, exceeding 300 mph.[17]

At this time, as Bill Gunston wrote in his book *The Development of Piston Aero Engines*:

> In the 1930s, the official view of the RAF was that quality was everything. Better aircraft, it was held, would 'slice through enemy formations like a knife through butter'. That is a natural viewpoint to adopt if your quantity is non-existent.[18]

Only the Hawker Fury biplane, of the previous generation of fighters, with its Rolls-Royce Kestrel engine, exceeded 200 mph – reaching 223 mph, which stood as the fastest speed obtained by a British fighter until the advent of the Gloster Gladiator (introduced into squadron service in 1937) which could reach 253 mph. The Gladiator's service ceiling was 32,800ft. The British biplane fighters of the 1930s (Gloster Gauntlet, Hawker Fury, Bristol Bulldog, Gloster Gladiator) had two, or at the most four .303 machine-guns as their main armament.[19] The two new British monoplane fighters had eight .303 Colt machine-guns as their armament, four in each wing.[20]

Of note during the inter-war period is the development of the fighter, due to design changes and development of them. Nowhere was this more apparent than in the development of engines. In 1903, the four-cylinder engine, which powered the Wright Brother's 'Flyer' at Kittyhawk had developed between 8–10bhp; fifteen years later, in 1918, the best engines powering fighters were developing close to 200bhp. In the subsequent fifteen years engines were developed which, by 1933, were developing 2,350bhp. Now granted that these were pure 'sprint' racing engines, but by 1937, just four years later, the early production Rolls-Royce Merlin V12 engines were developing, in reliable, service trim, over 1,000bhp.

In that same year, the new Messerschmitt Bf 109B went into Luftwaffe service and saw action in the Spanish Civil War. This new monoplane fighter could attain 292 mph, and reach 31,200ft. This new Messerschmitt was directly related to its predecessor, the Bf 108 Taifun. 'Bf' stood for Bayerische Flugzewerke, or 'Bavarian aviation factory', of which Willy Messerschmitt was the chief designer. His head of the drawing office was one Walter Rethel, who drew out the practical solutions of Willi Messerschmitt's fertile brain. The Taifun was a four-seater monoplane and would be used as a communications aircraft between the Luftwaffe staffeln during the war, a military trainer and a private touring aircraft. Its engine was of only some 220–270hp, yet with this the new Bf 108 produced outstanding performance due to its lightness.

Bayerische Flugzewerke, along with Heinkel, Arado and Focke-Wulf, were invited in 1934 to tender designs for a new, high-speed fighter, using the Junkers Jumo 210 V12 engine of 610hp but only Focke-Wulf was able to get hold of one of these new engines, the other three using, ironically, the British Rolls-Royce Kestrel V12.

The Messerschmitt design proved to be the best performing aircraft of the four tested, with the Heinkel He 112 only just behind it in terms of performance. The RLM ordered ten more development prototype from each company.

Technically, the new low-wing fighter from Bayerische Flugzewerke was a stressed-skin monoplane with only the high-mounted tailplane requiring bracing struts underneath, attaching to the fuselage. The wing itself consisted of one box spar, with leading and trailing spars, the whole covered in aluminium. Leading edge slats were used to help slow speed manoeuvrability. It was a clever design, using the profile of an inverted V12 engine to help shape a fuselage that was narrow towards the top, where the pilot's head would be, and wide right behind the engine, to give strong mountings for the wing attachment and undercarriage mounting points.

The first of the developed Bf 109s took to the air in January 1936, now fitted with a Jumo 210a V12 engine of 610hp, inverted in the way of most German liquid-cooled engines. The Kestrel engine had been mounted in the upright position.

Armament was first of all two 7.92mm machine-guns fitted ahead of the cockpit and synchronised to fire through the airscrew, shades of the First World War fighter armament. This was swiftly augmented first of all by another 7.92mm MG17 firing through the hollow prop shaft, then with a 15mm, later a 20mm, cannon mounted in the same way, but with strengthened mountings. The 'V' series of Bf 109s were all tested in 1937 and the Bf 109 V12 and V13 had the new Daimler-Benz DB600A engine giving 960hp; now the maximum speed of the two machine-guns and one cannon-armed fighter reached 323 mph and it could climb to 31,170ft. Throughout its long career, the Bf 109 would have a slight advantage over its enemies in having its armament mainly in the nose, giving a 'straight ahead' shot for its pilots, while most other fighters, with their guns situated in the wings, meant that they had to be aligned to converge at a given range. The Bf 109 pilot was able to operate his guns as if he were firing a rifle on a range. Where he aimed, the shots went.

The first Bf 109 to see combat was the 'B' model of 1937, in the Spanish Civil War, on the Nationalist side. This had reverted to using the Jumo, ("Junkers Moteren"), 210E engine of 680hp. By July, there were twenty-four Bf 109B-2s of J88 of the German Condor Legion in Spain and they swiftly proved their superiority over the Russian built Polikarpov I-15 biplane and I-16 monoplane fielded by the Republican air force. In all, between 1937 and 1939, some fifty-seven Bf 109s, of the 'B' and 'C' types saw action in Spain and aces such as Mölders, Harding, Lützow, Balthazar and Galland all experienced air combat in Spain (although Galland was flying the Heinkel He 51 ground attack aircraft) and so they would start the Second World War from a position of having superior fighting experience over French and British pilots.[21]

Their main opponent on the Republican side was the Polikarpov I-16 'Mosca' (fly) or 'Rata' (rat), as it was called by the Nationalists. The I-16's pilots called it a mule; it was a stubby, radial-engine low-wing monoplane fighter with a retractable undercarriage that could reach some 273mph, so it was not that much slower than the early Bf 109s.

What turned out to be invaluable to the pilots of the Condor Legion, and later on in the Luftwaffe, was being able to formulate tactics more suited to the faster fighters in vogue at this time, compared to those of the First World War. For instance, the German pilots learned to use the 'rotte' (pair) and 'schwarme' (formation of two rottes), or 'finger-four' as they became known when adopted by British fighter pilots in 1940/41.

The Bf 109 had its problems. Probably the major one was its narrow undercarriage, which made ground handling by the pilot critical and resulted in many ground-looping incidents. The wing structure of the Bf 109 was never as strong as the Spitfire or Hurricane and the leading edge slats could snap open when nearing the stall and cause the pilot more problems, especially when turning tightly. Accidents at training schools were frequent.

Another drawback that the Bf 109 suffered from throughout almost all its career was the cramped confines of the cockpit, which prevented its pilots from using all of the available sideways movement of the control stick. In addition, the 109's cockpit canopy was a side-hinged, heavily framed affair, which made vision to the rear difficult. In an emergency, the canopy could be jettisoned, preparatory to the pilot baling out.

The Bf 109 'D' model of 1938 reverted to the Daimler-Benz engine, now the 601A, fitted with fuel injection and giving 1,000hp. This engine, coupled to a three-bladed airscrew, gave the Bf 109D a top speed of some 345 mph in service trim.[22]

Most of Germany's aircraft immediately prior to, and during the war were fitted with Bosch-built mechanical fuel injection pumps, whilst the British aircraft industry was still using carburettors. The latter did investigate the possibility of using fuel injection during the 1930s but came to the conclusion there was not one single British company capable of machining the necessary injection pumps to the tolerances required.

On 11 July 1938, Willi Messerschmitt became Chairman and Managing Director of the previously named Bayerische Flugzewerk factory, which was now renamed as 'Messerschmitt A.G.' Henceforward, all new designs would be referred to as Messerschmitt Me …, but aircraft designed before this date were still referred to as: 'Bf …'. However, the war saw the designation 'Bf 109', and 'Me 109', becoming interchangeable. Just 250 Bf 109Ds were built before they were superseded by the 109E variant in 1939, which had extra machine-guns, one in each wing, to supplement the nose armament. This was the fighter that the Allies would face in the Battle of France and of Britain.[23]

The new Hurricane and Spitfire were introduced into squadron use in 1937 and 1938 respectively. Each had eight .303 machine-guns, four in each wing, giving them a heftier punch than any previous British fighter. The British biplane fighters of the 1920s and early 1930s had used two of the now venerable Vickers machine-gun, which needed its cocking handles within the cockpit, so that a pilot might clear a jammed round. Obviously, with eight machine-guns in the wings, this was going to be impossible, so the American Colt machine-gun, which rarely jammed, was chosen to supplant the Vickers. It was made under licence in Britain by BSA in Birmingham, and was now called the Browning, being slightly larger in British service, from its previous .300 calibre in American service.

The Hurricane I's top speed was quoted as being 330 mph at 17,500ft. The Spitfire Mk I's maximum speed was 367mph, altitude not specified. Fortunately, the RAF was mainly equipped with this new breed of fighters when war was declared on 3 September 1939.[24]

The Hawker Hurricane was a logical development of the previous Hawker fighter with the RAF, the Fury biplane. Construction was very similar with a fuselage of welded tubing, with aluminium sheeting covering the forward part of the fuselage and with fabric covering aft of the cockpit. The wing (fabric-covered to begin with but later covered with aluminium), although cantilever in construction, was quite thick, which mitigated against top speed and meant that the performance fell off quickly at altitude. This was something that Hawker's next fighter, the Typhoon of 1942, also suffered from. It wasn't until the advent of the Hawker Tempest in 1944 that Hawker's design staff managed to correct this fault and then they came up with a design that had a much thinner wing, which allowed greater speed.[25]

The Spitfire, although designed in the same period by R.J. Mitchell (who had designed the Supermarine S4, S5, S6 and S6b monoplanes that took part in and won the Schneider Trophy) was a quantum leap, particularly in construction, over the Hurricane. It was also far more complicated and time-consuming to build than the Hurricane. It had a fuselage built upon the monocoque principle, with the flush-riveted stressed aluminum skin providing its strength. Its beautiful elliptic, thin wing planform gave it superb manoeuvrability. By 1941 the Hurricane was obsolete, barely able to cope with the Bf 109E and being completely outclassed by the Bf 109F, and the Fw 190. The major problem with the Spitfire was the time taken to build it, some 13,500 hours, when compared to that of a Bf 109, just 5,000, later on reduced to 4,000 hours.[26]

The Hawker Hurricane was heavier than the Spitfire at 6,610 pounds (loaded), versus the Spitfire's svelte 5,800 pounds. The Hurricane was 32ft 3in long and its wingspan was 40ft. The Spitfire's length (Mk I) was 29ft 10in with a wingspan of 36ft 10in. By contrast, the Bf 109E was smaller than either of its opponents in 1940. It was 29ft in length, with a wingspan 32ft 7in and it weighed 5,500 pounds, so was a considerably smaller and lighter aircraft than its British counterparts.

The prototype Spitfire, K5054, first flew from Eastleigh airfield, near Southampton, on 5 March 1936 and was a success from the start, although it would go through many developments during its production life, nearly all to do with the installation of successively more powerful Merlin and then Griffon engines than the previous mark. Mitchell saw the prototype fly before dying of cancer; his place at Supermarine was taken by Joe Smith, a talented development engineer.

Dowding himself visited Eastleigh on 15 March and reported back to the Secretary of State for Air, Viscount Swinton, that the Spitfire flew 'remarkably well'. On 3 June 1936, the Air Ministry placed their first order for Spitfires with Supermarine, for 310 Mk Is, which would cost the British taxpayer £1.25 million. Due to production difficulties, the order was almost cancelled, and delivery was late.

Both the Spitfire and the Hurricane were powered by the Rolls-Royce Merlin V12 engine of 27 litres. The design of the Merlin had begun in 1932.

The Rolls-Royce Merlin started life being known as the PV12 (Private Venture 12 cylinders). The Merlin was basically a scaled-up Kestrel and, despite a problematic start, when the designers departed from the original Kestrel type of head design, by July 1934 it was giving 790hp at 12,000ft and 625hp at sea level. Weight was 1177 pounds.

The Merlin engine had started off with four valves per cylinder in what was called the 'ramp head', with two of the valves per cylinder upright, as in the Kestrel but with the other two in a 45-degree configuration and this configuration didn't work well, suffering from detonation and cracking of the head. This engine gave 950hp at 11,000ft. Development went on and, in November 1936, the Merlin F, known internally as the Mk I, passed its 100-hour test for military aircraft at 890hp. Most of these early Mark 1s were fitted to the Fairey Battle single-engine day bomber. Still, this did not stop the Rolls-Royce engineers from developing the Merlin still further and on they went, changing the cylinder heads to the tried and trusted four valves in an upright position, and forsaking the 'ramp head' design of the Mark I. So fast did development of the Merlin proceed that in 1937, the designers and development engineers produced a 'sprint' engine that was intended for a record-breaking Spitfire, and which developed 1,800hp for fifteen hours at 3,200rpm with a maximum of 2,160hp if revved even higher to 3,500rpm.[27]

The Merlin II, which was fitted to the Spitfire Mk I and the Hurricane Mk I, was delivered in August 1937 and could deliver some 1,030hp in combat. These early Spitfires and Hurricanes used a two-bladed wooden propeller. The Spitfire and Hurricane Mk Is built after July 1938 featured the Merlin III, now giving up to 1,310hp and now using the constant speed propeller, either made by de Havilland or Rotol.[28]

Where German engine development was concerned, Daimler-Benz in 1937 built a highly developed version of their inverted V12 DB601 of 33.9 litres, with fuel injection to power the Messerschmitt Bf 109 V13, which took the world speed record at 379 mph. To achieve its rated power of 1,660hp, the DB601 'Rekordmotor' had its compression ratio increased to 8:1, its rpm to 2,650 and was running on a 'special brew' of fuel.

By April 1939, the engine was developing 2,770hp and it was installed in a clean little aeroplane called the Heinkel He 112U, and this claimed the world speed record at 463mph. Imagine Heinkel's chagrin when, just a month later, Flugkapitän Fritz Wendel, flying what was euphemistically named the Messerschmitt 109R, left the record at 469.22mph. This record-breaking aircraft had little to do with a Bf 109 in service at the time, being a 'one off', strictly meant to go fast but the Germans believed that having the '109' appellation would make the people at the Air Ministry worry about how fast their front-line fighters were. Indeed, as we have seen, Supermarine and Rolls-Royce had been developing both a more powerful Merlin engine and a stripped and lightened Spitfire for an attempt on the world air speed record, but gave up when they realised that they could not match the speed of the '109R'.[29]

The 'standard' DB601, weighing in at 1,452 pounds in its 'N' form would be to the Luftwaffe what the Merlin was to the RAF and there was a horsepower race between them throughout the war, each variant outstripping the other, type by type and year by year. As well as the Daimler-Benz inverted V12s, there was also the Junkers Jumo 211 and 213 of the same basic layout. All possessed cast cylinder and crankcase blocks and were cooled by a water and glycol mixture. The Daimler-Benz engines had four valves per cylinder, while the Junkers engines had three. They all possessed Bosch-made fuel injection, as opposed to the carburettors used on British engines. When a Bf 109 dived away from a Spitfire in 1940, the Merlin engine in the Spitfire would cut out under negative G and the aircraft would be unable to follow the fleeing 109, unless it half-rolled onto its back first, thus losing even more initial distance to the fleeing 109.[30]

Fortunately for Britain, there worked at the Royal Aircraft Establishment at Farnborough a lady engineer, Miss Beatrice Shilling, who had raced motorcycles at Brooklands before the war. She designed a small restrictor to fit inside the Merlin's carburettor float, which prevented the fuel from being drawn away from the fuel inlet under negative G. Known as 'Miss Shilling's orifice', it cured the problem. From March 1941 Spitfires were fitted with this modification in the field, sometimes by Miss Shilling herself, who would arrive at a front-line airfield on her racing motorbike, suitably de-tuned for the road, with the necessary tools on board.[31]

The other engine worthy of note on the German side was the air-cooled radial BMW 801 (a radial engine has its cylinders grouped around the crankshaft, as against an in-line engine, which had its cylinders grouped behind one another longitudinally), and which powered the Fw 190, when that fighter was introduced into service in August 1941. This engine had started out as a fresh design, following that of the radial BMW 132, which had in turn been based upon the

American-made Pratt and Whitney Hornet, for which BMW had taken out a licence to produce in Germany in the 1930s.

The BMW 139, as it was known, of 54.44 litres, powered the prototype Fw 190 that first flew in January 1939, but then BMW redesigned the engine to become the BMW 801 of 41.8 litres. Even though the 801 had to go through several different versions, with different cooling and engine mountings, it swiftly became a formidable power unit, particularly when used in either the Fw 190, or the Junkers Ju88. When this latter aircraft in night-fighter form, was re-equipped with the 801, from Junkers Jumo liquid-cooled V12 form, it reached a claimed 404 mph. However, the engine did weigh 3,960 pounds. Although at first glance this appears so much more than any of the contemporary liquid-cooled engines, all their associated radiators, header tanks and cooling lines weight would need to be added on to their bare weight in order to get a fair comparison.[32]

In their turn, the British built some very good air-cooled radial engines during the Second World War, specifically those designed and built by the Bristol Company. Their sleeve-valved two-row Hercules engines powered multiple British bombers, including the Wellington, Stirling, Halifax and Lancaster, and the company's own Beaufort and Beaufighter. But strangely, where fighters were concerned, Bristol had little input until the even larger Centaurus was designed and developed; that powered a version of the Tempest, the Mk V, in 1944 and its seagoing cousin, the Sea Fury. It was rated at 2,500hp.[33]

Russia lagged behind Britain and Germany in aero-engine design in the lead up to the Second World War. Where liquid-cooled V12s were concerned, Andre Mikulin built a licence production version of the BMW V1 and developed this 44.66-litre engine through the years, using twin overhead camshafts per bank operating on four valves per cylinder. Supercharged, this engine, which powered the revered Ilyushin IL-2 'Sturmovik' ground attack aircraft in its AM-38 form, gave some 1,782hp. In summary, they were large and somewhat overweight, but worked reliably and well, particularly in the cold of the Eastern Front.[34]

Recognising that Britain had few defences against incoming raids by day or night, British scientists, led by Robert Watson-Watt, invented 'Radio Direction Finding', or RDF for short, which became known as Radar. In the 1930s, Dowding saw that the new RDF (Radar) system was what was needed to detect incoming raids by enemy bombers, by both day and night. In daytime, bomber/bombers could be detected either forming up over France or on the way across the Channel by the new 'chain home' system, which consisted of radar masts constructed and positioned around the British coast. These masts sent signals to a plotting room, where the plot of the incoming attack was shown by WAAF operatives moving indicators across an enormous map which showed the number of aircraft, plus their altitude and heading, in the incoming raid. These plotting rooms were situated at the various Group Headquarters, who would then decide which fighter squadrons/ wings would intercept the incoming raid.

The group controller in the appropriate section then took that information and vectored the intercepting fighters to attack the bombers. However, it was not until mid-1941 that the system started to be used fully by the RAF by night as well as by day. It took until then for the airborne radar (AI) when mounted in an aircraft to work effectively, and that was when radar equipped Beaufighter night fighters started to take a toll on the German bombers carrying out the nightly raids known as the Blitz, which were occurring over Britain on most nights in the early part of 1941.[35]

The new German Luftwaffe, formed in the early 1930s, had a completely different strategy from Britain in case of war, in how to use their aircraft in any foreseeable conflict. Not for them strategic bombing as favoured by the British, at least not until it was really too late in the war for them to develop and manufacture a strategic bomber in any numbers in a Germany constantly under attack by the British and American bombers.

No, the Luftwaffe's purpose was supporting the Heer, the ground troops. To this end, they developed the dive-bomber for pinpoint bombing accuracy. Ernst Udet, the minister in charge of aircraft production of the Luftwaffe before the outbreak of war in 1939, was a great proponent of this, having visited America and watched their Curtis Helldivers practising in the early 1930s. Udet was the guiding force behind the introduction of the Junkers Ju 87 Stuka dive bomber. In fact, so obsessed did the Germans become with the idea of dive bombing, they stipulated that every one of their bombers had to be strong enough to carry out dive bombing, even the twin-engine Junkers Ju 88, which turned out to be perhaps the best of all the German 'twins', being not only a fast medium bomber but also a night-fighter, night-intruder, long-range fighter, and even being used for reconnaissance missions.

The Germans produced a plethora of twin-engine medium bombers, such as the Heinkel He 111, the Dornier Do 17 and the aforementioned Ju 88 in the 1930s, all twin-engine monoplanes. With these, the Germans expected to be able to blast any impediments to the German army, such as tanks, artillery emplacements and troops out of the way of the Wehrmacht's advance. Initially, of course, they succeeded. In Poland and then France and the Low Countries, the siren-equipped Stukas destroyed all opposition to Germany's ground forces, while the Luftwaffe's medium bombers attacked the populace in the cities and towns, forcing their population to join the growing throngs of refugees, who blocked the roads and further held up the defending armies. Until the Battle of Britain, the German strategy succeeded, but when their Panzers came to the Channel coast, matters changed.[36]

During the 1930s, the RAF appeared to have forgotten all the lessons learned in air fighting in the First World War. Their commanders at this time thought that their fighters would only be attacking formations of bombers, with German fighters not having the range to escort the bombers to the target.

Therefore, they instituted tight 'Vic' formations, each of three aircraft, tasked with holding formation as they attacked the bombers and then all three aircraft firing their guns at their leader's command, with their eight guns synchronised for their fire to meet at 400 yards range. Fortunately, by the time the Battle of France was in progress in May/June 1940, RAF pilots realised that this type of formation flying in battle was impractical and they started taking note of what the German pilots, with their experience of battle during the Spanish Civil War, were doing; consequently, their guns were resynchronised so that their bullets now converged at 250 yards.[37]

Chapter 3

1940

The good fighters of old put themselves beyond the possibility of defeat, and then waited for an opportunity of defeating the enemy.

Sun Tzu

The real start of the Second World War in the air and on the ground in Western Europe came on 10 May 1940, when the Germans invaded France, Belgium and Holland, known collectively as 'the Low Countries', thus ending what had come to be known as the 'Phoney War', which had started when Britain and France declared war on Germany on 3 September 1939.

In the next eight months, little of note militarily happened, except that German forces invaded and occupied Norway, needing the iron ore that that country could supply for her war munitions. The British, who had hoped to forestall them, were summarily ejected. The French army had advanced to take up position on the border between France and Germany but were halted by the Wehrmacht and went no further, while a British Expeditionary Force, as in the First World War, had taken up positions in France and then sat to await further orders. The Royal Navy resumed their blockade of Germany, as they had in the previous war.

So fast and successful were the German armoured columns' assaults on Belgium and France in May and June, that their forces reached the Channel coast within a month and the British were extremely fortunate to be able to repatriate over 300,000 of their, and their allies', soldiers back to Britain, mainly through Dunkirk. But they left all their heavy weapons, their tanks and artillery behind them in France, for the Germans to do with as they pleased. Many of the French and British tanks were dismantled for various parts for the Wehrmacht to use, particularly in their forthcoming self-propelled artillery and anti-tank guns.

After the evacuation of Dunkirk in June 1940 there was a short lull in the fighting during which Hitler attempted to make peace with Britain, which Churchill and his War Cabinet spurned.

In the air, the Luftwaffe had proved all-conquering, its dive-bombing Junkers Ju 87 Stukas, as intended, blasting all opposition to the German army spearheads out of their way. Their medium bombers, Dornier Do 17s, Heinkel He 111s and the newly introduced Junkers Ju 88s, droned over France with virtual impunity, French and British fighter defences were almost cursorily dismissed by the German Bf 109E fighters, either escorting the bombers, or on 'Frei Jagd' (Free Hunt) missions.[1]

The British had sent a few squadrons of Hawker Hurricane fighters and Fairey Battle day-bombers to France to oppose the Luftwaffe but their pilots and crews were almost completely overwhelmed by the speed and ferocity of their attackers. The French air force did not have enough modern fighter aircraft to give much more than token resistance to the Luftwaffe. The Fairey Battles, in particular, intended to be used as light day bombers, suffered horrendous losses; 100 per cent on 11 May alone, for example. At the end of the French campaign, those few that were left were relegated to operations by night.[2]

Although believing the strategic bomber would be its main effort in bringing an enemy to its knees, before the war the RAF seems not to have considered using aircraft to support the ground operations of the army very much, if at all. In fact, it was only when they realised the shattering effect that the German Junkers Ju 87s had had in the campaigns in Poland and France that Britain began belatedly to equip Hurricanes and American supplied P-40s with under-fuselage and wing bomb racks, so that they could be used as Army Co-operation machines, particularly in the Western Desert.[3]

French airfields were bombed and strafed; inexperienced fighter pilots were shot down by experienced German fighter pilots in their Bf 109s. The French government cried out for more RAF fighter squadrons to be sent to their aid in their faltering defence against Germany, but Britain could not afford to lose more aircraft.

The men in control of Fighter Command, in particular Air Chief Marshal Dowding, as Air Officer Commanding (AOC) Fighter Command, saw that he would need to conserve every fighter aircraft that he had available, both Spitfires and Hurricanes, for the forthcoming Battle of Britain that would clearly be the next battle to be fought when France fell.

Fortunately for Britain, Dowding's view won the argument, even though the country's new Prime Minister, Winston Churchill, had wanted to let the French have more British fighters, particularly Spitfires, for their defence. When granted permission to address the War Cabinet in May 1940, Dowding managed to convince Churchill that the RAF's fighter squadrons could not afford to lose many more fighters, as they would be needed to face the German bombers when it came to Britain's turn to be attacked.

Dowding presented a graph which showed the rate of losses that Hurricanes in France were suffering. He pointed out to the War Cabinet, and particularly to Churchill, that Britain could not afford to send more fighters to France without depleting her own defences. He persuaded Churchill that Fighter Command could initiate patrols from English-based fighters over the beaches at Dunkirk and Calais, to intercept the German bombers, who were even then trying to prevent the evacuation of the British army from France, and that is what happened. For the first time, the German fighter pilots, in their Bf 109Es, met the Spitfire in combat and found it to be a much tougher enemy than the French-based Hurricanes or French fighters had been.[4]

When first delivered most Spitfires and Hurricanes had two-bladed, fixed-pitch wooden airscrews. By May 1939 these had been replaced by two-pitch three-bladed de Havilland airscrews, with Hurricane squadrons being the first to be equipped with these new propellers.[5]

During June and July 1940, most of the Spitfires and Hurricanes of Fighter Command were converted from these de Havilland airscrews to the constant speed de Havilland/Rotol propeller, which increased a Spitfire Mk I's climb rate by 730 ft/minute. Not only that, but the Rotol constant speed propeller also gave a shorter take-off distance, as well as giving the Spitfire Mk I a faster climb to a higher ceiling than previously. Apparently, the new propeller also gave the Spitfire increased manoeuvrability and greater endurance. By June 1940, all the fighters in Britain had been converted thus giving them some useful extra performance.[6]

The hydraulically operated Rotol three-bladed metal constant speed airscrew became a standard fitting on Spitfires and Hurricanes just in time for the Battle of Britain. It worked by allowing the pilot to select the rpm that suited his engine by movement of the throttle lever, and this automatically changed the pitch of the propeller blades to suit the engine's rpm, thus freeing the pilot from having to remember to make those changes manually which – especially in the heat of combat – was not an easy task, particularly to a beginner. Rotol was a company founded by both Rolls-Royce and Bristol, hence the name. Rolls-Royce now supplied an engine for the Spitfire and Hurricane to accept the new variable-pitch propellers, the Merlin Mk III (although this wasn't strictly necessary to have the constant speed propellers fitted) which had the oilways to provide the hydraulic pressure to operate the variable pitch mechanism.

Germany then threw its bombers by day against Britain and, from July to October, the Battle of Britain was fought. For the first time, the German military might in the air was defeated. Using radar detection to see the German bombers forming up over France, Fighter Command HQ were able to vector the Spitfires and Hurricanes of 11 Group, commanded by Keith Park, guarding the South East, and sometimes 12 Group, commanded by Trafford

Leigh-Mallory guarding the Midlands, into positions from where they could strike the massed bombers and their fighter escorts of Messerschmitt Bf 109Es.[7]

The Battle of Britain officially started on 10 July 1940. 'Luftschlacht am England' was intended to bring the British Government to sue for a negotiated peace. After the Luftwaffe's presumed success in bombing raids, Operation *Sea Lion* was intended to bring the Wehrmacht across the Channel in barges, which were commandeered from all over occupied Europe and brought to French ports, where in turn they were subjected to bombing raids by British night bombers.

The first bombing raid on Britain itself took place on 28 July. At the beginning of the battle, the Luftwaffe attacked shipping in the Channel but then, on 12 August, turned to bombing Fighter Command's airfields. It was during this time that the Junkers Ju 87, so dominant in previous campaigns of the Luftwaffe, was first faced by modern fighter aircraft and suffered severe losses, leading it to be withdrawn, as the British Fairey Battle had been in the French campaign.

The first few Spitfire Mk IIs, designated as such to differentiate them from the previous Mark Is, which had been built by Vickers-Supermarine, were built in June 1940 at the new shadow factory at Castle Bromwich and were introduced into squadron service on 16 August 1940. The engine in the Mark II was now the Merlin XII, which had its supercharger uprated to +9lbs, instead of +6 ¼lbs of the previous Merlin Mk II/III. It gave some 190 more hp than the previous Mark of Merlin, 1,175. A larger spinner was needed to encompass the mechanism of the Rotol three bladed propeller, now of 10' 9" diameter.[8]

Thus equipped, the service ceiling of a Spitfire went up by 4,000ft and the Mk II was faster than the Mk I below 17,000ft. Climb rate of the Mk II was superior to the Mk I also, at seven minutes to 20,000ft. Many pilots who flew the Mk II and later Marks of Spitfire, such as the Mk V and Mk IX rated the handling of the Mk II as the best of all the various Marks. It started reaching the squadrons of 11 Group in numbers in August 1940.

The Luftwaffe was winning the battle by bombing and strafing the RAF's fighter airfields when, a few days after the German attacks on fighter airfields had begun, a small British bomber force of just ninety-one aircraft managed to get through to Berlin on the night of 25 August. Hitler was so enraged by this that he ordered Göring to switch his bombers to raiding London and therefore took the pressure off the airfields. The first big raids on British cities began on 7 September, thus giving the airfields time to recover from the bombing and strafing that had been inflicted on them. This was the crucial move of the battle; it is probable that, had the Germans carried on bombing the airfields, Fighter Command would have been completely crippled within a few weeks.[9]

However, little attention by historians has been given to the fact that the Royal Navy was superior, certainly in numbers, to the Kreigsmarine (German Navy) in capital ships. Therefore, even if the Germans had gained air superiority over the Channel, it is doubtful that the barges carrying German soldiers in an invasion attempt would have been left to make their voyage in peace, despite the attentions of the Luftwaffe. There is also the fact that RAF Bomber Command, by night, had carried out extensive bombing of the barges meant to carry the Wehrmacht over the Channel, now assembled in French ports, destroying many of them.

Comparisons Of The Spitfire Versus The BF 109E

Jeffrey Quill, Chief Test Pilot for Supermarine, who flew with the RAF in combat during the Battle of Britain, compared the Bf 109E to the Spitfire I as follows:

> My experience in fighting against the Bf 109E in a Spitfire
> Mk. I was mostly around or above 20,000ft and led me to
> the conclusion that the Spitfire was slightly superior both
> in speed and rate of climb, that it was a more 'slippery' or

lower drag aeroplane, and that it was outstandingly better in a turning circle.

In October 1940 I flew a captured Me 109E; to my surprise and relief I found the aileron control of the German fighter every bit as bad – if not worse – at high speed as that of the Spitfire I and II with fabric-covered ailerons. They were good at low and medium speed, but at 400 mph and above they were almost immovable. I thought the Me 109E performed well, particularly on the climb at altitude, and it had good stalling characteristics under g, except that the leading-edge slats kept snapping in and out. But it had no rudder trimmer – which gave it a heavy footload at high speed – while the cockpit, the canopy and the rearward vision were much worse than in the Spitfire. Had I flown the Me 109 earlier I would have treated the aeroplane with less respect in combat.[10]

An article in *Flight* magazine on 5 February 1942 detailed the flight tests of a captured Bf 109E. The article praised the aircraft's behaviour at altitude, maximum height being given as 37,500ft and also said that the 109 had 'an excellent rate of climb'. The author particularly mentioned the steep angle of climb that the 109E could adopt. It also praised the aircraft's short take-off and the fact that the engine did not cut out when negative G was used, as in a dive. Landing was called 'somewhat tricky' and the article said that the controls had excellent response and feel at low speeds, but were much too heavy 'for manoeuvring at high speed'. The report also described how the ailerons were connected to the flaps, such that the ailerons drooped by eleven degrees when the flaps were lowered. *Flight* reported that this interconnection was not present on the later Bf 109F.

The article described the cockpit as 'too cramped for comfort. It is too narrow, has insufficient headroom and a tiring seating position.

The cramped position seriously restricts the force, which the pilot can exert on the control column, particularly in the lateral direction for aileron operation.' It praised the positioning of the control column, but thought that the lack of fore and aft adjustment of the rudder pedals was 'a bad feature'.

Where the engine controls were concerned, *Flight* were impressed by the 'extreme simplicity afforded by the degree of automaticity achieved. Thus, the throttle arrangements comprise only a single lever with no gate or over-ride.' Fuel mixture, supercharger speed, coolant and oil temperature were all controlled automatically and some versions of the Bf 109E had an automatic propeller pitch control installed while some versions had a manual control for this. Aircraft weight was given as 6,090 pounds and maximum speed was given as 365 mph with the rpm gauge indicating 2,600rpm at 20,000ft. This compares with the factory figures, which in 1938 gave the Bf 109E a maximum speed of 358 mph at 15,800ft.

Although the intercepting Spitfires Mk Is and IIs could not usually climb high enough to get above the escorting Messerschmitt Bf 109s they could usually hold them off because their performance equalled, if not surpassed, the Bf 109Es, while the slower Hurricanes tackled the bombers. By this stage of the war, both the British and the Germans were using reflector gunsights which helped their gunnery, although Adolf Galland, an ace with JG 26 'Schlageter', at one time tried using a telescopic sight in his Bf 109E, but he found it unsatisfactory and reverted to his previous Revi reflector sight.[11]

Captain Eric 'Winkle' Brown was a test pilot in the Royal Navy and probably flew more captured German aircraft than anyone else in Britain. He tested a Bf 109E-3, that had landed in France in November 1939 and here are some of his observations:

> From the handling viewpoint, the 109E had two pluses
> and four minuses. On the credit side, it had a steep angle

of climbing that made it difficult to follow, and it could also bunt into a dive without its direct-injection engine cutting out under negative G, thus leaving a pursuing British fighter behind, as its carburettor-fed engine faltered. On the downside the 109 had poor harmony of control: no rudder trimmer, which meant that it was easy to inadvertently pick up skid and ruin ones sighting aim; in tight turns, the slats snatched open, giving lateral twitching and again ruining the pilot's aim. Finally, when the speed was allowed to build up rapidly in a dive, the elevators became increasingly heavy until at 440 mph, they became virtually immovable.

The cockpit was claustrophobic in the extreme, as it was small and was closed by a cumbersome hood that was quite difficult to open from the inside. Once the 109 was airborne, the main wheels retracted quickly but the electrically actuated airscrew pitch changing was slow. The flaps were raised manually by means of the outer of two concentrically mounted wheels to the pilot's left; the inner wheel adjusted the tailplane incidence. Thus the wheels could be moved simultaneously to counteract the trim change as the flaps came up. Stability proved excellent in the longitudinal and lateral planes and was almost neutral directionally.

Control harmony was poor because the rudder was light, the ailerons moderately light and the elevators extremely heavy. Control harmony in a fighter should be achieved with light ailerons, slightly heavier elevator and the rudder heaviest.[12]

Major Werner Mölders, the Commander of JG 51, tested a captured Spitfire in this period, and compared the British fighters to his own Bf 109E prior to the Battle:

It was very interesting to carry out the flight trials at Rechlin with the Spitfire and the Hurricane. Both types are very simple to fly compared to our aircraft, and childishly easy to take-off and land. The Hurricane is good-natured and turns well, but its performance is decidedly inferior to that of the Me 109. It has strong stick forces and is 'lazy' on the ailerons.

The Spitfire is one class better. It handles well, is light on the controls, faultless in the turn and has a performance approaching that of the Me 109. As a fighting aircraft, however, it is miserable. A sudden push forward on the stick will cause the motor to cut; and because the propeller has only two pitch settings (take-off and cruise) in a rapidly changing air combat situation the motor is either overspeeding or else is not being used to the full.

Mölders was obviously flying an early Mk I Spitfire, without the Rotol or de Havilland constant speed airscrew.[13]

On flying a captured Spitfire Mk II, Oberleutnant Hans Schmoller-Haldy of JG 54 commented:

My first impression was that it had a beautiful engine. It purred. The engine of the Messerschmitt 109 was very loud. Also the Spitfire was easier to fly, and to land than the Me 109. The 109 was unforgiving of any inattention. I felt familiar with the Spitfire from the start. That was my first and lasting impression. But with my experience with the 109, I personally would not have traded it for a Spitfire. It gave the impression, though I did not fly the Spitfire long enough to prove it, that the 109 was the faster especially in the dive. Also I think the pilot's view was better from the 109. In the Spitfire one flew further back, a bit more over the wing.[14]

For fighter-versus-fighter combat, I thought the Spitfire was better armed than the Me 109. The cannon fitted to the 109 were not much use against enemy fighters, and the machine guns on top of the engine often suffered stoppages. The cannon were good if they hit; but their rate of fire was very low. The cannon had greater range than the machine guns. But we were always told that in a dogfight one could not hope to hit anything at ranges greater than 50 metres, it was necessary to close in to short range.[15]

Incidentally, one thing that is hardly ever mentioned in comparisons of British and German aircraft is weight of firepower. With a three-second burst, a Hurricane and Spitfire, each with eight .303 machine-guns, could deliver 10 pounds of firepower. By contrast, a Bf 109E, with its five guns in total, could deliver 18 pounds of lead in the same three-second burst.

Günther Rall, who served with III./JG 52 during the Battle of Britain, reflected on the strengths and weaknesses of the adversaries at that time:

The elliptical wings of the Spitfires had fantastic characteristics, great lift. They were very manoeuvrable. We couldn't catch them in a steep climb. On the other hand they could stall during inverted manoeuvres, cutting off the fuel because the force of gravity prevented the flow of fuel. But they were still a highly respected enemy. In contrast, our Bf 109s had shortcomings. I didn't like the slats and our cockpits were very narrow, with restricted rear visibility. Fighter pilots need a good all-round field of vision and we didn't have it.[16]

Oberleutnant Gerhard Schöpfel, Gruppenkommandeur of III./JG 26, wrote the following regarding the Bf 109 E:

It was superior to the Hurricane above 6,000 metres, faster than the Spitfire also. I believe that our armament was the better, it was located more centrally which made for more accurate shooting. On the other hand, the British fighters could turn tighter than we could. Also I felt that the Messerschmitt was not as strong as the British fighters and could not take so much punishment.[17]

Adolf Galland wrote of the match-up that 'the Bf-109 was superior in the attack and not so suitable for purely defensive purposes as the Spitfire, which although a little slower, was much more manouevrable'.[18] Hugh Dundas thought the antagonists to be evenly matched:

There is no doubt that Goering and his commanders overrated the effectiveness of their fighters in relation to our own. In fact the Messerschmitt 109 and the Spitfire were extraordinarily evenly matched. Their duel for supremacy lasted throughout the war, as each plane was constantly improved and given increased power and performance. At times the Germans, by rushing out a new version before our own next improvement was ready, would get one jump ahead. At other times the advantage would be to the RAF. But on balance the Spitfire was, I believe, slightly the better aircraft. And so it was in 1940. In particular, such advantages as it enjoyed over the Me 109 at the time were enhanced by the circumstances of the battle.[19]

Leutnant Max-Hellmuth Ostermann of 7./JG 54 wrote the following in his diary for 31 August 1940:

Utter exhaustion from the English operations has set in. Once more I lost contact with my squadron. The Spitfires showed themselves wonderfully manoeuvrable. Their aerobatics display – looping and rolling, opening fire in a climbing roll – filled us with amazement. I did no shooting but kept trying to get into position, meanwhile keeping a sharp watch on my tail.[20]

A word here about the actual flying of a Spitfire (or a Hurricane). Before 1940, not only did the British pilots have to worry about the throttle position, where the engine rpm was concerned in the early Spitfires (and Hurricanes), but also about the airscrew control, whether it was in fine or coarse pitch, before 1940. The Rotol constant pitch airscrew, introduced in mid-1940 alleviated this problem, to a great extent.

The German fighter pilots in their Bf 109Es also had to think about using their engine and airscrew controls, all this as well as actually flying the aircraft. In the Bf 109E, there was a propeller pitch control situated close to the throttle control on the left-hand side of the cockpit, giving the pilot control over the pitch. Being able to fly (and fight) the aircraft without thinking about where the engine and airscrew controls should be, only came with the experience of many flying hours. At the height of the Battle of Britain, however, this luxury of time was not possible, with some British fighter pilots being allocated to squadrons with very little flying time on single-seat fighters.

Fuels Used by Both Sides in The Battle of Britain

During 1940, 100 octane fuel, developed by Dr Bill Sweeney for Esso became available to RAF fighter squadrons, replacing the previous 87 octane fuel used. With this came an increase in the boost pressure of the Merlin's supercharger to 12 lbs/sq. inch, which was available for five minutes, the engine now giving some 1,310hp from its 27 litres at 9,000ft.

In comparison, the DB601A engine used in the Bf 109E gave some 1,036hp from its 33.9 litres at 5,250ft, but the Bf 109 was slightly smaller and lighter than the Spitfire, so performance was broadly similar. However, numerous tests by several agencies in Britain, America, Switzerland (!), France and Germany broadly agreed that maximum speed of the Spitfire 1 and II at circa 16,000ft was in the 360 mph range, while that of the Bf 109E was around 340 mph plus. Certainly, most RAF pilots who flew Spitfires in the Battle of Britain felt that their aircraft was faster, especially in the climb, than a Bf 109E. The Bf 109E used a three bladed, variable pitch aluminium propeller, whose pitch, as we have seen, was manually controlled by the pilot. It was in this configuration that Spitfires and Bf 109Es first met each other in combat in May 1940, over the Dunkirk beaches.

Pilot Officer Art Donahue's account of using +12 boost during his first combat of 5 August 1940, while flying Spitfires with 64 Squadron out of Kenley, is typical:

> 'There are bandits approaching from the north.' In quick response to this information, our leader sang out a command: 'All Tiger aircraft, full throttle! Full throttle!' That meant to use the emergency throttle that gave extra power to our engines. I was flying in our leader's section, on his left. As he gave the command 'full throttle', his plane started to draw ahead, away from me. I pushed in my emergency throttle in response to the command, the first time I had ever used it, and my engine fairly screamed with new power. I felt my plane speeding up like a high spirited horse that has been spurred.[21]

Flying Officer Hugh Dundas (later group captain) flying Spitfires with 616 Squadron out of Leconfield, in the northern part of 12 Group, wrote of scrambling to intercept Ju 88s, operating from Denmark, on 15 August 1940:

> I set a course and rammed the throttle 'through the gate', to get the maximum power output, permissible for only a very

limited time. Some of the others were ahead of me, some behind. We did not bother to wait for each other or try to form up into flights and sections. We raced individually across the coast and out to sea. About fifteen miles east of Bridlington I saw them, to the left front, and slightly below – the thin, pencil shapes of German twin-engine bombers, flying in loose, straggling, scattered formation toward the coast.[22]

Pilot Officer Ronald Berry of 603 Squadron shot down Oberleutnant Helmut Rau of I/JG 3, who was at the controls of a Me 109 E-4, on 31 August. He recorded the following in his Combat Report:

As I had no oxygen, I had to leave the squadron at 22,000ft and waited below in the sun for straggling enemy aircraft. After patrolling for thirty minutes, I saw a Me109 proceeding very fast. To overhaul him I had to press the emergency boost – indicated speed – 345. I caught the enemy aircraft off Shoeburyness. I opened fire at close range and fired all my ammunition until the enemy aircraft streamed with smoke and pancaked on the mud at Shoeburyness.

Pilot Officer Roger Hall, of 152 Squadron based at Warmwell in 10 Group, described a scramble on 4 September:

We were travelling at full throttle and climbing at nearly 3,000ft a minute in the general direction of the enemy formation, which was just visible high up above and in front of us. I could see Yellow Section in front and above us also, going at full boost. Black streams of petrol vapour were coming away from their engines. 'Better use your energy boost, Roger,' Ferdie called out to me, as he started to increase speed himself. The makers stipulated that the emergency boost must not be used for more than five consecutive minutes, but now the occasion seemed to warrant the risk. I throttled back, pushed the red half-lever forward and then opened up the main throttle again. Immediately the aircraft seemed to leap forward with a jolt, hitting me in the back as it did so, and the engine started to vibrate – black smoke pouring out of each exhaust port. The engine vibration transmitted itself to the entire aircraft and I began to appreciate the maker's instructions.[23]

German Reaction

Hermann Göring, the Commander-in-Chief of the Luftwaffe, berated his fighter pilots for not flying closer to the bombers and ordered his pilots to do so, which severely restricted their freedom to intercept the attacking Spitfires and Hurricanes.

At one point in September, when meeting with Adolf Galland and Werner Mölders, the two leading German 'experten' at the time, and also the leaders of JG 26 and JG 53 respectively, Göring asked each of them what they would like to increase their Gruppe's effectiveness, and which would improve their performance. Mölders replied that he would like some Bf 109Es, fitted with the new DB601N high compression engine. When asked the same question, Galland replied that he would like 'some Spitfires' for his geschwader. Göring was not amused, replying that: 'We have the best fighter in the world! Don't blame me!' In vain, Galland tried to tell Göring that the Spitfire could decelerate, and turn tighter than the Bf 109Es, whose main advantage over the Spitfires lay in speed and height but Göring wouldn't listen.[24]

Oberleutnant Ulrich Steinhilper of III/JG 52 flew a cannon-equipped Bf 109E-4 in October 1940 and, by this late stage of the battle, wrote:

The British have, in part, a new engine in their Spitfires and our Me can hardly keep up with it. We have also made improvements and have also some new engines, but there is no more talk of absolute superiority. The other day (12 October) we tangled with these newer Spitfires and had three losses against one success. I got into deep trouble myself and my Rottenhund (Sigi Voss) was shot down. I ended up against two Spitfires with all weapons jammed. There was no alternative but to get the hell out of it.[25]

In Germany, as in Britain at this time, the news reports were full of how many aircraft each air force was shooting down. In September, however, General Erich Quade of the Luftwaffe gave a talk on German radio about the battle. Contrary to the usual news reports in Germany, the general bestowed praise upon the Spitfire, surprising his audience, who had believed the Bf 109 to be superior. The numbers of aircraft shot down by either side that he quoted were also different from the usual newspaper reports, making many who were listening begin to doubt the information they had previously been given.

Over-claiming on both the British and the German side was already rife; for instance, on 31 August, Fighter Command lost thirty-nine aircraft, but the German Air Force claimed to have shot down 115. German losses were thirty-nine aircraft, but the RAF claimed ninety-four. It was a pattern that was to be repeated by the British fighters over France in 1941 and 1942.[26]

This over-claiming was due mainly to the excitement of a pilot in battle, particularly when new to combat. It was often difficult to see what really happened to an opponent, after a pilot could see that his ammunition was scoring hits on the enemy. Many fighter pilots would take violent evasive action, sometimes deliberately inducing a spin, or diving away, leading the attacking pilots to believe that they had scored a victory, even though they had not followed it down to see if it crashed or pulled out.

Around this time, several staffeln were equipped with the Bf 109E-4, which were fitted a rack to carry a 250kg bomb. Thus armed, they could climb for height over France, cruise over England at altitude, release their bombs (which were not usually well aimed), and then dive for home at speed, thus making them almost uncatchable.

The first 'Jabo' (Jagdbomber) raid occurred on 15 September, when twenty-two Bf 109s of II/JG 2, escorted by many 'fighter' Bf 109Es, crossed the English coast at 25,000ft, descended to 12,000ft over London, released their bombs and dived away, crossing the Channel at low altitude and maximum speed. The controllers of 11 Group were completely fooled, believing that the formation, as it had no twin-engine bombers in it, posed no danger and so had not tried to intercept it.[27]

After the daytime battle ended in defeat for the Luftwaffe on 30 October, Germany took to bombing Britain by night. Until the end of 1940 Britain had almost no defence against this tactic except by using anti-aircraft guns, which on the whole were not very effective. During December, however, the first German bomber losses from interception by British night-fighters took place. It was a start; but the Blitz only really ended when Hitler withdrew his bomber fleet to the east of Germany in preparation for his assault on Russia in June 1941.

When the Luftwaffe turned from day to night bombing in what later became known as the Blitz, Dowding and the RAF were ill-prepared to combat the raids. Dowding had already foreseen the possibility of bombing by night and had thrown his weight behind the development of the radar-equipped night fighter, but this new invention would not be ready for operational use until early in 1941 and Dowding had to accept the many criticisms that he received about this seeming neglect of Britain's defences, although he had more than enough to cope with, looking after Britain's fighter defences by daylight.

Such was the shortage of pilots in Fighter Command towards the end of the Battle of Britain, that pilots in Operational Training Units (OTUs) were declared battle-ready and operational. These were the squadrons to which recently trained pilots were sent in order to improve their flying and fighting skills, and to become battle ready so that they could then join a squadron equipped with fighters on operations.

RAF Training in 1940

Training in the RAF in 1940 had been cut down to between 130 to 150 hours from the previous 200 for a pilot, before being sent to a squadron, such was the demand for new pilots. After lessons on theory, which would include navigation, particularly needed for the pilots of single-engine fighters, a pupil pilot would then be expected to fly some twelve hours on de Havilland Tiger Moth biplanes or the Miles Magister monoplanes. He would then transition, after soloing, to an Elementary Flying Training School, where further instruction was given in stall recovery, and simply accumulating more hours of flying time, learning to turn properly, diving and climbing and level flight and, of course, landing.

Having successfully logged some fifty more hours flying time, a student now progressed to a Service Flying training school, where they now flew an advanced monoplane trainer, usually the AT-6 Texan, or, as it was known in RAF parlance, the Harvard. The Miles Master with an 870hp engine was also used in this training period. Both of these aircraft were two-seater monoplanes. After a further 120 hours of flying time, provided the student had mastered all that the Harvard or Master could do, they were judged competent to fly a Hurricane or a Spitfire.

After several hours in Spitfires and/or Hurricanes, pilots would be posted to a squadron and, as Hugh Dundas recounted about his own battle-weary squadron in October 1940:

> To set the scene I should explain that, after the daily expeditions to join the 12 Group Wing came to an end,

616 was turned temporarily into a 'C' Class squadron. That was the role given, at that time, to most squadrons in 13 Group [north of England] and also those, like ourselves, in the northern sectors of 12 Group.

It was an expedient made necessary by the grievous wastage of pilots in 11 and 10 Groups [South/South West of England]. New pilots emerging from operational training units were posted to 'C' Class squadrons in each of which was maintained a hard core of more or less experienced men who could put the newcomer through an intensive course of battle training before they were sent to fill gaps in squadrons based in the south, where the Germans kept up a certain amount of activity, mainly in the form of fighter sweeps, throughout October and November.[28]

Operational Training Units were beginning to be established by 1940 and it was there that pilots trained on Spitfires or Hurricanes, often in simulated combat scenarios. Theoretically, by the time a pilot was allocated to a squadron he should have had some 270 hours to his credit, but some pilots were still being allocated to Spitfire-equipped squadrons with only 130 hours in their logbooks. Of course, the real test came when the new pilots went into action for the first time.

After eighty-seven hours on Tiger Moth biplanes and some 100 in a Miles Magister monoplane, Air Vice-Marshal James 'Johnnie' Johnson, who became Britain's top scoring ace, recounted in his classic book *Wing Leader* his time at an OTU at Hawarden:

The unit at Hawarden had only been formed a short time before and lectures on combat tactics had not yet been devised. How we longed for this knowledge! What went on when flights of Spitfires and Messerschmitts met?

When squadron met squadron and wing encountered wing? Could the 109s turn inside us? What about their new cannon, that fired through the hub of their propeller? What happened when they hurtled down out of the sun? Were they aggressive, these pilots who had inherited the traditions of the 'Red Knight', Baron Manfred von Richthofen, of the First World War? All these, and the hundreds of other questions remained. I set off to my new squadron at Duxford with a total of two hundred and five hours flying time, including twenty-three on Spitfires. I left Hawarden with anything but a clear idea of what took place when Spitfire met Messerschmitt.[29]

Johnson also recounted that he never fired the guns on a Spitfire while at the OTU. In *One of the Few*, Johnny Kent recounted his experiences of attending the OTU at Hawarden in 1940:

I kept after Bill Kain, about air firing, explaining that I had never fired eight guns and I wanted to find out what they sounded like – and what effect they had on the aircraft.

Finally, in desperation, he allowed me one shoot. My target was a spit of sand in the Dee estuary and on my first attack I got a neat group with a half second burst, but on my second dive, the guns failed to fire. I tried several more times, but just nothing happened so, in a bit of a temper, I returned to the airfield and told Bill Kain what I thought of an installation which could produce stoppages in all eight guns at once. Bill then explained that there had been no stoppage, that was all the ammunition they could spare me!

I knew that both the country and the Air Force were in a pretty bad way, but this brought home to me just how desperate the situation was. It did not matter so much in my particular case as I had done so much front gun firing before, although not with eight guns, but many of the new boys never fired their guns at all until they went into action for the first time – a sobering thought when one considers the task before them. It was a great tribute to their grit and determination that they carried themselves into the violent battles all over the next few months, and inflicted the damage they did, with virtually no instruction or practice.[30]

While the Battle of Britain ended in defeat for the Luftwaffe on 30 October, Germany, during late September, had started raiding Britain by night. Until the end of 1940 Britain had almost no defence against this tactic except by using anti-aircraft guns, which on the whole were not very effective. During December, however, the first German bomber losses from interception by British night-fighters took place. It was a start; but the Blitz only really ended when Hitler withdrew his bomber fleet to the east of Germany in preparation for his assault on Russia in June 1941.

When the Luftwaffe turned from day to night bombing in what later became known as the Blitz, Dowding and the RAF were ill-prepared to combat the raids. Dowding had already foreseen the possibility of bombing by night and had thrown his weight behind the development of the radar-equipped night fighter, but this new invention would not be ready for operational use until late in 1940 or early in 1941, and Dowding had to accept the many criticisms that he received about this seeming neglect of Britain's defences, although he had more than enough to cope with, looking after Britain's fighter defences by daylight.

Once the night bombing by the Luftwaffe started in earnest, a committee set up by Churchill was chaired by John Salmond to investigate what could be done to combat the nightly bombing raids being carried out on Britain. This committee came up with seventeen suggestions, but after going through them Dowding pointed out at a meeting in early October that there were only two suggestions worth pursuing. The Prime Minister, Winston Churchill, was upset by this seeming lack of action.

Arguments Within RAF Fighter Command

During the summer of 1940 an 'anonymous' memorandum entitled 'A Weak Link in the Nation's Defences' had been circulated among influential people in government, parliament, and in the RAF. A copy went to a junior Conservative Member of Parliament, Irene Ward. She sent it on to Winston Churchill in August, together with a covering letter in which she wrote that she had been 'kept informed about the views of many people in the Air Force', and that their 'overwhelming desire' was that Charles Portal should be appointed to succeed Newall as Chief of Air Staff, '*and that on no account should the post be offered to the current C-in-C of Fighter Command, Sir Hugh Dowding*' (author's italics). One wonders who she spoke to, or even if she spoke to anyone except a few ambitious officers. She even wrote that '*the RAF would consider it a disaster*' (author's italics) if the latter took place. Again, one has to wonder who in the RAF Irene Ward spoke to – probably not Dowding's pilots. Before receiving Miss Ward's letter, Churchill had wanted Dowding to succeed Newall as CAS, but those responsible for the memo pressured him into changing his mind.

The actual writer of this memo was Wing Commander Edgar Kingston-McCloughry, a staff officer at the Air Ministry. He was looked on with favour by Lord Beaverbrook, who headed up the Ministry for Aircraft Production. This ex-newspaper boss (the equivalent of today's Rupert Murdoch) may have helped McCloughry in the writing of the memorandum. It would seem that Beaverbrook also did not think that Cyril Newall should remain in charge at the Air Ministry.

A meeting had been called at the Air Ministry on 17 October 1940, to discuss 'Major day fighting tactics in the fighter force'. Present were AOC Fighter Command Hugh Dowding, 11 Group's commander, Air Vice-Marshal Keith Park, 12 Group's commander, Air Vice-Marshal Trafford Leigh-Mallory, and Air Vice-Marshal William Sholto Douglas, then Deputy Chief of the Air Staff. By this time, Charles Portal (known to Sholto Douglas and his friends as Peter) had become Chief of the Air Staff and was a supporter of Sholto Douglas's ideas, which coincided with Leigh-Mallory's idea about the use of the Big Wing.[31] The Air Chief of Staff, Air Chief Marshal Cyril Newall, was unable to attend due to illness, and Sholto Douglas chaired the meeting. It was Sholto Douglas who compiled the report of this meeting, which went to Churchill.

For some time, there had been an argument brewing between Leigh-Mallory, the leader of 12 Group, based in the Midlands, and Keith Park, the leader of 11 Group, about how best to defend the South East of England and London, 11 Group's domain. Park turned out to be an excellent tactician, not sending up his Spitfires and Hurricanes when the Germans flew 'Frei Jagd' missions over the UK. These were composed entirely of Bf 109Es and Park kept his Spitfires and Hurricanes on the ground, conserving his fighters to intercept the German bombers later.

Because of its proximity to France, over the coast of which the German bombers formed up during the Battle of Britain, 11 Group – which bore the brunt of the defence of Britain during the Battle – rarely had the luxury of getting more than one squadron in a position to intercept the German bombers before they managed to drop their bombs. The British fighters were too busy struggling for height because the radar could only give warnings of an incoming raid as the German bombers and their fighter escorts formed up over the French coast, with only the short dash across the English Channel before they reached Britain.

Hugh Dowding was, by all accounts, a man of few words and sometimes spoke without tact, which did not endear him to certain people in positions of power, such as Archibald Sinclair, then the Secretary for Air, John Salmond and Hugh Trenchard. As we have already seen, Trenchard had long harboured animosity towards Dowding although Sholto Douglas later claimed that this was patched up before Trenchard retired from the Air Ministry.

There was also personal animosity between Leigh-Mallory and Keith Park, perhaps stemming from the fact that Keith Park was a New Zealander and had joined the British Army as a Non-Commissioned Officer (NCO). Park had fought at Gallipoli and had then been wounded while fighting at the Battle of the Somme in 1916. Upon recovering from his wounds, he joined the RFC, flying Bristol F2B Fighters and shooting down five German aircraft before the end of 1918, making him an 'ace'. He too was shot down twice during this time, being lucky to survive the war. Ralph Dundas, a pilot in the Oxford University Air Squadron in the 1930s, had this to say about Park:

> During WW1 Park was so severely wounded in the New Zealand army, in the Dardanelles and on the Somme, that he was invalided out as unfit for further service. His papers were then lost whereupon he joined the RFC to become a fighter pilot of distinction. He must have been 40 in 1932, 48 in 1940. Park was not very popular in the Oxford University Air Squadron nor good with undergraduates who were after all just civilians: too much of a service man for OUAS. He lacked the human touch, had no sense of humour or fun, and was, we thought, a prim, officious, fussy, prosaic fellow, half governess half old woman, perhaps. A bit of a bad joke, a stern bore in

the air. But that was his job. He had a reputation for being a gingerman to keep people on their toes. I don't think the officers liked him or trifled with him either. Wing Commander Park, then DSO, MC, Croix de Guerre, was very much the boss. He was of course a disciplinarian and rightly, though in OUAS a bit tricky.[32]

Leigh-Mallory, the son of a Church of England Rector, had been to Cambridge University before volunteering for the army in 1914 and being commissioned. After being wounded in the Second Battle of Ypres, in 1915, he had joined the RFC as a pilot and flew on bombing, reconnaissance and photographic missions during the battle of the Somme in 1916. After this, he flew on army cooperation missions until the end of the war. Thus, he had never been a 'fighter boy', with all the glamour that this connotation implies.

This difference of rank and class between Park and his colleagues in 1940 is important because they – Leigh-Mallory, William Sholto Douglas, Dowding and Hugh Trenchard – had all been commissioned officers when they had joined up and Park had not. The class system ran deep in the British military.

As we have seen, Sholto Douglas had served in the First World War as a pilot, becoming a squadron leader in 1918. Related to the Marquess of Queensbury, he had been born to an upper-class family and gone to a public school (the equivalent of a private school in the USA) and Lincoln College, in Oxford. It was this upbringing which enabled him to be commissioned as an officer when he joined the British Army in 1914. The standard line for the sons of the aristocracy (still in vogue up to and past the Second World War) was that the eldest son inherited the family estate, the second in line joined the army as an officer, and the youngest joined the Church.

Where tactics between the various Fighter Command groups in Britain were concerned, there was considerable disagreement between Keith Park, in charge of 11 Group, and Trafford Leigh-

Mallory, commander of 12 Group. The October meeting had been called in an attempt to sort this out.

It was Leigh-Mallory's belief, bolstered by Douglas Bader (an acting Squadron Leader in 12 Group, who had lost his legs in a flying accident before the war and who was brought to this meeting to give the point of view of an 'ordinary' pilot), that the fighters should form themselves into a formation of not less than three, and preferably five, squadrons, even if this meant delaying intercepting the bombers until after they had dropped their bombs. This became known as the 'Big Wing' theory.[33] Leigh-Mallory claimed at the meeting on 17 October that it only took six minutes for the squadrons to form up but reality was that it was more like fifteen.

As a background to the meeting of 17 October, it should be pointed out that at this time 12 Group was tasked with defending 11 Group's airfields during the battle, something that Leigh-Mallory's squadrons pointedly failed to do, much to Park's annoyance. Jon Diamond, on the website warfarehistorynetwork.com, wrote that before the Fall of France, it had been foreseen that Leigh-Mallory's 12 Group would be the one facing the Luftwaffe across the North Sea, but after the French surrender it became apparent that the attack would have to be intercepted by Keith Park's 11 Group, something that upset Leigh-Mallory; he asked Dowding to allow him to take over 11 Group, and Dowding refused to do so.

The upshot of this meeting was that no agreement was reached on whether to keep on using the squadrons in a piecemeal fashion, as Park was forced to do, or to form them up into a 'Big Wing' before attacking the bombers, and Dowding did not impose a decision upon his two group commanders, who, as we have seen, also personally disliked one another. Perhaps he should have done.

As can be seen with Trenchard's policies during the First World War, the RAF had been committed to the idea that the strategic bomber would be a war-winner in the next conflict; now here was 1940, and the fighter defences of Britain had beaten the bombers of the Luftwaffe. The higher reaches of the RAF did not want a man such as Dowding to perhaps rise to command the whole of the RAF, as he may well have favoured fighter production over their beloved bombers.

Neither Dowding nor Park had much interest in the politics of the RAF, but Trenchard, Portal, Leigh-Mallory, and Sholto Douglas certainly did. Portal, Sholto Douglas and Leigh-Mallory were proteges of Trenchard – indeed, Trenchard referred to Portal as his 'favourite disciple'.[34]

Later in October 1940, and ominously for Hugh Dowding, Newall was removed from his post by Winston Churchill and replaced by the close friend of Sholto Douglas, Charles Portal. Newall's then age of 54 was given as the reason for his 'retirement'. Dowding, on the other hand, was 58 and had already had his retirement date put back twice by Winston Churchill.

Air Chief Marshal Sir Cyril Newall was almost at the retirement age of 56 anyway, but he became the victim of an orchestrated campaign that led to his dismissal in October 1940. Ominously for Hugh Dowding, Newall was replaced by the close friend of Sholto Douglas – Charles Portal. Newall's age was given as the reason for his 'retirement'.

Although Churchill appreciated the part played by both Dowding and Park in the Battle of Britain, Dowding was dismissed from his position on 25 November 1940, as his retirement date had been put back several times, and on 18 December Keith Park was relegated to a training position due to his continued disagreements with Sholto Douglas, who had taken Dowding's position as A.O.C. Fighter Command. Dowding's reaction was to write later:

> Churchill told me that I was to be replaced as C-in-C Fighter Command. He told me of his surprise that this recommendation should have been made 'in the moment of victory', but did not indicate any personal opposition.

It seemed natural enough to me. The Air Council had been anxious to be rid of me since before the start of the war, and this seemed to be an appropriate moment.

Dowding's farewell letter to his squadrons is poignant:

My dear Fighter Boys,

In sending you this my last message, I wish I could say all that is in my heart. I cannot hope to surpass the simple eloquence of the Prime Minister's words, 'Never before has so much been owed by so many to so few.' The debt remains and will increase.

In saying goodbye to you I want you to know how continually you have been in my thoughts, and that, though our direct communication may be severed, I may yet be able to help you in your gallant fight.

Goodbye to you and God bless you all.

Air Chief Marshal Hugh Dowding
24 November 1940

Dowding was finally fully retired in 1942. This followed a tour of America where he tried, unsuccessfully, to persuade American industry to produce the Napier Sabre engine (already condemned by American aircraft manufacturers for its use of sleeve valves, Pratt and Whitney in particular favouring the two poppet valved radial type engine), advised against the use of the heavy bomber, and promoted fighter development. Ironically, Keith Park was replaced by Leigh-Mallory as commander of 11 Group, but later became the RAF Commander during the defence of Malta and re-emerged as the fine tactician that he was. Sholto Douglas took over Fighter Command after Dowding retired in November 1940, and almost immediately had to listen to what Portal had told him of Trenchard's advice on what the next move by Fighter Command should be.

In a BBC radio interview in 1968, Dowding said that his one overriding memory of the events of 1940, during the Battle of Britain, was of how tired he, and most other people in the RAF were at that time. He pointed out the fact that he had many late nights that year because he was attending to Britain's night fighter defence as well as the day fighters, and involved himself with the development of AI radar. He went on to become a spiritualist, many times commenting to friends about how he could see some of the dead pilots he had commanded and called them 'his chicks'. He married again later in life, to Muriel Whiting in 1951. Dowding died on 15 February 1970.

When Charles Portal took over overall command of the RAF in December 1940, he invited Trenchard to the Air Ministry and asked him for his advice about what to do next with the RAF, now that the Battle of Britain was over. Trenchard advised Portal to send RAF fighters on the offensive, against the Germans in occupied France. He referred to this policy as 'Lean towards France'.[34]

Portal subsequently met with Sholto Douglas to discuss Trenchard's advice and expressed his doubts about the wisdom of repeating the same tactics over France as the Germans had unsuccessfully employed during the Battle of Britain. Sholto Douglas rightly saw the prospects of high casualties among his pilots as they would have two crossings of the Channel, there and back, in addition to possibly engaging the German fighters now stationed in France – all at the limit of their endurance.

Portal told Sholto Douglas to write a paper on this possible employment of Fighter Command; when it was complete, he presented it to Portal, and Sholto Douglas found that he had changed his mind and that, in his opinion, it would be a good thing for Fighter Command to go on to the offensive over France. Quite what his reasoning was behind his change of mind has never been revealed. Portal concurred and so the stage was set. The first indication of this new 'Lean towards France' policy came on 20 December 1940 when a pair of Spitfire Mk Is of 66 Squadron strafed the airfield at Le Touqet.[35]

At the beginning of 1941, war games were held by the RAF, giving Leigh-Mallory the chance to prove his 'Big Wing' theory, had he been in charge of 11 Group during the Battle of Britain. The squadrons took too long to form up and missed intercepting the bombers. Leigh-Mallory was not deterred in his determination to use 'Big Wings' in the future use of Fighter Command.

In November 1940, the Axis powers of Nazi Germany, Fascist Italy and Imperial Japan signed the Tripartite Treaty. This assumed, in December 1941, an ominous clause for Germany. It was one which stated that in the event of war between any of the three partners and America, the other two would declare war themselves upon America. As a result, Hitler declared war on America on 10 December 1941 in support of Japan following the raid on Pearl Harbor three days earlier. It was one of the factors that would lead to Germany's downfall, particularly in the West.

Chapter 4

1941

*Trenchard follows the good military principle of
repeating any tactics that have not been actually
disastrous – and often those that have – again and
again, regardless of the fact that the enemy will
probably think out some very good reply, until they
really are so disastrous that they have to be abandoned.*
Lieutenant Thomas Hughes, RFC, 1916

By the end of the Battle of Britain, daylight raids on Britain by massed bomber formations from Occupied Europe had all but ceased.

Towards the end of 1940, German Bf 109E fighter-bombers, 'Jagdbombers', as we have seen, had flown across the Channel at altitude to England, but their bomb aiming accuracy was not good. They carried on with these attacks on Britain sporadically but came to realise, in the new year, that they needed to attack at low level to have any chance of bombing accurately, and of escaping interception by diving away, now bomb-less, across the Channel.[1]

During this time the Germans switched over to bombing Britain, mainly London, by night; the period became known as the Blitz. British night defences, including the anti-aircraft guns, were mostly ineffective. After trying to defend Bristol at night in his Hurricane while with 87 Squadron, then Flight Commander Roland Beamont, a fighter pilot with some six victories during the Battles of France and Britain, suggested to his commanding officer that it would be worth raiding enemy bombers' bases in France to catch the enemy when landing after a raid in early to mid-1941. I was fortunate to have been able to interview Beamont, during which he told me that:

> The lighting inside the cockpit was adjustable and we obviously turned it down, so that we could see better at night. As we knew where most of the raiding bombers were based, it was relatively simple to wait for a raid to take place on Britain and then fly to France and await the bombers' return. We destroyed several Heinkels and Dorniers while they were on their final approaches.

The Hurricane's night intruder task was later (1942) taken over by de Havilland Mosquitoes, which had the advantage of carrying a navigator/radar operator to assist the pilot.

The Blitz lasted until May 1941, when Germany moved many Luftwaffe aircraft from France to bases in the east in preparation for Operation *Barbarossa*, the invasion of Russia in June. Once this happened, Winston Churchill ordered that the RAF had to do all that it could to force the Luftwaffe to send more squadrons away from the Russian front, in order to bolster JG 2 and JG 26, stationed in France. Despite the mass of British aircraft that would be thrown against the Luftwaffe over France in the next two years, the German fighter groups never seemed to need reinforcements.

Each Jagdgeschwader (Jagd – hunting/fighter, geschwader – group/wing) consisted of three gruppen. A gruppe each commanded by a Kommandeur, in the Luftwaffe was the equivalent of a wing in the RAF and USAAF, comprised of some three 'staffeln' (squadrons) each commanded by a Staffelkäpitan (squadron leader) with twelve aircraft in each staffel. The gruppen were each numbered as, for instance, I/JG 26 consisted of Staffeln 1, 2 and 3, II/JG 26 consisted of Staffeln 4, 5 and 6, III/JG 26 consisted of Staffeln 7,8 and 9. The Jagdbombers (fighter bombers) were an extra staffeln, 10/JG 26.

There was also a 'stabschwarm' (staff flight/organisation) which comprised the Jagdgeschwader's Kommodore, usually with the rank of Oberstleutnant. He led the four aircraft stabschwarm, with his adjutant, each with their own wingmen, making up a separate fighting group, and which commanded the geschwader in the air.

To defend the French coast for most of 1941 and 1942, the Luftwaffe left just two fighter Jagdgeschwaders, JG 2 'Richthofen', and JG 26 'Schlageter', each with some 120 plus Messerschmitt Bf 109Es ('Emil') to begin with and then 109Fs ('Friedrich') from early 1941. Later, from August 1941, the staffeln of these Jagdgeschwaders, first of all JG 26, were re-equipped with Focke-Wulf 190s. JG 26 was assigned to the area of Belgium and northeast France, while JG 2 guarded the Channel coast west of the river Seine, down to the Atlantic. It was no accident that these two groups contained some of the top German aces (experten) of the Luftwaffe. On 7 December 1940, JG 26 had moved from the Pas de Calais area to Abbeville-Drucat, which had recently been the home of JG 53 and ZG 26 (ZG – Zerstorer – destroyer group using Messerschmitt Bf 110s).[2]

These would be spread out over the several airfields in the area to which they were assigned. Thus, each geschwader usually consisted of some 124 aircraft and 1,800 men for its nominal strength.

Each of the three gruppes that made up the geschwader usually had its own stabschwarm of four aircraft each, backed up by the 'stabskompanie' of some 200 men, who looked after maintenance, transportation, communications, flak (to protect each airfield) and for general duties. In the following few months, Adolf Galland would rotate each of his staffeln through Audembert, in order to evaluate and guide the pilots through the forthcoming struggle.

Until April 1941, JG 1, JG 51, two staffeln of JG 52, and JG 53 had also flown from Northern France on defence missions, with JG 52 having one staffel, I./JG 52, mainly operating over the Dutch coast, out of range of Spitfires and Hurricanes, and II./JG 52 operating from Belgium, but all except JG 2 and JG 26 were moved to the East for the forthcoming invasion of Russia during April and May. On 9 February, JG 26's officers and men vacated their bases in France to go on leave, turning them over to JG 51. The men had been granted leave simultaneously, the officers first of all going on an all-expenses paid skiing trip to Austria, while the men had to settle for home leave.[3]

All except Staffel 7./JG 26. They were posted to Sicily, to escort Luftwaffe bombers raiding Malta. Apart from a short break spent in Yugoslavia, they were there from February until June, when they transitioned to Libya, where they remained until the end of August, when they returned to France, to join the rest of the geschwader. 7./JG 26 was assisted in the desert of North Africa by III/JG 27. During their time flying from Sicily, and in Yugoslavia and the Western Desert, 7./JG 26 claimed fifty-two enemy aircraft destroyed, for no pilot being lost from their staffel. They virtually destroyed the then fighter defence of Malta, which consisted mainly of 261 Squadron, flying outdated Hurricane Mk Is, which the Messerschmitts could out-speed, out-climb and out-dive. Add to this the fact that their leader, Oberleutnant Joachim Müncheberg, gave instructions to his men never to tackle the Hurricanes in anything other than an attacking dive from above, and certainly never to engage in a turning battle and this gave the Germans their tremendous victory score ratio. 261 Squadron was shot out of the Mediterranean skies.[4]

Of all the warring air forces, the Luftwaffe adopted probably the most stringent rules to corroborate claims; every claim by a pilot or gunner required written confirmation from at least one of their fellow pilots in the action. Ground observers of the action (if any) also had to submit their confirmation of a shoot down in writing.

The Messerschmitt Bf 109's main victims in the Malta and Western Desert campaigns were Hurricanes and Curtiss P-40 Tomahawks and Kittyhawks. These aircraft were employed primarily as ground-attack aircraft, many armed with bombs, to assist the British army and thus flew low, rendering themselves vulnerable to diving attacks by the higher flying German fighters, who racked up considerable scores against the slower, more vulnerable British fighter bombers, whose pilots were frequently not English but Canadians, South Africans and Australians.

It took time for the fighter bombers' pilots to work out efficient tactics against the marauding Bf 109s. The early marks of the P-40, called the 'Tomahawk' by the RAF, only had a single stage supercharger for its Allison V12 engine and was inferior to the Bf 109, in both 'E' and 'F' specification, below 14,500ft, but as that was where most combats over the desert took place, it was not such a disadvantage as it first appeared. As well, like the Spitfire and Hurricane, the P-40 could turn tighter than a Bf 109E and could absorb considerable punishment, while still getting its pilot home. The German's real advantage was in the quality, experience and the tactics that their pilots employed.[5]

Lord Tedder, at that time in command of the Desert Air Force, wrote of this period:

> The Germans, even with their Me 109Fs, were still refusing to fight, except on very rare occasions. Their game was on jumping the occasional straggler, or of making a single stab at an outside aircraft in a formation. This despite the fact that both the Tomahawk [P-40 – Author] and the Hurricane II were outclassed in speed and climb by the enemy aircraft. *One Squadron of Spitfire Mk Vs would have been worth a lot* [author's italics].[6]

By 26 March, JG 26 had begun its return to France from its home bases, at Dortmund and Bonn-Hangelar to airfields in the Pas de Calais area in Northern France. On 1 April, the Jagdgeschwader transferred to airfields in Brittany. Adolf Galland's own base for his 'stabschwarm' (headquarters flight) was now at Brest-Guipivas. For the next three months there were few actions in the war in the air over France, perhaps eight to ten 'Circuses', and there were occasional raids by the British on the battlecruisers *Scharnhorst* and *Gneisenau*, in Brest harbour, but they caused little damage.[7]

A 'Circus' consisted of six to twelve medium bombers (usually Bristol Blenheims) with an escort of many squadrons of fighters. Johnnie Johnson, in his book *Wing Leader* wrote: 'Our longest penetrations to Lille, Roubaix and Tourney were bitterly opposed, and as far as I was concerned the air fighting was more ferocious than at any other time of the war.'

A 'Ramrod' consisted of fighter escorted Hurricanes, armed with bombs, usually at low-level, while a 'Rodeo' was a fighter sweep, with no bombers to escort. A 'Rhubarb' was a low-level attack by a few fighters over France, usually in pairs, looking for targets of opportunity, such as trains or staff cars, in cloudy weather. They were not popular with the pilots, mainly due to the efficient German anti-aircraft ('flak') guns, and were discontinued in late 1943, unless exceptional circumstances dictated them. A 'roadstead' was an attack on German shipping, whether in port or at sea.

About 'Rhubarbs', Johnnie Johnson once wrote:

> Apart from the flak, the hazards of making a let down
> over unknown territory and with no accurate knowledge
> of the cloud base seemed too great a risk for the damage
> we inflicted. Hundreds of pilots were lost on either small
> or large 'rhubarbs'.[8]

Apart from a few desultory combats in this area, JG 26, under the command of the formidable Oberstleutnant Adolf Galland, did not achieve much until subsequently, on 1 June 1941, when JG 26 moved again. This time, Adolf Galland and his staff moved to Audembert, where he was able to use a converted chateau for his headquarters. I Gruppe went to Clairmairas, near to St Omer, II Gruppe were stationed at Maldegem, in Belgium and III Gruppe went to Liegescourt, near to Abbeville. Not for nothing were the

Bf 109Fs of JG 26 to become known to the Spitfire squadrons as the 'Abbeville boys'.[9]

JG 2 first of all moved their Ist and IIIrd Gruppes to Cherbourg-Theville and Caen-Roquancourt respectively, while II Gruppe went to Brest, in the Brittany peninsula. The move of II Gruppe meant that they were now available to cover the harbour of Brest, in which sheltered the two battlecruisers, *Scharnhorst* and *Gneisenau*. In the coming eleven months, these two ships were to suffer more than sixty bombing raids, although none permanently crippled either ship. On 1 June 1941, JG 2 took over the airfields that JG 26 had just vacated. From this date JG 2 was given the responsibility of guarding the French coast from the Seine estuary to Cherbourg, while JG 26 was to guard the coast from the Seine to Holland.[10]

As already noted, JG 26 had the seasoned and charismatic Adolf Galland for its kommodore; he had been promoted to this command on 22 August 1940, while JG 2 was commanded at this time by Wilhelm Balthasar. Following Balthasar's death in combat on 3 July, JG 2 was commanded by Walter Oesau. Both Galland and Balthasar had been flying and fighting with the Luftwaffe since the Spanish Civil War and were very experienced as fighter pilots – particularly Balthasar, with many victories to his credit – and both were experienced leaders. Galland had flown nearly 300 missions in Spain, using Heinkel He 51 ground attack biplanes. Despite longing to fly the newly introduced Bf 109 in combat in Spain, he was not able to but his successor, Lieutenant Mölders did and swiftly started scoring victories over the Republicans' Russian supplied aircraft. Mölders and Galland would soon be locked in a friendly rivalry in the early part of the Second World War, to see who could shoot down the most Allied aircraft.

In overall command of the Luftwaffe force's fighters in France and the Low Countries, which contained JG 2 and JG 26, was Major General Theo Osterkamp (Jagdfliegerführer), based at Le Touquet. Osterkamp had been a fighter ace in the First World War, having entered the naval flying service. For the first two years of that war, he had been an observer in two-seater aircraft patrolling the Belgian coast. After training as a pilot in the first half of 1917, he went on to become an 'ace' by shooting down more than five Allied aircraft. He was one of the very few German pilots to fly the Fokker DVIII (the 'flying razor blade'), a parasol monoplane, in late 1918 and at one point had been shot down, having to take to his parachute – one of the lucky few in the First World War to have such a device. He claimed thirty-two victories and was one of the last pilots to receive the *Pour le Mérite*, Germany's highest decoration in the First World War, before the armistice of 11 November 1918.

Osterkamp had also led JG 51 during the Battles of France and Britain in 1940 from the air, claiming six victories. In July 1940, he was replaced by Werner Mölders, was promoted, awarded the Knight's Cross (which replaced the *Pour le Mérite* as the most sought after decoration in the German military in the Second World War) and given his new command post in France.[11]

Facing the French coast across the English Channel was 11 Group, who looked after the South Eastern sector of Britain. The majority of the fighting during the Battle of Britain had been carried out by the squadrons in this group, and it was mainly from this group that the attacks on Northern France would originate in 1941. The airfields' names roll off the tongue now as the names of Agincourt, Crecy and Poitiers did to generations after the fourteenth century. At the beginning of 1941, the squadrons, each nominally of twelve aircraft, based on each field were composed as follows (in alphabetical order):

Biggin Hill	2 x Spitfire I + 1 x Spitfire IIa
Croydon	1 x Hurricane IIa
Debden	2 x Hurricane I
Hawkinge	1 x Spitfire IIa
Hornchurch	1 x Spitfire I/IIa, 1 x Spitfire IIa
Kenley	2 x Hurricane I

Northolt	2 x Hurricane I
North Weald	2 x Hurricane I
Tangmere	1 x Spitfire I, 1 x Hurricane I.

Seventeen squadrons of fighters were based on these nine airfields, so approximately 244 fighter aircraft were in 11 Group. Numerically, the RAF and Luftwaffe fighters opposing each other across the Channel were almost evenly matched at the beginning of 1941, with perhaps a few more fighters on the Luftwaffe's side than with the RAF.[12]

Gradually, these squadrons became integrated into 'wings', usually comprising three squadrons of twelve aircraft, each commanded by a squadron leader, the wing itself being commanded by a wing commander, the first of which were appointed in March 1941. A wing commander had command over all the personnel in each wing, including the ancillary staff such as ground crew, anti-aircraft gunners and the transportation and administration necessary to keep the wing operating. In time, groups were formed under a group captain, these comprising five squadrons each.[13]

As the Luftwaffe was raiding Britain almost every night during this time, the first task Sholto Douglas had after taking command of Fighter Command in November 1940 was to find a way to locate and shoot down enemy bombers. This was a hard job, but the task was made much easier for Sholto Douglas with the earlier decisions made by Hugh Dowding over the use of Airborne Interception radar, or AI for short, particularly in the twin-engine Bristol Beaufighter.

With this AI-equipped night fighter, a solution had been found to the problem of detecting and shooting down the nocturnal raiders; but not until later in 1941 did the new British night fighters make a severe impact upon the German bombers. Daytime operating Spitfires and Hurricanes were used on some evenings, in the hope that their pilots might be able to spot the incoming bombers, but it was a forlorn hope and not many of them succeeded in even spotting an enemy bomber. However, the fact is that the raids on Britain virtually stopped in May, when the Luftwaffe moved east, in preparation for the invasion of Russia in June.

As discussed in the previous chapter, Air Vice-Marshal Sir Charles Portal had taken over the job of Chief of the Air Staff in place of Cyril Newall on 25 October 1940. Portal was another ex-First World War pilot, having flown BE2Cs in 1916 and RE8s in 1917, both types being two-seater reconnaissance/artillery observation machines. As mentioned earlier, in November 1940 Portal and Sholto Douglas discussed the meeting Portal had recently had with Trenchard, commander of the RFC/RAF from 1916, during and after the First World War, until his retirement in 1930.

It was Trenchard who had suggested to Portal that it was time for Fighter Command to go onto the offensive, 'Lean towards France', as he put it. The idea was that the RAF should adopt much the same offensive policy as in the First World War, that is always on the attack against the Germans, even though the Germans now occupied the north of France completely. The Channel now became the equivalent of the First World War's trench lines and thus was born the 'Non-Stop Offensive', as it was known in some quarters.[14]

Trenchard appears always to have disregarded the number of casualties suffered in the conflict of 1914 to 1918, when compared to the losses of the German Air Force in the same period. Dowding had been very careful to try to keep the number of fighter pilot casualties down as much as was possible during the Battle of Britain, as he probably never had more than 600 aircraft and their pilots ready to do battle over Britain at any one time. Although the supply situation was improving, both in terms of pilots and fighters, Fighter Command still needed to build back up to strength after the Battle of Britain was over.

Many of the newer pilots in the RAF in 1940 were not British. Pilots came from Poland, Czechoslovakia, Norway, France, Belgium (one pilot, originally from Belgium, R.G.C. de Grunne, had actually flown Bf 109s in the Spanish Civil War for the Nationalists). These pilots had escaped from their countries as the Nazis had attacked and then occupied them. Then there were the pilots from Britain's dominions, Canada, Australia and New Zealand, and many other places. Several 'Eagle' Squadrons featured volunteer pilots from America. Fully 20 per cent of the pilots flying and fighting with Fighter Command during the Second World War did not count Britain as their home country.[15]

At this time, the RAF formalised a tour of operations for a pilot flying fighters to be 200 combat hours flown. Previously, the amount of flying and fighting time a pilot could withstand had been down to his commanding officer but in 1941, a new regime was instituted by the Air Ministry.

In 1941/42, the average time spent in the air by an escorting Spitfire Mk V flying to France was one-and-a-quarter hours from take-off to landing. Sometimes, it could stretch to one and a half hours but by then the aircraft would be almost out of fuel.[16] So the average pilot would have to complete some 150 combat missions or more to end his tour of operations. During the period that the Circuses, Ramrods and Rodeos were flown, the British fighters were sometimes flying in combat up to three times a day.

Where the pilots of the Luftwaffe were concerned, they flew until either being killed, wounded, or being promoted to a desk job.

Like the Messerschmitt Bf 109Es that had escorted the German bombers during the Battle of Britain, the RAF's Spitfires and Hurricanes suffered in the new escort fighter role. They were interceptor fighters, built to shoot down incoming bombing raids, not to escort bombers over long distances. In order to conserve weight, a Spitfire's fuel tank only held some eighty-five gallons, with provision for an extra twenty-nine-gallon tank available for ferry flights only. These British fighters were limited to being able to penetrate only some sixty miles inland once over the French coast, to Paris and not much further than that, not including fuel used in any combats they might get into. Their fuel consumption limited their range to circa 470 miles.[17]

To accomplish even these fuel/time-limited sorties, the Spitfire Mk II/V pilot needed to learn how to manage his fuel consumption, before combat, to eke out every gallon of fuel his aircraft consumed. This meant keeping the fuel mixture lean, the throttle fully open and the propeller in coarse pitch. If the Spitfire pilots had the advantage of spotting the enemy early, something not usually achieved, then he set the propeller pitch to fine, opened the throttle and gained speed as quickly as possible. When entering combat, a pilot had to get up to fighting speed fast. The higher the initial rpm, the faster would be the engine's response.

During the Spanish Civil War of 1937–39, the Heinkel He 51s of the German Condor Legion had started using drop tanks, suspended under their bellies, to increase their range. These could be dropped when the enemy was sighted. By 1940, the Junkers Ju 87s were also using them to extend their range, and by August 1940 the Bf 109E-7 was also using them.

The RAF did not adopt drop tanks until late 1942. The only exception was a small use of 'slipper' type auxiliary fuel tanks beneath the fuselage, which was used for ferry flights from late 1941. Expendable drop tanks would probably have helped a lot in the Circuses of 1941, as the escorting Spitfires were always at the limit of their range over Northern France at that time. Apparently, this modification would have interrupted the delivery of Spitfires and the Air Ministry judged that unacceptable.

By the beginning of 1941, with the Battle of Britain over, it is probable that the German fighter pilots of the Luftwaffe were at the peak of their profession. They had the advantage of some of them having fought in a modern monoplane fighter, the Bf 109, for years and had learned new tactics, the 'rotte' (pair) and 'schwarme' (two pairs in a finger-four formation) forming their efficient tactical fighter unit when on patrol. Many of those pilots had fought through the Spanish Civil War, the campaigns in Poland, France and over England had racked up high scores, and even those who hadn't scored highly, probably through being wingmen detailed to look after their leader, were now extremely experienced at flying in combat.

By contrast, the fighter pilots of the RAF, even if they had joined and learned to fly pre-war, had had little experience of fighting the Germans until the latter stages of the battle of France and then the Battle of Britain. They had had to try and fight the German fighter escort in unsuitable formations (the 'Vic' of three, or in line astern) and their opponents, in their Bf 109Es, had the advantage not only of using better fighting formations, but also in flying an aircraft that could climb faster and dive faster, particularly with their fuel injection equipped Daimler-Benz engines, than either the Spitfire or the Hurricane. Nevertheless, those British pilots who had survived the Battles had themselves now racked up experience of air fighting and had gained confidence.

But by the beginning of 1941 a lot of experienced British fighter pilots had been killed, were 'rested' by being sent to an operational training unit or given a desk job. They had been replaced with a new intake of hurriedly trained young men, who were simply not experienced enough, or well enough taught, by the operational training units in fighting tactics, to be able to take on the German fighters on anything like equal terms. It's probable that where tactics were concerned, the RAF instructors were as much in the dark as their predecessors, unless they had learned the hard lesson during the Battles of France and Britain that German fighter tactics were superior to those being employed by the RAF in 1939/40. This illustrates completely how right L.J.K. Setright was when he wrote that by this time, the best pilots of the RAF had gone.[18] At least by June 1941 training bases were opening in America for the RAF, under the lend-lease agreement, and pilots now had the advantage of good weather conditions in places like Florida and California to learn to fly in.

In 1938 an RAF pilot had received 200–300 hours flying time before seeing squadron service. His German equivalent would have done a minimum of 240 hours over eighteen months to two years, those extra hours being spent in the aircraft that he would fly on operations, giving him much needed time to acclimatise himself to its vicissitudes. Along the way, as well the practicalities of flying he would have been taught navigation, the theory of aeronautics, meteorology and even the law as it pertained to flying.

Incidentally, as regards pilot training 'on the job', Leigh-Mallory, commenting on an operation to Boulogne in March 1941, where 610 Squadron lost four Spitfires for no claims wrote:

> The average number of experienced war pilots in squadrons I have visited lately is five and I don't think squadrons are being allowed nearly enough training from their experienced pilots. Squadrons ought to go up and carry out surprise attacks on each other, and especially practise regaining formation after being split up. I think perhaps fighter pilots are so busy keeping formation that they are not able to keep a good enough lookout.

He was right, but he still kept sending these inexperienced pilots out over France.

In March 1941, Sholto Douglas's senior air staff officer, Air Commodore Douglas Evill, told his superior officer that he thought that the Circus operations were ineffective and should not be continued. He contended that a better use should be found for the aircraft involved. Sholto Douglas did not see things Evill's way, even though he agreed that further training of the pilots was necessary.[19]

By this time, the Germans had recognised their need for a far simpler and faster pilot training schedule and introduced a system that concentrated primarily on the practicalities of learning to fly. Their final training time came in older Bf 109s and particularly concentrated on how to fly in the rotte and schwarme formations employed by the German fighter force. Upon being directed to a Jagdstaffel, a new pilot underwent further training by the more experienced pilots in the staffel, particularly in the use of the tactics being employed in the particular sector to which they had been posted.

It was not until 1944 that, due to their critical lack of fuel, a German fighter pilot's flying training hours were reduced to 160 only.

Apart from the perils of being shot down over land, hopefully being able to parachute out of their crippled aircraft (about one in every five pilots in a damaged fighter managed to bale out) or force land in a field, the pilots of Fighter Command flying over the Channel might now face falling into the Channel. Flying clothing in those days was basically a pilot's RAF uniform, over which he wore a 'Mae West', as a flotation device. The temperature in the Channel, even in the summer, seldom rose above 64°F and during the winter months dropped to around 46°F. Air-Sea rescue boats were ready to pick up downed fliers, but even so they had to be quick to save them because, apart from the risk of drowning, they could die of hypothermia before being found and recovered.

New Fighter Aircraft in 1941

As well as ordering the raiding Circuses, Sholto Douglas does not seem to have considered the pending introduction of better German fighters coming on stream either, though his intelligence services may have told him about them. For instance, the improved Bf 109F-2 ('Friedrich') was introduced into general service in early 1941, just in time to meet the new Spitfire Mk V. It was probably overall a slightly better performer than the Spitfire Mk V, which, truth be told, was somewhat of a disappointment to Fighter Command's pilots. That Mark of Spitfire had first of all replaced Spitfire Mk IIs in 92 Squadron in December 1940.

Newly introduced into Luftwaffe service in late 1940/early 1941, the Bf 109F was a substantial redesign of Messerschmitt's fighter and had a much more streamlined nose than the previous Bf 109E, with a bigger spinner. The wings now had rounded, instead of squared-off tips and this increased the wing area; the external bracing struts under the now cantilevered tailplane had gone and the tailwheel was semi-retractable. The armament in the first versions was composed of two MG 17 7.92mm machine-guns in the cowling in front of the pilot and a 15mm cannon in between the 'V' of the Daimler-Benz DB601N inverted V12 engine of 33.9 litres, which was rated at 1,270hp, thanks to its redesigned cylinder heads, increased compression ratio (mainly due to the use of flat-topped pistons, instead of the previously used concave type), a higher permissible rev limit and an improved supercharger.

The cannon fired through the hollow propshaft, which was geared from the engine's crankshaft. Later models, including the Bf 109F-4 introduced in July and August 1941, had the more powerful DB601E engine, which, with the permissible rev limit raised to 2,800rpm, produced some 1,350hp, which gave the model a 20 mph+ speed advantage over the Spitfire Mk V. A maximum speed of 387 mph in level flight at 33,000ft was quoted in the specifications, with a service ceiling of 39,350ft. At 20,500ft, this new variant of the Bf 109 was timed at 415.4 mph. The new DB601 engine was over 17 inches longer than the engine of the 'Emil' had been, necessitating a complete redesign of the nose, and this gave Messerschmitt's designers the opportunity to clean up the nose area, giving it a much more streamlined appearance and thus helping it to achieve its new top speed increase.

What is remarkable, when comparison is made with the Rolls-Royce Merlin, is how much bigger in capacity the Daimler-Benz DB engines were, at the aforesaid 33.9 litres, compared to the Merlin's 27.0 litres. Rolls-Royce truly were the masters of the art of supercharging. Throughout the war, the power outputs of the engines in the Spitfire and the Bf 109 remained remarkably similar.

Into this redesigned Bf 109F also went changes to the cooling system and a new self-sealing fuel tank, increased armour protection and a new hydraulic system. The wings no longer carried any armament, as had the earlier 'Emil' series but as well as the rounded wingtips, they also featured reshaped ailerons, flaps and slats. Later marks of the 'Friedrich' carried the very good MG151/20 (20mm calibre) cannon, firing through the propshaft. This could fire 750 rounds per minute at a muzzle velocity of 1,040ft per second.

The new Bf 109F 'Friedrich' was tested in April 1939 and was ready for production by January 1940, but an order from Hitler stopped aircraft development at this time, as he believed that Germany would not need any newer designs in the coming year. At the end of May, that order was rescinded and the production lines at Regensburg and other factories that built the Bf 109F under licence commenced rolling again in November.[20]

Initially, although well-liked by the pilots who received the new Mark of the Bf 109 (the F-2) there were some teething troubles, as in any new aircraft. Tyres needing replacement early on in their lives, loose ammunition boxes were reported, there was inadequate oxygen equipment for high altitude flying, plus sundry other modifications were needed, which were addressed by the introduction of the Bf 109F-4. Some early models also had a distressing habit of losing their tails (shades of the Hawker Typhoon, then just near to being introduced into service with No 56 Squadron), but a redesign of the tail structure with the addition of strengthening plates riveted to the rear of the fuselage cured this problem.

Engines wore out after less than forty hours, as two major problems reared their heads for Germany in 1941. Nickel was now impossible to get, due to the blockade of Europe and so valve life was threatened. In fact, this became such a problem that German fighter pilots were instructed not to use emergency boost, thus hobbling their aircraft's potential high performance in combat. As well, the correct fuel for the DB601N became unavailable and, coupled with the problem of the new, rubberised bag type fuel tank now being used which tended to fragment on the inside when fuel was left in it for any amount of time, meant that this engine particularly could suffer from engine-destroying detonation at wide throttle openings.

The Germans, having no oil supplies of their own, had to rely on synthetic fuels, mainly made in Romania during the war and, although the equivalent of 100 octane fuel became available to the Luftwaffe, it also brought with it problems with oil dilution of the fuel, which severely hampered the full throttle use of the engines. By 1941/42, commanders were having to tell their pilots not to use the emergency boost system for maximum power, even when in combat.[21]

Oberstleutnant Adolf Galland, the commander of JG 26 and himself already an established 'Experte', thought the 'Friedrich' could use more guns and later in 1941, he flew a Bf 109F-2, which had two extra 20mm MG FF cannon, one in each wing. Galland also had the armament of two other Bf 109Fs modified. These carried bigger machine-guns of 12.7mm in the cowling. These larger guns would be carried in the later Bf 109G ('Gustav') when that was introduced in February,1942.[22]

Performance-wise, the 'Friedrich', even in its earlier models, was a big improvement over the previous 'Emil'. It could climb to 16,400ft in 5 minutes 12 seconds, nearly a minute faster than the 'Emil' it replaced, handily out-climbing the Spitfire Mk V. More importantly, it could turn tighter than an 'Emil', though still not as tight as a Spitfire. Incidentally, II/JG 26 did not have its 'Emils' replaced until August 1941, when the staffel was re-equipped with the new Fw 190A.

The new Bf 109F also had the advantage of a service ceiling some 4,000ft higher than the Spitfire Mk V and was thus able to bounce the escorting Spitfires from out of the sun over France when the situation permitted.[23]

The Bf 109F now had a new electro-mechanical three-bladed constant speed VDM propeller, made of aluminium, whose pitch was automatically changed electrically. This meant one less control for the pilot to worry about, replacing the manual propeller pitch control that had been fitted to the Bf 109E. Even so, a manual override was still fitted, in case of a failure of the constant speed unit. This was designed to automatically change the pitch of its blades, so as to allow it to maintain constant engine rpm, irrespective of the aircraft's airspeed or altitude, or of the amount of engine torque.[24]

The Spitfire Mk V was faster and could fly higher than the previous Spitfire Mk II, which had seen front-line service during the Battle of Britain and also for the first part of 1941. That aircraft had had a maximum speed of 361 mph at 18,500ft. The Mk V went only slightly faster, to 375 mph at 20,000ft. Climb rate was ground level to 20,000ft in 7.1 minutes. Its service ceiling was given as 35,000ft, though it was touted that some could get to over 36,000ft in service trim.[25] However, RAF pilots, in their memoirs, disagree about this.

Walter Johnston, who flew a Mk V with 92 Squadron, recounted that in the summer of 1942:

> We used to get up to 25/26,000ft quite regularly, but 30,000ft and above was really stretching it. On those occasions, it was bitterly cold. On one trip we were up high and all of us were really hanging on our props. I was flying number three behind James Rankin and we were at the point where, if we were to have fired our cannon, we would have stalled. Then I looked up to starboard and, completely unannounced, a 109 came up alongside us. He was slightly above and he knew damned fine that he was as safe as houses. He looked over and gave me a wave and then pulled up and climbed merrily away, and I thought 'My God, what would I give for that?'[26]

By all accounts, the pilots of the Spitfire Mk V rated it as a delightful aeroplane to fly but it didn't appear in numbers until May 1941, almost a year after the introduction of the Mk II, which had, with the earlier Mk I, born the brunt of the battle over England. It had been intended that the new Spitfire should have been the Mark III, with the more powerful Merlin XX engine and a redesigned, strengthened wing and fuselage. The prototype first flew on 16 March 1940, but production of this Mk III was put on hold when the Air Ministry made the decision to allocate the Merlin XX to the Hurricane Mk II and the Bolton Paul Defiant turret-armed two seat fighter.

It was the introduction of the Bf 109F, however, which necessitated the hurried advent of the Mk V. Incidentally, the Spitfire Mk V introduced metal-covered ailerons, which greatly reduced the amount of force that a pilot had to apply when turning, or rolling. Mk II pilots, seeing this great improvement over their fabric covered ailerons, sometimes short-circuited official channels and 616 Squadron flew directly to the factory to get their Spitfires so modified![27]

This decision, to produce the new Mk V Spitfire, had been taken after a meeting at the Airplane and Armament Experimental Establishment at Boscombe Down on Christmas Eve 1940. At this meeting, Rolls-Royce told representatives of the Air Ministry that they would not be able to deliver the Merlin XX for use in Spitfires for several months, but believed that they could deliver the simpler Merlin 45, which could be retro-fitted into current Spitfire Mk Is and IIs in ten days each, plus be able to deliver 300 new Merlin 45s by March 1941 with 200 more to follow in April. The Air Ministry followed up this meeting with a contract that formalised this.[28]

Quickly, because Supermarine needed more time to tool up for the new Mk III, the company developed the Mark V, a stop-gap Spitfire which was really a Mk I/II, powered by the Merlin Type 45, 46, or 50, with a simpler, single-stage supercharger configured for performance at altitude, instead of the two-stage supercharger of the Merlin XX, and this new Merlin was also optimised for faster production.

The Merlin 45 developed 1,440hp at take-off and 1,515hp at 11,000ft, using +16 pounds of supercharger boost, on 100-octane fuel. A further variant, the Merlin 45M, powered some Mk Vs. This engine had a smaller diameter supercharger impeller and could run at +18 pounds of boost. This helped the engine deliver 1,585hp at

2,750ft and boosted the Spitfire's climb rate. Although the Spitfire Mk V was introduced into squadron service in February1941, only one squadron was thus equipped until May, when another four squadrons replaced their old Mk IIs with the new Mark.

The Merlin XX had had a two-stage supercharger, one for low and one for high altitude but the Spitfire Mk III, for which the Merlin XX was intended, was taking too long to bring into production and only the prototype was ever built. Most Merlin XXs, when they started being produced, were actually used in bombers, such as the Vickers Wellington. The sole Spitfire Mk III was later re-fitted with a Merlin 61 and became the prototype Mk IX. A hundred Mk I/IIs were modified to take the Merlin 45, while Mk Vs were being readied to be built new on the factory's production lines and these were the first Mk Vs introduced into squadron service in February 1941.[29]

Once in service, the first Spitfire Mk Vs displayed low oil pressure and high oil temperature at altitude, as the oil cooler of the Mk Is and IIs had not been uprated to cope with the increased power of the Merlin 45. The cooler's matrix was made larger and fitted beneath the port wing and this cured the problem.

The airscrew for the Mk V was, first of all, the three blade metal hydraulic de Havilland variable pitch propeller, which had also been used on the Mk II, which was later replaced by the Rotol compressed wood airscrew, both replacing the fixed pitch two bladed airscrew fitted to the first seventy-seven Mk Is. Early Mk Vbs suffered problems with their airscrews, when they found cold temperatures when the Spitfires came close to their new, higher ceilings. The oil that operated the de Havilland contact speed units congealed. Pilots with these airscrews were urged to change pitch frequently at altitude to prevent this until the engineers at de Havilland came up with a solution. The airscrews by Rotol did not seem to suffer from this problem.[30]

There were three main versions of the Spitfire Mark V, the 'standard' Mk Va, fitted with eight .303 machine-guns in the wing; the Mk Vb, with two 20mm cannon and four .303 machine-guns and the Mk Vc, which could carry four 20mm cannon, all in the wings. To accommodate the larger ammunition feed motors of the cannons, bulges were fitted over them, which slightly interrupted the airflow over the wings.

The Circuses Begin

JG 26's records alone show that from January to the end of June 1941, the pilots of that unit had shot down ninety-four British aircraft, mainly Spitfires, for the loss of just thirty-one Bf 109s. This, despite the fact that one staffel, 7/JG 26, had been posted to Tunisia during late January, not returning to France until September, and they were therefore not fighting over France during this period.[31]

The 'Lean towards France' policy really got underway just before the invasion of Russia on 22 June 1941. Fighter Command, primarily 11 Group, now commanded by Trafford Leigh-Mallory, sent 'Circuses' of a few Bristol Blenheim bombers, escorted by many squadrons of Spitfires and Hurricanes, as the Luftwaffe often ignored the 'Rhubarbs' and 'Rodeos', which were pure fighter sweeps made by Fighter Command over the Channel. 'Roadsteads' were anti-shipping strikes, attempting to deny use of the Channel to the shipping being used by the Germans. At the beginning of the year, Churchill had agreed to Trenchard's proposed 'Lean towards France' plan but had warned both Sholto Douglas and Leigh-Mallory to 'Watch your losses'.

For instance, five squadrons of Spitfires and Hurricanes made a sweep over Calais on 10 January 1941, but the German fighters did not bother to take off to intercept them. Squadron Leader Johnny Kent wrote that the Biggin Hill wing plus two other squadrons formed up and set course for Le Touquet where they were to turn and fly north, sweeping in behind the main force, or 'Beehive' as it was called, just over the French coast. Kent spotted the raiding Blenheims by the amount of flak bursts that followed them. After mentioning that he saw no German fighter opposition on this trip, Kent pointed out that this trip marked the point at which RAF Fighter Command went from the defensive to the offensive. [32]

On 28 January 1941, Reichsmarschall Hermann Göring summoned the leaders of his fighter geschwaders then stationed in France to a meeting, whereby they received a tremendous telling off from the head of the Luftwaffe, mainly on account of the poor results obtained by the German fighters when the RAF had carried out their sweep on 10 January. A secondary criticism was that noted by Hitler when he had spent Christmas Day with JG 26, to the effect that there was a lack of martial bearing and a general slovenliness about the appearance of the men of the Jagdwaffe. Göring went on to say that he was going to appoint younger, more vigorous men to command the various Geschwaders from now on.[33]

The first official 'rhubarb', which consisted of six Hurricanes in three separate pairs, took place on 12 January. Two Hurricanes failed to return.[34] On 22 January the RAF had one of their rare successes: two Hurricanes strafed the airfield of 1/JG 26, wounding one pilot and destroying his Bf 109. One ground crew member was killed and two others wounded. Both Hurricanes returned safely.[35]

Initially, the usual formation of a Circus was the Blenheim bombers at about 17,000ft with the escorting fighters on either side, and slightly higher, at 18,000ft for a 'close escort'. Then there was what was called the 'lower escort' at 20,000ft, the 'higher escort' at 22,000ft, the 'lowest high cover' at 25,000ft, 'middle high cover' at 27,000ft and a 'top high cover', at anything up to the ceiling of the Spitfires that performed this task, usually 30,000ft – if they could get there.

There was usually a 'withdrawal wing' of three squadrons of Spitfires as well, sent out later to shield the returning aircraft, and to try and help those aircraft which, by dint of having been in combat, were running low on fuel.

All this was laid out in operational orders, coming from Headquarters 11 Group, on 16 February. These orders were copious, detailing even the duties of the Air-Sea Rescue boats and Lysander Army Co-operation aircraft to circle, if at all possible, downed pilots in the water to help the boats find them.[36]

Just before these orders were sent out, on 16 February, Chief of the air staff, Air Chief Marshal Sir Charles Portal had replied to a letter written to him by Air Marshal Sir Richard Peirse, then Commander in Chief of Bomber Command, at High Wycombe on 13 February. Apart from writing that he did not like the word 'bait' when applied to the crews of the Blenheim bombers being used, Portal also said:

> I regard the exercise of the initiative as in itself an extremely important factor in morale, *and I would willingly accept equal loss or even more in order to throw the enemy on to the defensive, and give our own units the moral superiority gained by doing most of the fighting on the other side.*[37] [Author's italics]

As the sweeps carried on, the number and position of the squadrons changed in response to the German fighters' tactics. The Jagdgeschwader's usual tactic was to stalk the 'Beehive', from a height advantage and try to get into a position from where, if possible, the German fighters could attack ('bounce') from out of the sun and dive from their altitude, through the top screens of Spitfires, to attack the bombers directly, trying not to engage the escorts on the way down. If successful, the Messerschmitt Bf 109Fs and later on the Fw 190s, could then use the speed gained in the dive to climb back up above the British formation to try again when they thought they had the advantage. These were essentially the tactics dictated by Oswald Boelcke and Manfred von Richthofen, and could be summed up as: 'Always above, seldom on the same level, never underneath', the creed of Adolph 'Sailor' Malan, one of Britain's high scoring aces.

Just as in the Battle of Britain the year before with the German fighters, the British close escort found themselves to be hampered by lacking the room to manoeuvre freely against the German interceptors. However, if the German fighters attempted to bounce the British fighter escort, and the Spitfires saw them coming, by timing matters well they could 'break' (turn) into their opponents' attack. This would usually turn into what was called a dogfight, each pilot seeking an opening to gain a good firing position, usually through each one attempting to out-turn the other.

For the Spitfires, the best manoeuvre was to turn as tightly as possible as neither the Bf 109E/F, nor the Fw 190A appeared capable of matching its ability to turn tightly, in the hands of a capable pilot. The problem for the Spitfire pilots was that sooner or later, they would have to make a break to escape the turn in an attempt to get back across the Channel before their fuel ran out, this giving the German pilot an opportunity to gain the advantage. But the German fighter pilots also had to keep an eye on their fuel gauges, particularly in their Bf 109s.

By 26 February, Fighter Command had flown six Circuses, nearly all of them featuring between six and twelve Blenheim medium bombers, escorted by between five and eight squadron of Spitfires and Hurricanes, some giving close escort to the bombers, others acting as top support, forward support and withdrawal cover. Combat with the defending Bf 109s ensued on several occasions but on the whole, casualties on both sides were light.

March, probably due to the cold winter weather, saw only two Circuses being flown and it was obvious that Fighter Command was gaining experience in how to stage the escorts for the medium bombers they were looking after. For instance, the first Circus had no less than nine squadrons of fighters with the usual six Bristol Blenheims carrying out the bombing; the bombers carried out their raid unscathed, but four Spitfires were shot down by Bf 109s from JG 51 while just one Bf 109 was claimed as damaged.[38]

The second Circus, on 13 March, saw six Blenheims, again heavily escorted, attacking enemy airfields at Calais-Marck fairly uneventfully, apart from the flak. Top cover squadron, at 28,000ft was 'bounced' by Bf 109s from 33,000ft, suffered no casualties but scored no victories either; some of the 109s were said to be at 36,000ft. One Spitfire was lost, its pilot becoming a prisoner of war and another crash landed near Dungeness.[39]

It was not until 16 April that the next Circus took place, and the one after that was not until 21 May. This time the Blenheim force numbered seventeen, but no less than sixteen RAF fighter squadrons were involved in the operation. The British lost five Hurricanes, three Spitfires and a Blenheim.

The next month, on 9 and 11 June, JG 26 was back in action, shooting down seven British aircraft, including two Spitfires, engaged in Rhubarb missions.[40]

On 16 June, six Blenheims of Coastal Command were escorted by six squadrons of Hurricanes and Spitfires; in the confused melee that ensued when 8/JG 26 and Galland's stabschwarm intercepted them, the RAF lost eight aircraft, with three more being seriously damaged. The RAF claimed eleven German fighters shot down, five 'probables', and four damaged; but actual German losses were just four, a Heinkel He 59 floatplane engaged in attempting to pick up downed aircrew, and three Bf 109s.[41]

The next day, no less than fourteen RAF fighter squadrons escorted twenty-three Blenheim bombers on a Circus against a chemical plant at Chocques, which later on became a favourite target of the RAF. This time the whole of JG 26 scrambled to intercept them. Fifteen Spitfires and Hurricanes were lost while just one Bf 109 was shot down; Fighter Command claimed that their escorting fighters had shot down fifteen Bf 109s, 'probably' shot down another seven and damaged eleven. It was during this period that the B109 pilots of JG 26, with the noses of their BF 109Fs painted bright yellow, began to be known as the 'Abbeville Boys', and they were treated with the respect they deserved by the fighter pilots of 11 Group.[42]

One day later still, sixteen RAF fighter squadrons from their airfields at Tangmere, Manston, Biggin Hill and Northolt escorted just six Blenheims to France. JG2 lost just one Bf 109, while the RAF claimed ten destroyed and five probables, while losing four Spitfires.[43] Incidentally, these Circuses tended to arrive over France in the afternoon or late evening because, during full summer, visibility was usually good at these times with often little cloud to escape into.

In the latter half of June, JG 2's pilots alone claimed some sixty-nine Spitfires and Hurricanes shot down for the loss of just twenty-one Bf 109s. At least by this time the British pilots flying their Spitfires had ditched their previous fighting formation of a 'Vic' of three aircraft, with the leader looking for the enemy while it was all the two flying behind him and alongside each other could manage to formate on one another, without sparing any time searching the sky for the enemy. Now, the squadrons had adopted the finger-four formation used by the Germans, so called because of its similarity to the spread-out fingers of one hand, in which two pairs could support one another with the leader of each pair charged with spotting and attacking the enemy while his wingman protected his tail. As well, the gun harmonisation distance for the RAF had been brought down from the pre-war recommended distance of 400 yards to 250 yards, giving a greater concentration of bullets at the average range then being used.

One area in which Fighter Command was woefully deficient was in the shooting ability of its pilots. The RAF simply didn't pay enough attention to the art of deflection shooting at this time (that is aiming ahead of an enemy aircraft crossing the nose of an attacking fighter) to help to make their pilots better shots. It was something that they had to learn 'on the job'.

Johnnie Johnson recounted his thoughts on the shooting abilities of RAF pilots in 1941:

> The majority of our pilots could fly reasonably well. They were trained sufficiently to hold their own in a dogfight, but when it came to the ultimate test, judging the range

and deflection angle of their opponents, the average pilot failed, and this was because we paid too little attention to the science of air gunnery. Perhaps I should qualify this statement to apply only to those of us who completed our training during the war years.

The fact remains that the average pilot could knock down a 109 when he overhauled it from dead astern and hose-piped his opponent with two cannons and four machine-guns. But give him a testing deflection shot at angles of more than a few degrees and he usually failed to nail his opponent. Personally, I found my own game and wild fowling experience to be of the greatest value. The fighter pilot who could hit a curling, down wind pheasant, or a jinking head-on partridge, or who could kill a widgeon cleanly in a darkening sky, had little trouble in bringing his guns to bear against a 109. The outstanding fighter pilots were invariably excellent game shots.

On taking over a wing composed of Canadians in early 1943, Johnson had this to write about the standard of shooting of RAF Fighter pilots at this stage of the war:

It was standard procedure for our guns and cannon to be harmonised to give a fairly large 'shotgun' pattern at the best firing range. The theory behind this was that, as the average pilot was not a good shot, the open pattern would give him the best chance of hitting the Huns. But a far more lethal method of obtaining a kill, provided the pilot could aim and shoot, was to harmonise the guns to give a 'spot' concentration of fire. [Here Johnson names the previous wing commander] had had his guns set on the spot principle, and since his combat films were some of the best ever taken, I followed his example.[44]

Two Circuses were flown on 21 June, again just six Blenheims in each escorted by seventeen RAF fighter squadrons. Twelve Spitfires, Hurricanes and Blenheims were shot down. For once, JG 26 suffered real casualties with nine going down including Galland, who was forced to make a crash landing in his damaged Bf 109F.

Adolf Galland was actually shot down twice on 21 June, and survived both occasions; the first time was in combating Circus 16. After Galland had shot down a Blenheim, he was in turn shot down, by Pilot Officer H. Drobinski for his third victory. With his radiator damaged and his engine seized up, Galland was fortunate enough to be near to Calais-Marck airfield and belly-landed there. In the dogfight, his wingman, Unterfeldwebel Hegenauer, was shot down also, parachuting to safety. Squadron Leader J.A. 'Johnny' Kent DFC was the RAF fighter pilot credited with this victory, but the RAF account indicates that Wing Commander Douglas Bader shot down Hegenauer, and Lieutenant H.O. Mehre, a Norwegian, shot down Galland.

Having been picked up from Calais-Marck in the Gruppe's Messerschmitt Bf 108 'Taifun' communications aircraft, Galland was in time to scramble again to attack Circus 17 later that same afternoon. Galland was without his usual wingman in this battle as Hegenauer still hadn't returned after being shot down earlier in the day.

After shooting down a Spitfire but without a wingman to confirm his victory, Galland committed the cardinal fighter pilot sin of following it down to see it crash, and was jumped by another Spitfire, being flown by Reg Grant, a New Zealander, for his first victory. Galland parachuted to the ground with injuries to his face and arm and with a twisted ankle. Upon his return to his headquarters he learned that he had been awarded the swords to the oak leaves of his Knight's Cross for achieving seventy victories, but he had also been ordered by Hitler not to fly on operations again.[45]

Incidentally, it wasn't just the British who over-claimed; on 21 June, II./JG 2 had claimed ten Spitfires destroyed, while JG 26 had claimed eight. The actual losses to Fighter Command were three Spitfires.

The very next day saw Circus 18 flown and at the end of it, when they returned home, the British fighter pilots put in claims for thirty-one Bf 109s destroyed, five 'probables' and seven damaged. The British lost one Spitfire, together with its pilot. Reality was somewhat different, although the Germans also overclaimed but not quite on such a grand scale. They claimed to have shot down ten Spitfires and two Blenheims. None of the latter had been lost. German Bf 109 losses were just four.[46]

With the invasion of Russia on 22 June 1941, Churchill and the Air Ministry came under pressure from Stalin, who was very keen for the Luftwaffe to send more fighter squadrons over to France, away from the fighting in Russia; he called for even more British aircraft to be committed to the struggle over Northern France and the Channel in order to take pressure off the Russians, but the Germans felt no need to add more squadrons to JG 2 and JG 26. It was shades of June 1940 over again but now the other way around, and Dowding was no longer at Fighter Command to stand up to the Prime Minister's wishes.

On 3 July 1941, the Deputy Chief of the Air Staff, Air Vice-Marshal N.H. Bottomley, changed the previous policy, as stated on the 13 February 1941, about the purpose of the Circus operations. This now read:

> In light of the present strategical situation it is necessary to modify the aim of these operations. Their primary aim should now be the destruction of certain important targets by day bombing, and incidentally, the destruction of enemy fighter aircraft.

From this time on until the end of July, Fighter Command sent Circuses to France almost every day. From 5 July, they sometimes used Britain's first wartime four-engine bomber, the Short Stirling, as 'bait' in these raids. The Stirling's ceiling was a lowly (literally) 16,500ft, so the German fighters had no problem, if vectored in time, to climb above the top cover of the escort and then to attempt to dive down through the various layers of escorting Spitfires and Hurricanes, to launch their attacks on the bombers, be they Blenheims or Stirlings.

Hugh 'Cocky' Dundas, a Spitfire pilot serving in 616 Squadron, wrote of his impressions of a typical operation over France that July:

Up the line D.B.'s [Douglas Bader] motor starts. 610 have formed up and are beginning to move off across the airfield as we taxi out …

Twenty-five thousand. 'levelling out'. Puffs of black ten thousand feet below show where the bombers are crossing between Boulogne and le Touqet. Six big cigars with tiers of protective fighters milling above them.

'Hello Douglas, Woody calling. There are fifty plus gaining height to the east.'

'Okay Woody.'

'Put your corks in boys.' Stan.

Over the coast at Harlow we nose ahead without altering course.

'D.B. there's some stuff at 3 o'clock, climbing round to the south west.'

'Okay I see. Stan, you deal with them if necessary.'

'Okay okay don't get excited.'

Usual remarks. Usual shouts of warning. Usual bad language. Usual bloody Huns climbing round the usual bloody way.

St Omer on the left. We fly on, straight and steady in force, towards Lille.

Stan's voice: 'They're behind us, Walker squadron. Stand by to break.'

Then: 'Look out Walker. Breaking starboard.'

Looking over my shoulder to the right and above I see the specks and glints which are Stan's planes break up into the fight, a quick impression of machines diving, climbing, gyrating. Stan, Ian, Tony, Derek and the rest of them are fighting for their lives up there.

Close to the target now. 'Billy here, DB. There's a lot of stuff coming round at 3 o'clock, slightly above.'

Quick look to the right. Where the hell? Christ yes! There they are the sods. A typical long fast climbing straggle of 109s.

'More below, D.B., to port.'

'Okay going down. Ken, watch those buggers behind.'

'Okay D.B.'

'Come on Cocky.'

Down after DB. … Getting in range now. Wait for it, wait for D.B. and open up altogether. 250 yards … 200 … wish to Christ I felt safer behind … 150. DB opens up. I pull my nose up slightly to put the dot ahead of his orange spinner. Hold it and squeeze, cannon and machine-guns together … correct slightly … you're hitting the bastard … wisp of smoke.

'BREAK, Rusty squadron, for Christ sake break!'

Stick hard over and back into tummy, peak revs and haul her round. Tracers curl past … orange nose impression not forty yards off… slacken turn for a second … Hell of a melee … better keep turning, keep turning, keep turning.

There's a chance, now. Ease off, nose up, give her two lengths lead and fire. Now break, don't hang around, break! Tracers again … a huge orange spinner and three little tongues of flame spitting at me for a second in a semi-head-on attack. Round, round, so that she nearly spins. Then they're all gone, gone as usual as suddenly as they came.

'Cocky, where the hell are you? Are you with me, Cocky?' There he is, I think. Lucky to find him after that shambles. 'Okay D.B., coming up on your starboard now.'

'Right behind you Cocky.' That's Johnny calling.

'Okay Johnny I see you now.'

Good show; the old firm's still together.

Dundas went on to relate that his squadron suffered 'grievous losses'. Between 20 June and 10 August, it lost 12 pilots, over half of its full establishment. In return, the squadron claimed 21 enemy planes definitely destroyed, 12 probably destroyed and 21 damaged. But overall, morale remained high.[47]

The war diary of JG 26 alone for this same period admitted losing twenty-five Bf 109s in combat but claimed the shooting down of seventy-nine British aircraft, mainly Spitfires.

During this next seven-week period, the RAF lost 163 Spitfires and Hurricanes to JG 26 alone, together with a few Blenheims. JG 26's losses were just forty-six Bf 109s.

Wing Leader Johnny Kent was very critical of these close escort Circuses, with the slow cruising Bristol Blenheims at their centre. He pointed out in his book that there were two major mistakes committed by RAF fighters: The first mistake was in tying the fighters too close to the bombers, allowing the German fighters to scythe through the formation to attack the bombers, whilst the escorting fighters were trying to get up to combat speed, whilst looking around to see if there were more enemy fighters attacking.

Kent went on to write:

The second mistake was really very similar in its effect to the first but, if anything, was accentuated in that operations carried out as far afield as Lille necessitated the fighters flying slowly not only to stay with the bombers but also to conserve fuel. The fact is that one could not afford to fight on such an operation as to do so properly meant that you would have insufficient fuel to get back across the Channel. All that we could do was to defend ourselves, but by so doing one failed to give sufficient protection to the bombers. This was something that we had noticed with the Germans in 1940 – the fighters were loath to join combat when escorting the bombers on the more penetrating raids. The significance was not appreciated by us – *or at least not by those who were more concerned with planning our operations than carrying them out.*[48] [Author's italics]

One notable result for the RAF fighters during this period was the loss of Hauptmann Wilhelm Balthasar, the Kommodore of JG 2, on 3 July. His Bf 109F lost a wing when it was hit by cannon fire from the Spitfire flown by the CO of 609 Squadron, Squadron Leader M.L. Robinson, DFC. Balthasar had scored forty-seven victories during his service career and was replaced by the commander of III/JG 53, Walther Oesau.

On 10 July, Hauptmann Rolf Pingel, a German 'Experte' with twenty-five victories of 1/JG 26 was shot down over Britain after having followed a Stirling Bomber back to its base. Over Kent, his engine was damaged, apparently by fire from the rear gunner of the bomber and he was forced down, helped on his way by Sergeant J. Smigielski of 306 Squadron, flying a Spitfire. However, no bullet holes were found in Pingel's newly delivered Messerschmitt, and it now appears that he suffered some form of engine failure.

Pingel had been flying a Bf 109F-2 and he belly-landed it in a Kent field. Captured, his 109 was swiftly repaired and flown in comparison tests by the Air Fighting Development Unit. Pingel had fought in the Spanish Civil War, as well as the aerial battles over Poland, France and Britain and had been awarded the Knight's Cross. His interrogation makes interesting reading, but probably made somewhat uncomfortable listening for his RAF interrogators.

Rolf Pingel told them first of all that he was glad that the RAF were now raiding France as that meant that any German pilot shot down there, if he managed to bale out or crash land, would not be taken prisoner as many of Pingel's friends had been in the Battle of Britain.

Pingel went on to say that over 100 Spitfires had been shot down over France so far in 1941, while the Germans had only lost some twenty to thirty Bf 109s. He told his interrogators that his gruppe alone had shot down some fifty British aircraft for the loss of only eight pilots.

When told that British pilots had claimed shooting down 125 Bf 109s in the same period, Pingel pondered it, then replied that that couldn't possibly be right as it would have meant that his Jagdgeschwader would have lost over half their fighter strength in France and there weren't enough Bf 109s available to replace such a loss. One wonders at Sholto Douglas and Trafford Leigh-Mallory's reaction when given this news.[49]

The captured Bf 109F-2 of Rolf Pingel was tested by the RAF in October 1941, against a Spitfire Mk Vb and was found to be some 21 mph faster than the Spitfire at 18,800ft. The tests also confirmed that the 109F could out-climb the Spitfire. Later on in October, this captured 109F-2 was crashed and that was the end of any more comparative trials.

Flight magazine featured Pingel's repaired Bf 109F-2 in the edition of 5 February 1942. It described the aircraft's maximum speed as being 371 mph at 22,000ft and its maximum rate of climb, measured at 5,000ft was 3,320ft/minute, which had fallen off to 2,370ft/minute at 20,000ft. Maximum power of the DB601N engine was given as 1,085bhp, at sea level, again at 2,600rpm. Weight was 6,090 pounds. Rate of climb at 5,000ft was 3,320ft/minute and at 20,000ft the maximum rate of climb was 2,370ft/minute. 'Reputed' ceiling was 40,000ft. Interestingly, the Messerschmitt factory's own tests gave a maximum speed for a Bf 109F-2 as 393 mph at 15,800ft and a Bf 109F-4, with DB601E engine was tested at 415 mph at 20,460ft. The factory gave this same aircraft a maximum altitude of 39,000ft.[50]

Wing Commander Johnny Kent test-flew a captured Bf 109F in 1943, while he was in the Middle East. In his book *One of the Few*, Kent recounted:

> I was lucky enough to fly the 109F and found it very pleasant but extremely blind, particularly downwards, and this probably explains why, during the Battle of Britain in particular, the German pilots did not attack even when we were only a few hundred feet below them. This happened on numerous occasions and they obviously did not know we were there.[51]

It was around this time that RAF Intelligence made an estimate of how many German single-engine fighters Fighter Command had to contend with in France. They estimated between 340 to 375 single-engine fighters. This was half as many again as the actual number.

There were two more Circuses on 23 July, with 59 and 60 being flown. JG 2 claimed fourteen Spitfires in No.59, plus fifteen more for No.60; JG 26 claimed thirteen aircraft shot down, of which eleven were confirmed. They lost three Bf 109s. True victories and losses were somewhat different: fifteen Spitfires were lost. On this day as well, 15 Squadron Short Stirlings bombed *Scharnhorst* in La Pallice docks. One was lost, while JG 2 claimed to have shot down three USAAF B-17s. Obviously at this time of the war, one four-engine bomber looked very like another.

On 31 July, the RAF held a review to measure the success (or otherwise) of their operations. One of those invited was Air Vice-Marshal 'Bomber' Harris, now the Commander-in-Chief of Bomber

Command. Although Leigh-Mallory argued in favour of continuing the sweeps, using Short Stirling four-engine bombers, Harris thought the sweeps were not accomplishing anything useful and withdrew the Stirlings from daytime use, leaving the crews of the obsolescent Bristol Blenheims to 'keep on carrying on'.

So it went on. On 9 August, for example, Fighter Command reported shooting down eighteen Bf 109s, probably destroying twelve, and damaging nine more. JG 26 actually lost just two Bf 109s.

According to Hugh Dundas:

> In the six weeks between mid-June and the end of July – the period of maximum activity by our squadrons – Fighter Command lost one hundred and twenty-three pilots and planes. Against this, we claimed the destruction of three hundred and twenty-two German planes. These figures were not compatible with the withdrawal of the Luftwaffe units from west to east. It had to be concluded that our claims were exaggerated – and considerably so.[52]

The new commander at Fighter Command does not seem to have learnt an important lesson from the Battle of Britain, still fresh in the memory of most RAF personnel at this time. Any British aircraft lost over France would mean its pilot lost to the war effort, either killed or captured.

No.129 Squadron had been formed at Tangmere in the summer of 1941, its new squadron leader, Dennis Armitage, had this to say about the operations undertaken by his squadron:

> It wasn't like fighting a battle on your home ground. It seemed to us very pointless. It was a political, psychological exercise so that the French could see British aircraft overhead. I didn't enjoy it. I didn't enter into it in the same way as I had the Battle of Britain.[53]

Victory Claims

One of the seemingly unforeseen problems that Fighter Command had was the confirmation (or not) of the pilots' claims. These were based upon combat reports taken by each squadron's intelligence officer, upon the pilots' return from an operation. Almost invariably, the British and their French, Polish and Czech allies over-claimed. The Germans were guilty of the same fault but at least their claims, except those that fell in the Channel, could be substantiated by ground troops manning the anti-aircraft guns in France.

Where the RAF's claims were concerned, a lot was down to wishful thinking, when an enemy aircraft under fire started to smoke. This might have been genuinely due to battle damage, but also might have been due to the German pilot ramming his throttle wide open to escape his assailant and the resulting full flow of fuel would mean more smoke from the exhausts. A British pilot might also have seen his victim fall in a spin and think he had destroyed that aircraft, whereas the German pilot, again, was trying to throw off his pursuer. Whatever the reason, the British believed that they were shooting down almost four times more aircraft than they actually were. It was a repeat of the German claims for their victories over RAF fighters in the Battle of Britain where, had they been accurate, all the aircraft of Fighter Command would have ceased to exist after the first few days of the battle.

On their side, the Germans demanded the corroboration of another pilot, or the crews of anti-aircraft guns stationed on and around the French coast. Their figures for British aircraft shot down in 1941 and '42 over the French coast were at least more accurate (but not always!) than the British claims. JG 2 seem to have been guilty of overclaiming more than JG 26.

From the beginning of June until the end of 1941, RAF fighters (mostly Spitfire Mk Vbs, as the Hurricane was becoming obsolete in the escort fighter role) performed massed sweeps escorting small forces of typically Blenheim bombers, tasked with bombing railway yards, dockyards, factories and airfields over the Channel in France, with the intent of drawing the German fighters into combat – and this they did.

The Hurricanes being used during this period of 1941 were mainly of the Mk IIC variety, which was almost universally known as the 'Hurribomber', it having provision for carrying two 250-pound bombs, one under each wing. The Mk IIc was well armed, having four 20mm Hispano-Suiza cannon fitted, but weight had increased over the Mk I and maximum speed given was 336 mph. This aircraft would stay in service until 1943, when it was steadily replaced in squadron service by Hawker Typhoons.

Interestingly, German fighter pilots, while perhaps actually shooting down a Hurricane, nearly always claimed that they had shot down a Spitfire, it obviously being seen as more of a feat to shoot down a Spitfire than a Hurricane. Adolf Galland once described the Hurricane as: 'A very nice aircraft to shoot down.'

The Germans, now using their 'Freya' and 'Wurzburg' radar and ground control in France, as the British had done during the Battle of Britain, could easily vector their fighters into an advantageous position over France in order to attack the incoming British bombers and fighters, and nearly always with the advantage of height. Additionally, the Germans, like the British, also had a section which intercepted and listened to R/T chatter from the British pilots and were able to use this to judge where and when the raids were coming, thus giving the German fighter pilots time to climb above the incoming Spitfires and Blenheims to perform their favourite diving attacks upon Allied formations.

Probably the best description, from a British pilot, of just what it was like to fly on these Circuses came from Johnnie Johnson in 1941, flying Spitfires Vs with 616 Squadron, at that time led by Wing Leader Douglas Bader. Johnson described a typical mission to Lille in July 1941 thus:

'Woody' Woodhall gave us our course to steer for home on the way out: 'Course for Dover – 310 degrees.' Woodhall fades out, for he has done his utmost to paint a broad picture of the air situation. Now it is up to our leader:

'Dogsbody (Bader's callsign) from blue one. Beehive at twelve o' clock below. About seven miles.'

'OK I see them.' And the wing leader eases his force to starboard and a better sun-up position.

The high-flying Messerschmitts have seen our wing and stab at Stan's top-cover squadron with savage attacks from either flank.

'Break port, Ken.' (From a pilot of 610)

'Keep turning.'

'Tell me when to stop turning.'

'Keep turning. There's four behind!'

'Get in, red section.'

'We're stuck into some 109's behind you, Douglas.' (This quietly from Stan.)

'O.K. Stan.'

'Baling out.'

'Try and make it, Mac. Not far to the coast.' (This urgently from the squadron commander.)

'No use. Temperatures off the clock. She'll burn any time. Look after my dog.'

"Keep turning, yellow section."

So far the fight has remained well above us. We catch fleeting glimpses of high vapour trails and ducking, twisting fighters. Two-thirds of the wing are behind us, holding off the 109s and we forge on to the target area to carry out our assigned task. We can never reform into a wing again, and the pilots of 145 and 610 will make their way home in twos and fours. We head towards the distant beehive, well aware that there is now no covering force of Spitfires above us.

The Stirlings have dropped their heavy loads of bombs and begin their return journey. We curve slowly over the outskirts of Lille to make sure the beehive is not harried from the rear. I look down at a pall of debris and black smoke rising from the target five miles below, and absurdly my memory flashes back to contrast the scene with those other schoolboy Sunday afternoons.

'Dogsbody from Smith. 109s above. Six o'clock. About twenty-five to thirty.'

'Well done. Watch 'em and tell me when to break.'

I can see them. High in the sun, and their presence only betrayed by the reflected sparkle from highly polished windscreens and cockpit covers.

'They're coming down, Dogsbody. Break left.' And round to port we go, with Smith sliding below Bader and Cocky and me above so that we cover each other in this steep turn. We curve around and catch a glimpse of four baffled 109s climbing back to join their companions, for they can't stay with us in a turn. The keen eyes of Smith saved us from a nasty smack that time.

'Keep turning, Dogsbody. More coming down.' From Cocky.

'OK. We might get a squirt this time,' rejoins Bader. What a man, I think, what a man!

The turn tightens and in my extreme position on the starboard side I'm driving my Spitfire through a greater radius of curve than the others and falling behind. I kick on hard bottom rudder and skid inwards, down and behind the leader. More 109s hurtle down from above and a section of four angle in from the starboard flank. I look round for other Spitfires but there are none in sight. The four of us are alone over Lille.

'Keep turning. Keep turning.' (From Bader.) 'They can't stay with us.' And we keep turning, hot and frightened and a long way from home. We can't keep turning all bloody day, I think bitterly.

Cocky has not re-formed after the last break and I take his place next to Bader and the three of us watch the Messerschmitts, time their dives and call the break into their attacks. The odds are heavily against us.

We turn across the sun and I am on the inside. The blinding light seems only 2ft above Bader's cockpit and if I drop further below I shall lose him. Already his Spitfire has lost its colour and is swallowed up by the sun's fierce light. I come out of the turn and find myself alone in the Lille sky.

The Messerschmitts come in close for the kill. At this range their camouflage looks dirty and oil stained, and one brute has a startling black and white spinner. In a hot sweat of fear I keep turning and turning, and the fear is mingled with an abject humiliation that these bastards should single me out and chop me up at their leisure. The radio is silent, or probably I don't hear it in the stress of trying to stay alive. I can't spend the whole day turning, Le Touquet is 70 hostile miles away; far better to fight back and take one with me.

Four Messerschmitts roar down from 6 o'clock. I see them in time and curve the shuddering, protesting Spitfire to meet them, for she's on the brink of a high-speed stall. They are so certain of my destruction that they are flying badly and I fasten on to tail-end Charlie and give him a long burst of fire. He is at the maximum range, and although my shooting has no apparent effect, some of my despair and fear on this fateful afternoon seems to evaporate at the faint sound of chattering machine guns. But perhaps my attack has its just reward, for Smith's voice comes loud and clear over the radio. 'One Spit behind, Dogsbody. Thousand yards. Looks like he's in trouble.' Then I see the aircraft with the lovely curving wings that can only belong to Spitfires. I take a long breath and in a deliberately calm voice: 'It's me Dogsbody – Johnny.'

'Okay Johnny. We'll orbit here for you. Drop in on my starboard. We'll get a couple of these —'

There is no longer any question of not getting home now that I am with Bader again. He will bring us safely back to Tangmere and I know he's enjoying this, for he sounds full of confidence over the radio.

A dozen Messerschmitts still shadow our small formation. They are well up sun and waiting to strike. Smith and I fly with our necks twisted round, like the resting Mallard ducks one sees in the London parks, and all our concentration focused on the glinting shoals of 109s.

'Two coming down from 5 o'clock, Dogsbody. Break right,' from me. And this time, mine is the smallest turn so that I am the first to meet the attack. A 109 is very close and climbing away to port. Here is a chance. Time for a quick shot and no danger of losing the other two Spitfires if I don't get involved in a long tail chase. I line up my Spitfire behind the 109, clench the spade grip of the stick with both hands and send short bursts into his belly at less than a hundred yards. The 109 bursts apart and the explosion looks exactly the same as a near burst of heavy flak, a vicious flower with a poisonous glowing centre and black swirling edges.

I reform and the Messerschmitts come in again, as this time Bader calls the break. It's well judged and the wing leader fastens on to the last 109 and I cover his Spitfire as it appears to stand on its tail with wisps of smoke plummeting from the gun ports. The enemy aircraft starts to pour white smoke from its belly and thick black smoke from the engine. They merge together and look like a long, dirty banner against the faded blue of some high cirrus cloud.

'Bloody good shooting, sir'

"We'll get some more."

Unbelievably the Messerschmitts, which have tailed us for so long, vanish and we are alone in the high spaces.

We pick up the English coast near Dover and turn to port for Sussex and Tangmere. We circle our airfield and land without any fuss or aerobatics, for we never know until we are on the ground whether or not a stray bullet has partially severed a control cable.[54]

Radio Interception

Britain's 'Y' section, which intercepted and decoded the German's W/T and R/T traffic was asked by the Air Ministry about why it always seemed that the German fighters knew where the Circuses were going. Aileen Clayton, a German speaking WAAF in the intelligence service later on wrote, in her book *The Enemy is Listening*:

> The keenest interest was always shown by Fighter Command in what the German Y Service (the Horchdienst) were reporting about British fighters preparing to attack a German formation. This was very much a case of forewarned being forearmed. We became so concerned about the amount of information the Horchdienst was obviously getting that in July 1941 we set up a watch at Kingsdown on British fighter R/T

on the 100 to 120 megacycle band, and from that we were able to give Fighter Command a few home truths, including issuing to them a comparison between British and German fighter security.

We knew that we were able to monitor Luftwaffe R/T up to 500 miles on the 2 to 6 megacycle band, and by this time we were covering the whole of the Western European coastline from Jutland to La Rochelle.

There was little reason why the Germans should not also have Y's extensive cover, indeed, we knew that they had. When it came to a general comparison of the signals security of the British and German fighters, we came to the conclusion that the Germans revealed more information by trusting to the inviolability of their code words and map systems, than by careless and unnecessary chance, while exactly the reverse applied to the British pilots and their controllers.

The very nature of the tight system of control employed by the RAF required more communication between aircraft and controller than was the case with the German day fighters. On the whole they were much more cagey than our pilots. It is no good having a code language if some idiot compromises it. One might as well just talk in plain language. I often wondered how long it took the German Y Service to decode our 'Gate' and 'Buster' (slow down and step on it)? What was the sense of a controller saying: 'Understand you are Popeye, increase angels and see if you come to quilt', since patently, angels (height) had been well and truly compromised very early on in the war. And how kind of one controller to advise the German Y station of the limit of his controls zone by warning a pilot: 'You'd better come back or you'll be getting out of my

Control,' or, 'Bandit (enemy aircraft) has turned north and he's going off of our table.'

A pilot, chatting to a friend, must also have proved helpful to the enemy when he divulged: 'A good way to find base is to fly up river,' we knew only too well how helpful this type of information was to one's enemy. We even have one controller telling a pilot: 'You are now crossing the river east of Gravesend. If you fly west, you will find the airfield 10 miles ahead.' And the pilot who, somewhat relieved, informed his ground controller that he: 'Nearly flew into the balloon barrage slightly north of base,' it would've been even more helpful to the Germans to have also given the height of the barrage.

For the month of August alone, JG 26 shot down sixty-six Spitfires, plus a few Blenheims and Hurricanes. The Jagdgeschwader lost only fifteen Bf 109s and two Fw 190s, which had just been introduced into staffel service. They were to prove an even more formidable foe to the British Spitfires than the already proven Bf 109F.

At least the RAF had the Air Transport Auxiliary (ATA) which consisted mainly of female pilots, who ferried their new and much needed Spitfires to the squadrons. To see an attractive woman, clad in full flying gear, step out of the cockpit must have brought some cheer to the pilots, not counting the ground crews![55]

One of the casualties of Circus 68, sent out on 9 August, was the proponent of the 'Big Wing' theory, Wing Commander Douglas Bader himself. The legless pilot was lucky to be able to parachute out of his doomed Spitfire after its tail was severely damaged by cannon fire. Sadly, it may not even have been cannon fire from a Bf 109, but from Bader's squadron mate, Flight Lieutenant 'Buck' Casson, who mistook Bader's Spitfire for a 109. He also failed to return from this Circus and spent the rest of the war in captivity.

After his capture, Bader was invited to have dinner in the officers' mess of JG 26 by Adolf Galland and before dinner, Galland showed Bader one of the staffel's Bf 109Fs. Bader asked to be allowed to sit in the cockpit and Galland allowed his request. Bader then asked Galland if he couldn't just take off and do a quick circuit, to which Galland replied, 'If I grant your wish I'm afraid you'll escape and I should be forced to chase after you. Now we have met, we don't want to shoot at each other again, do we? [56]

Shortly after Bader's capture, the ineptitude of the Air Ministry struck again. Squadron Leader Stan Turner's 145 Squadron, which usually accompanied Bader's wing as top cover on Circus operations, was ordered to Yorkshire for a 'rest'. They were replaced by a 'relatively inexperienced squadron, right in the middle of the shooting season'.[57]

JG 2 starred on 12 August, against Circus 69 and Circus 70. Their commanding officer, Walter Oesau, alone shot down five Spitfires. At least, that was what he claimed. Erich Leie claimed three Spitfires and Hans Hahn claimed three. True Spitfire losses were six.

Circus 72 was flown on 14 August and this time, all except one Blenheim returned safely, that one being shot down by a pilot from 9./JG 26. Spitfires managed to shoot two 109s down and two more were forced to crash land.[58]

Around this time, Wing Commander 'Johnny' Kent, a Canadian who had been one of the pre-war test pilots for the RAF, attended a conference being held at Northolt, presided over by Trafford Leigh-Mallory and including the other fighter and bomber wing leaders of the RAF. This conference was being held to discuss the various problems that were arising during the staging of the Circuses.

Kent disturbed Leigh-Mallory after the conference was over by asking what purpose the sweeps served; if, he said, it was for actually destroying the industrial potential of the various targets, then many more bombers would be needed. If it was 'merely' to bring up the

German fighters to fight, then the targets needed to be closer to Britain, as most of his pilots were having to fight with one eye on their fuel gauges in order to get home.

Leigh-Mallory 'looked rather taken aback' at this question, and asked Group Captain Victor Beamish, himself a very experienced fighter pilot and leader, for his opinion. Beamish agreed with Kent. So Leigh-Mallory, obviously seeking only the answer he wanted, asked one of his staff officers who had been a pilot in the First World War about this. That worthy replied: 'My answer is – we've done it!' Kent grew angry and argued with the staff officer, but Leigh-Mallory was unmoved. Therefore, as Kent recorded: 'we continued to fly to Lille and lose good men, all to little purpose'.[59]

Circus 73 was flown on 14 August and, as if to demonstrate by how much RAF fighter pilots were over-claiming, the Polish wing 'bounced' Bf 109s of III./JG 26 and claimed no less than thirteen (later upgraded to sixteen) 109s for four losses. JG 26, in actual fact, lost just two aircraft, one pilot baling out while the other was killed. Incidentally, it was on this date also that the newly delivered Focke-Wulf 190s made their first kills – two Spitfires.

As if to emphasise this over-claiming, two days later saw the escorting Spitfires claiming ten destroyed, and just one damaged, later upgraded to nineteen destroyed and three probables, while actual German losses were one 109 destroyed and four with various states of damage, but all these got back to their airfields. Four Spitfires went down.

At around this time, as if these losses were not enough to depress the pilots themselves and the staff officers at the Air Ministry, a report was circulated which showed that, of all the bombs dropped by Bomber Command so far in the war, hardly any had hit (or even dropped close to) their target. All those officers who had, for so many years, championed the bomber over the fighter, were aghast. How could this be? Their wonderful weapon, which they had trumpeted would bring Nazi Germany to its knees, simply wasn't working.

It was to take years before proper navigational aids and pathfinding techniques would finally make Britain's night bombing effort the terror to the German civilians that it became.

The Arrival of the Focke Wulf 190

As we have seen, in August, Germany's newest fighter, the Fw 190A had been introduced into Luftwaffe service, operating first of all on the Channel front with JG 26. When this aircraft was first encountered in combat, it came as a complete surprise to the British, having much superior performance to the Spitfire Mk V, then in general service. RAF Intelligence officers told the Spitfire pilots that these new German fighters were probably some old Curtis Hawks that the Luftwaffe had taken over but, as Johnnie Johnson wrote, 'No pre-war fighter had the performance of this brute!'

The Focke-Wulf Fw 190A-0 was an excellent fighter, with its BMW 801C-1 fourteen cylinder, two-row radial engine giving up to 1,600hp, which gave the Fw 190 a performance enabling it to outrun the Spitfire V easily and exceed that aircraft's maximum speed by up to 40 mph. Initial armament was four 7.92mm machine-guns but two 20mm cannon were soon added as the initial armament was thought to be too light. For the pilot, BMW had provided what the Germans called the 'kommandogerat', a radical single lever control in the cockpit, which combined throttle (for rpm control) boost pressure, mixture control, ignition timing, supercharger speed and airscrew pitch all in one control. Controls such as flaps and undercarriage retraction and lowering were electrically operated. This thus gave German pilots a simple aircraft to control, particularly when in combat; there were less things for the pilot to bother about.

To further help its pilot, the Fw 190 had a superb sliding cockpit canopy, giving very much improved pilot vision all round over that of the Bf 109. A true killing machine, the Fw 190 was known as the 'Wuerger', or 'Shrike/Butcher Bird' by its pilots. British intelligence was told of this new German fighter by a prisoner of war in February 1941 but refused to believe that a fighter powered by a radial engine could possibly match the performance of the Spitfire. They were to be proved wrong. The Fw 190 had been designed in 1937 and had first flown in 1939, before the outbreak of the war.

The Fw 190 proved that a radial-engine fighter, shunned by the British before the war, could be as fast, if not faster than an equivalent in-line liquid-cooled engine aircraft of the same power. The trick was in getting the cowling right. Yes, the inline engine appeared to be the right choice as it gave a smaller fuselage cross section, which helped it aerodynamically, but the cooling fluid had itself to be cooled, which meant radiators sprouting out of that smooth airframe, which all produced drag.

The Fw 190 was superior in climbing ability and speed to the then current Spitfire Mk V, being able to climb at 3,280ft per minute up to 17,500ft and was timed at 408 mph at 19,420ft, but performance fell off when the Fw 190A series climbed to over 20,000ft. This was not a problem in 1941/42 when the RAF first encountered the new Fw 190 over France, most combats seeming to take place at under 20,000ft but it was a big disadvantage when the Fw 190 fought the American B-17s and B-24s from 1942 onwards as they tended to fly at 25,000ft on their bombing raids. Maximum ceiling of the Fw 190 was given as 33,800ft.

The Fw 190A series had some problems initially, mainly to do with the engines overheating, not receiving enough cooling air, plus oil and fuel lines that tended to leak (!) but this was cured by Focke-Wulf and BMW's development engineers, aided by the Luftwaffe's own test pilots and engineers during intensive testing in 1941.

Back in March 1941, Oberleutnant Otto Behrens (later to lead 6/JG 26) was put in command of Erprobungsstaffel 190. He and Oberleutnant Karl Borris, the second Gruppe's technical officer, had led thirty engineers to the Luftwaffe Test Centre at Rechlin to sort out the initial problems, together with some thirty technical assistants. This small group was to look after and develop the new, but troublesome, fighter. They were given six pre-production Fw 190A-0 aircraft (Erprobungsstaffel 190) to 'trouble shoot' and develop. That they succeeded was to be proved in the months and years to come.

Borris recorded that:

> From the first take-off we were convinced of the robustness and the excellent flying qualities of the new aircraft. However, the BMW 801 engine, a new twin-row, 14-cylinder, air-cooled radial design, gave us nothing but misery. Whatever could possibly go wrong with it, did. We hardly dared to leave the immediate vicinity of the airfield with our six machines. Oil lines ruptured. The heavily armoured oil cooler ring in front of the engine often broke. The bottom cylinder of the rear row seized again and again, since the oil pump and the cooling surfaces were too small. Leaking fuel lines left the pilot in a dazed state from the fumes, unable to climb out of their airplanes unaided. The constant speed propeller often failed to work properly. Professor Kurt Tank tried to meet our demands in the most direct manner, avoiding the bureaucracy.

The development work was completed by the end of July and Erprobungsstaffel 190 was disbanded and the men returned to their units in France. After these six aircraft, only a hundred first production Fw 190A-1 aircraft were produced before the model was superseded by the Fw 190A-2, having the BMW 801C-2 engine and four 20mm cannon in the wings and two 7.92mm machine-guns in the cowling ahead of the pilot. The BMW 801C-2 engines, giving 1,560hp were 'lifed' for just twenty-five hours at the beginning of production. So unreliable were these early engines, including even the next 801D engines fitted to the Fw 190A-3, that JG 26 leader Adolf Galland stated, in December, that 'no missions over the Channel into England should be attempted'.

Oberleutnant Rolf Schrofter, III/JG 26's technical officer recalled later on that the chief culprit of the broken connecting rods in the BMW engine was one exhaust manifold, that of the bottom of the second row of cylinders, which was badly located. This allowed the cylinder to overheat, hence the conrod breakages. Apparently, this was something that could be fixed in the field. Oberleutnant Karl Borris, the eighth staffel's leader, was awarded a gold watch by the BMW company when the engine in his Fw 190 reached a hundred hours operating time, a record at that time.[60]

Ironically, what was to become part of the British answer to the Fw 190 made its first flight just seven days after the RAF's first encounter with the new enemy fighter. On 27 September, the Spitfire Mk IX had first flown in prototype form. This was the prototype Mk III, re-fitted with a Merlin 61, an engine originally intended for the Wellington bomber, and fitted with a much improved two-stage, two-speed supercharger, which helped the Merlin engine now develop some 1,565hp. But it took over four months, until 6 January 1942, before the second prototype, which originally had been a Mk I, flew. Now the proposed Mk VIII production order was cut back, pending the production of the Mk IX. However, it was to take another six months until the Mk IX was introduced into service – and then relatively slowly.[61]

The powers that be at the British Air Ministry had thought that the Spitfire Mk V was a fine fighter and would be able to best any German fighter in 1941. In this, they were sadly mistaken. With the introduction of the Bf 109F-4 in June, and then the Fw 190A-1 and A-2 in August/September, the aircraft performance advantage was most definitely with the Luftwaffe from the introduction of these two fighters, right through to July 1942, when the Spitfire Mk IX was introduced into service.

The Director of Technical Developments at the Air Ministry, a Mr Verney, had written the following for a meeting of the Air Staff on 24 June 1941:

I understand that Rolls-Royce have suddenly produced the Merlin 61 out of the hat and claim for it a performance equivalent to the Merlin 45 (which powered the Spitfire Mk V-Author) at lower altitudes, and at higher altitudes to the Merlin 60. If the engine is proved in service to be capable of this performance it will be a most valuable advance, but we must prepare trials before we can swing over to it entirely. *It is the ordinary Spitfire Mk V that I am worried about. This is the mainstay of the Spitfire first line strength for it is proving superior to the Me 109F* [author's italics] and we cannot run any risks with it. By the time the Merlin 61 is proved it seems to me we shall be in Spitfire F Mk IV production.

Just over four months later, Mr Verney was writing in another report to the Air Staff:

I want to recommend to the Air Staff for adopting a new version of the Spitfire, engined with the Merlin 61. The airframe is essentially the Spitfire Mk III (N3297*). It is essential that the immediate aim would be to transfer all Spitfire production by Supermarine from the Spitfire Mk V to the new aircraft, and production deliveries could begin by mid-1942* [author's italics].

Of course, this second letter was written once the performance of the new Fw 190 was realised.

In an attempt to improve the low-level performance of the Spitfire Mk V, some of them had 2ft 2in trimmed from each wingtip, and the supercharger's vanes of the Merlin 45M cropped to give better acceleration. These modifications gave the Mk V a much better rate of roll than the 'standard' variant, enabling the Mk V to gain some equivalence to the even faster rolling Fw 190. The pilots in the squadrons equipped with these Mk Vbs usually referred to them as 'clipped, cropped and clapped', referring to the clipped wings, the cropped supercharger, and the fact that the aircraft were, in their opinion, 'clapped out'. Later on, in 1942/43, some Mk Vs, modified as above, ran higher supercharger pressures for short periods, some with 16–18 pounds boost. This gave them a speed advantage over the Bf 109F of some 30 mph up to 14,000ft when any speed advantage disappeared. Incidentally, more Mk V Spitfires were built, some 6,487, than any other Mark of Spitfire.[62]

The Air Ministry issued recommendations after August 1941, as to the best engine settings to use in a Spitfire Mk V, while flying over enemy territory: Part of it read:

> At the present stage of the war, the enemy in France is equipped with the FW 190, a fighter with an excellent rate of climb and good acceleration. To defeat this aircraft and to avoid casualties on our side, our aircraft must fly as fast as possible whenever they are in the combat zone.

This was in response to the fact that to conserve fuel, particularly for the flight home across the Channel, British pilots had been flying on the leanest mixture setting that they could manage. Thus, when 'bounced' by enemy fighters, it could take a Mark V Spitfire several perilous seconds to accelerate up to combat speed.

John Rickard, a noted authority on the Spitfire, had this to say, when asked the question: 'Why didn't the Spitfires have drop tanks in 1941/2?' His answer was:

> The slipper tanks for the Spitfire V weren't approved for use until very late in 1941, but during 1942 they were sometimes used on operations as enough aircraft with the modified equipment to carry them entered service. However, they did reduce the Spitfire's combat performance, and were made of strategically significant

metals, so the RAF didn't like jettisoning them over German territory.

Squadron Leader Pete Brothers made mention of this when he remembered action in 1941:

It quickly became obvious to us in 11 Group flying sweeps over France that the FW 190 was clearly superior to our Spitfire Mk Vs right from the start.

Morale was affected to a certain extent, but we felt that on the whole we were better pilots than the Germans, and could just about cope with this new threat. We still had confidence in the soundness of our Spitfires and we simply treated the FW 190 with more respect than a BF 109F.

Our circus and rodeo sweeps were restricted to targets not too distant from the Channel, due to the limited legs of the Mark 5 Spitfire. One hour and 15 minutes sorties were the norm for 1941 to 42 although I did crack one hour and 30 minutes on several occasions and came home very dry. The furthest inland we would dare go on an escort mission was Paris, and even then you would have to manage the Merlin just right to ensure a frugal fuel intake – weak mixture, power set to cruise, full throttle to achieve low revs and coarse pitch on the propeller.

Because of the limited radius of action, if we were jumped we couldn't usually rush off after our opponents if they flew a diving attack through the bombers from their usual position several thousand feet above us. However, if they stuck around to press home an attack, or we saw them first, you immediately changed the prop pitch to fine and built up speed to enter the fray – having the throttle already at maximum revs helped us build up to combat speed quite quickly, and the clever pilot always kept one eye on the enemy and the other on his fuel gauge.[63]

At this time, September 1941, RAF fighter pilots would have received some 200 hours of flight, and the German pilots 240. However, flying time at OTUs had been drastically slashed down to just four weeks in August 1940, so this probably had a great bearing on why the new RAF pilots were shot down in such numbers when compared to the Germans in 1941. They simply did not have enough tactical knowledge in how to combat the German fighter defences over France.

By September 1941, the RAF's Wings had expanded to at least three squadrons each. The wings and squadrons were:

Biggin Hill	72, 92, 609
Duxford	52, 266, 601
Hornchurch	54, 603, 611
Kenley	452, 485, 602
Northolt	306, 308, 315
North Weald	71, 111, 222, 402
Tangmere	41, 129, 616

Still Circus operations carried on with predictable results. On 20 September, for example, JG 2 alone claimed fifteen Spitfires, their training staffel (!) 4/JFS alone claiming another ten, while JG 26 claimed eight Spitfires, six being confirmed. True Spitfire losses were seven.

During November 1941, flight training for British pilots was reorganised, so that the emphasis was shifted on how to fly and fight in current conditions. Admittedly, both JG 2 and JG 26 were composed mainly of 'experten' (aces with five or more victories) but they were no more supermen than the British. As we have seen, the

Bf 109, in both 'E' and 'F' forms and the Spitfire I, II and V were evenly matched. The Fw 190 was another matter.

The answer was probably this: just as L.J.K. Setright wrote:

> By the time the Napier Sabre came into service [engine of the Hawker Typhoon – 1942] all too many of the really good pilots of fighter command had gone, and those who had taken their places were generally of poorer quality and were given only the most hasty and superficial of training before being sent out to do battle.

Setright is referring to the initial batch of British fighter pilots during the war who had been trained in peacetime, which had its own advantage in that these pilots had been able to rack up a lot of flying hours without anyone shooting at them. This in itself would have given the pilots confidence in being able to handle their aircraft instinctively, without having to think consciously about every control in the cockpit.

Contrast this with a pilot who joined the RAF in the first years of wartime; because of the demand for replacements for those who had been shot down and killed or captured in 1940, they would have received the bare minimum of training, particularly when it came to handling a sophisticated aircraft like the Spitfire, with its comparatively complex throttle and airscrew pitch controls, as we have touched on in the previous chapter. The Focke-Wulf Fw 190, by contrast, used their single lever control, 'kommandogerat', so that the pilot did not have to worry about always having the right combination of engine controls to suit any given situation.

Now consider the pilots of JG 2 and JG 26; many of these men had had the luxury of having trained in peacetime and they had accrued many hours of flying time. Several of these pilots had fought in the Spanish civil war of 1937–39 and then many had taken part in the French campaign in 1940, before (if they survived) taking part in the Battle of Britain.

So confident were the leading 'experten', such as Adolf Galland, the leader of JG 26 in 1941, that, if Galland had to fly to visit anywhere in France on official business, he would sometimes go by way of the English Channel, in order to surprise a Spitfire or two and perhaps add them to his score. This, by December 1941, had reached ninety-four confirmed victories. Compare this with the victory score of Britain's official highest scoring 'ace' Wing Commander Johnnie Johnson. By war's end in Europe, on 8 May 1945, Johnson had shot down a total of thirty-eight German aircraft. Of course, the air war had shifted after 1942 away from Britain's RAF and it wasn't until mid-1944 that the Spitfire-equipped squadrons of the RAF had, once again, many German aircraft to combat once the invasion of France had taken them there.

'Pat' Pattle, a South African who was killed in an air battle over Piraus Harbour, Athens, in 1941 claimed over fifty mainly Italian aircraft shot down, flying first of all a Gloster Gladiator and then a Hawker Hurricane. Due to the paucity of record keeping in that theatre, it is difficult to confirm all these but certainly his score exceeded forty.

September's Circuses carried on, Nos. 93 to 103; 93 was a typical raid, twelve Blenheims bombing the Mazingarbe power station. Almost 200 Allied fighters acted as escort. Running battles took place and at the end, the British pilots put in claims of seven destroyed, ten probables and five damaged, for losses of eight Spitfires and a Blenheim. Actual Luftwaffe loss was one Fw 190, which damaged its undercarriage when landing back at base. Circuses 97 and 99 became entangled together and the British lost five pilots and claimed sixteen shot down, plus eight probable and seven damaged. The Germans claimed twelve and lost none.

Circus 100B had the RAF pilots claiming fifteen Bf 109s destroyed, two probable with six damaged. German losses were two 109s shot down and two damaged. By the end of September, the RAF had lost some ninety-four fighters, while German losses in JG 26 were just thirteen, JG 2 three. The British had claimed eighty-three German aircraft downed.[64]

On 18 September, Chief of the Air Staff, Charles Portal, dictated his own memo about what he saw as happening over France. Among his points was a comparison of aircraft lost (265) to sorties carried out (16,307). He pointed out that amounted to a loss rate of between 1.6 and 1.9 per cent.

In the same memo, Portal wrote that the Jagdwaffe had lost 'at least' 430 fighters. He admitted that the RAF operations had not forced the German High Command to move any fighters from the Eastern Front to the Channel front, but then went on to claim that the operations by the RAF had been 'highly successful' in that, as well as damage that had been caused to German naval ships, and to the coal producing areas of Lille-Lens, 'Greater losses in aircraft have been imposed on the German fighter force than we have ourselves incurred.'

Portal went on to state that 'the cumulative effect on German morale is reported to have been considerable, *and the morale of our own forces is undoubtedly raised by taking the offensive.*' (Author's italics). He also claimed that 'the morale of the population in the occupied territories has been sustained'. One wonders where he got this information from.

A typical Circus sortie was No. 101, which resulted in the loss of eight Spitfires and a Hurricane. One of those Spitfires shot down was that of Squadron Leader Dennis Armitage of 129 Squadron. He afterwards remembered:

> I bought it some ten or twelve miles from Boulogne. We were doing fighter sweeps over France – a job I never liked very much. It seemed rather useless and costly for what it did – quite different from the Battle of Britain. I was also getting tired after nearly two years in Fighter Command, the last fifteen months without leave except the odd 48 hours snatched when I could fit it in.

Anyway, I bought it trying to get the squadron together after a little mix up with some 109s and spent the next three and a half years digging tunnels. My machine was only slightly damaged, but a stray incendiary must have got into the petrol system, for just as I was rounding on the cause of the trouble, the tank went up in flames and I got out quick, going straight through the Perspex canopy, which I had no time to open.

Winter was coming in now and the waters in the Channel were getting colder, not an inviting thought for any poor pilot shot down into it, but the 'season' was not yet over. There were six more Circuses to be flown to France and back.

On 7 October, Sholto Douglas wrote to Leigh-Mallory: 'I do most definitely want you to scale down on your "Circus" effort.' One of his reasons was: 'We are going to be desperately short of fighters for the next six months and we cannot afford heavy losses, however large the gain.'

Exactly what, apart from the shortage of fighters, compelled Sholto Douglas to request the scaling down of the Circuses is clear: he had received a direct order from the War Cabinet, led by Winston Churchill. Sholto Douglas subsequently wrote:

> In our offensive operations over France, we were finding both the multiplicity of the actual operations, as well as the stiff German defence that called for strenuous fighting on our part, and at one stage, late in 1941, I received orders, based on a Cabinet decision, to put the brakes on large-scale operations.[65]

It is possible that Sholto Douglas had, at last, begun to realise that his fighters were on the losing side of the equation. Certainly the appearance of the Fw 190 may have made him realise that offensive operations had to be scaled back until the RAF could come up with an improved aircraft to combat the new German fighter. Despite his request to Leigh-Mallory to scale Circuses down, that worthy carried on with planning for the remaining ones to be flown before the end of the year.

Just four more Circuses would be flown in 1941. On the first, 107 on 12 October, losses were even on both sides, two Spitfires and two Bf 109s. The second and third Circuses were both flown on 13 October and the British side claimed twenty 109s destroyed and four 'probables', plus many damaged. JG 26 lost just one pilot and that to a Blenheim gunner, while one Fw 190 made a crash landing.

On 21 October Sholto Douglas wrote to Nos. 10, 11 and 12 Groups. To 11 Group, he directed that only one Circus per week, or a maximum of six per month, would be flown, each operation to use 18 to 24 Squadrons. He followed this up with another letter on 24 November, allowing just three Circus operations per month. It is possible that Sholto Douglas was at last beginning to have some serious doubts about the victory claims that his pilots were submitting.

By this time, the ULTRA and signals intercepts had probably been brought to his attention, showing that the Germans were not asking for as many new fighters to replace their losses as he had hoped. (The codebreakers at Bletchley Park had broken the Luftwaffe's enigma codes in May 1940.) The interrogation of Rolf Pingel in July 1941 had probably also been brought to his attention, and Sholto Douglas might have realised that the German pilot's answers to his interrogators' questions made sense. These are suppositions, but certainly towards the end of 1941, Sholto Douglas had decided that it was time to call a halt to the Circuses and regroup.

In the event, 11 Group flew just one more Circus in 1941, that of 8 November. Before this they had flown some low Rodeos, using Hurricane fighter bombers, escorted by Spitfires, and a Rodeo on 1 November, with Blenheims bombing enemy airfields.[66]

Incidentally, it does seem strange that the RAF raids did not concentrate on the Luftwaffe's airfields, as this form of attack had almost crippled Fighter Command's airfields in the Battle of Britain in 1940. Cratering the enemy's landing and take-off fields could be as debilitating to them as shooting them down in the air.

Of one of these Rodeos, Squadron Leader Al Deere later wrote to Wing Leader Johnny Kent:

> 602 with me leading and 485, with Norman (Ryder-Author) leading rendezvoused at Manston with nine Hurricane bombers for the first low flying attack under this bloody scheme we are now working on. We 'peed' out to Dunkirk, of all places at 50ft and there's no need to explain the reception we got from ground defences. Could have stepped out of the machine and walked on the shells.
>
> Quite a few people received hits and we lost two Hurricanes and Norman. No 109s appeared at any time there or coming back. Norman was last seen at 500ft by his number two, who was hit fairly badly, just near Dunkirk and inland...
>
> That's the story and I consider it a bloody poor way for an experienced pilot to buy it. How the hell any of us got back is a miracle. To cap the party off, we were ordered off at five minutes notice from availability not even having done a similar show before. I can tell you, Johnny, we are all pretty sore about it and Group received no soft soap from me.[67]

Kent added: 'I probably made matters worse (afterwards) by being intolerant of what I considered the complete lack of understanding on the part of many Group Staff Officers, *very few of whom had operational experience*' [author's italics]. Incidentally, Norman

Ryder, of whom Deere wrote, survived his actual shoot down and became a prisoner of war.

Circus 110, on 8 November, was comprised of one Circus, plus a Rodeo and a Ramrod. Four squadrons of Spitfires comprised the Rodeo, which was intended to attack Dunkirk. In the event, they patrolled aimlessly between Deal and Dunkirk and then flew back to base and landed without loss.

Five Spitfire squadrons escorted twelve Hurricane fighter-bombers for the Ramrod, to attack a distillery near to St Pol. They carried out the attack, saw no enemy fighters and flew back to base.

The main Circus itself consisted of twelve Blenheims, escorted by thirteen squadrons of Spitfires. Almost incomprehensibly, the operation was led by an overage Wing Commander, D.R. Scott, AFC, who had never flown on a combat operation before. One has to ask oneself, what on earth was an inexperienced in combat wing commander doing leading such an expedition against the combat experienced pilots of JG 2 and JG 26? Some staff officer made a bad decision on this.

The Circus was a fiasco, and the wing commander was one of the victims. The Blenheims bombed Gosnay by mistake. In all, the operation lost sixteen Spitfires, including two squadron leaders and the wing commander. Just two German pilots were lost, one killed, one severely injured.

This was the first time that 616 Squadron had met the Fw 190s. Johnnie Johnson wrote:

> The Canadians were heavily engaged, and Roy Marples, flying next to our inexperienced wing leader, quietly reported a dozen Messerschmitts well above us. When they slanted down to attack us, Roy called the break and Nip and I, leading our finger fours on either flank, drove our Spitfires around in steep turns to meet the threat. But Roy was horrified to see the Wing Leader still flying

straight and level, quite unaware of the danger. Roy yelled over the radio and as the cannon shells streamed at them, all except the wing leader took desperate evading action.

Johnson then went on to write:

> Whatever these strange fighters were, they gave us a hard time of it. They seemed to be faster in a zoom climb than a 109, far more stable in a vertical dive, and they turned better than the Messerschmitt, for we had all our work cut out to shake them off. One of our Canadian sergeants, Sanderson, who was in the leading section, was set upon by two or three of these enemy fighters, was chased and harried all the way across the Channel and barely managed to crash land his Spitfire on the east coast near Southend.[68]

The next day, Trafford Leigh-Mallory wrote one of his multi-page memorandums, the essence of which was to blame the 'Poor judgement on the part of the leader.' Of course, the leader had died so wasn't able to defend himself. Leigh-Mallory artfully made it appear as if only four aircraft were lost for three enemy destroyed. The reality was very different.

Fighter operations were now finally restricted to patrols over the English coast in an attempt to stop the Bf 109 and Fw 190 Jagdbomber raids.[69]

Almost too late, by December 1941, Spitfire Mk Vs had been equipped with thirty, and then forty-five gallon drop tanks, enabling them to extend their range, if they hadn't been forced to drop them earlier when going into combat as they crossed the French coast.

On 10 December 1941, three days after the Japanese attack on Pearl Harbor, a comparison test was carried out at the Luftwaffe test centre at Rechlin between the recently introduced Fw 190A-2 and the Bf 109F-4. The Bf 109F-4 was then rated as attaining 393.7 mph on 87 octane fuel, but by February 1942, on 100 octane fuel, it could achieve 414.4 mph at 37,500ft. Climb performance of the Fw 190A-2 was considerably inferior to that of the Bf 109F-4; it took six minutes longer to climb to 33,000ft than the Bf 109F-4. Maximum speed was given as 401 mph.

Before the year came to an end, JG 26 completed their re-equipping with the new Fw 190A-2, which featured the wing root mounted MG17 machine-guns being replaced by MG151 20mm cannon, giving the new fighter an even deadlier punch than before. The BMW 801 engine was also a newer version than in the earlier 190A and most of its earlier problems had been ironed out plus it also gave a little more power than the earlier version.[70]

Introduction into Service of the Hawker Typhoon

It was in September 1941 that the new Hawker Typhoon, seen by the RAF as a possible answer to the Fw 190, was introduced into service with 56 Squadron, they being used very much in the development of the Typhoon but it did not make its first 'kill', a Junkers Ju 88, until 9 August 1942. The Typhoon was a troublesome aircraft in its introduction to squadron service, with some airframes having a tendency to lose their tails in a dive.

The Napier Sabre engine that powered the Typhoon was a compact and complex piece of machinery. It had its twenty-four cylinders divided into two horizontal flat-12s, one above the other, each one driving the prop shaft in between the two banks via gearing. The Sabre eschewed poppet valves in favour of sleeve valves, which required skilled machining. The use of sleeve valves had the advantage of making the two flat-12 banks narrower than the equivalent engine would have been, had it been fitted with the more normal overhead camshafts with poppet valves, thus narrowing the engine's frontal area and, therefore, drag in a closely cowled airframe. So complex was the Sabre that its production cost alone was four to five times greater than the Rolls-Royce Merlin engine. However, despite having twice as many cylinders as the Merlin V12 engine, the Sabre actually had fewer moving parts, due it not having poppet valves, tappets, camshafts etc.

Despite giving the promise of being very powerful, at over 2,200hp, the Sabre in the early production aircraft was unreliable. The root problem, among several others, was in the close machining tolerances required in the manufacture of the sleeves. In the end, it was found that Bristol's sleeves for its Hercules radial engine, suitably shortened, would work and this expedient was used, as Bristol had conquered the problem of making their sleeves to the correct tolerances, so that they did not tend to seize up as the Napier-built ones did.

Because its pistons were comparatively small, and because the stroke was also short, the Sabre could safely achieve much higher rpm than a comparable Daimler Benz 601/605, or a Rolls Royce Merlin, its maximum rpm being given as 4,200rpm. Reputedly, in the heat of battle, some were taken to 4,500rpm. This was at a time when the Merlin's maximum rpm was given as 2,900, and the DB605 as 3,200. As mentioned, the Sabre's maximum power was given as 2,200hp, but one example was run at 3,750hp for 175 hours, on test at Napier's factory in Acton, London.[71]

By 31 December 1941, JG 26 alone had shot down a confirmed 916 RAF aircraft since the beginning of the war, for a loss of ninety-five pilots killed fighting, twenty-two killed in flying accidents and thirty-four being captured since the outbreak of War in September 1939.

From 14 June until 31 December 1941, JG 26 and J G2, the only German fighter forces in occupied France, had shot down 411 RAF aircraft, mainly Spitfires, over the Channel and the French coast. The RAF claimed to have shot down 711 German fighters but in reality, the two German fighter groups stationed in France lost only

103 fighters during that period. From the beginning of the year up until 13 June, JG 2 and JG 26 had lost a total of eleven Bf 109s, six of them in flying accidents That was a win/loss ratio of almost four to one to the Germans, in combat with the British.

An order from the British War Cabinet to Fighter Command towards the end of 1941 told Sholto Douglas to cease offensive patrols and limit Fighter Command to take up a defensive stance for the immediate future, referring to it as 'a disagreeable necessity'. Sholto Douglas once wrote that by the end of 1941, he had lost 426 fighter pilots, over thirty-five squadrons of Spitfires and their pilots gone from the strength of Fighter Command. He makes no mention of the over one hundred crewmen who had also been lost in the obsolescent Blenheim bombers of Coastal Command on these almost useless sweeps.

Sholto Douglas went on to say that, in his opinion, it was worth the casualties incurred to gain what he called 'air superiority'. But for what? The start of 1942 saw the butcher's bill at Fighter Command rise at an alarming rate, while the two German Jagdgeschwaders in France had minimal losses.

Below is a list of losses to RAF Fighter Command in 1941, with the losses of German fighters from JG 26, their principal opponent, shown at this time:

RAF and JG 26 Losses in 1941:

February–August
7/JG 26 was in North Africa. They claimed 67 Allied aircraft shot down for no combat losses.

JG 26 in France:

April
8 Allied aircraft, including Spitfires   4 Bf 109s.

May
1 Spitfire   3 Bf 109s.

June
Start of the 'Lean towards France' Offensive.
85 Allied aircraft, mainly Spitfires   26 Bf 109s.

July
96 Allied aircraft, mainly Spitfires.   19 Bf 109s

August
92 Allied aircraft, mainly Spitfires.   15 Bf 109s, 2 Fw 190s.

September
75 Allied aircraft, mainly Spitfires   12 Bf 109s, 1 Fw 190

October
38 Allied aircraft, mainly Spitfires.   6 Bf 109s

November
30 Allied aircraft, mainly Spitfires.   5 Bf 109s, 4 Fw 190s.

December
10 Spitfires   2 Bf 109s, 7 Fw 190s.

Chapter 5

1942

*The past is a foreign country; they do
things differently there.*

L.P. Hartley

For Fighter Command, as 1942 went by, its losses increased over those of the previous year. The reason was simple: the Focke-Wulf Fw 190.

Various small-scale sweeps had been flown by the British over the Channel at the beginning of the year, but it was not until 3 March that Winston Churchill gave Sholto Douglas approval to carry on with large scale Circus raids, in the hope that the British would at least be able to shoot down the German fighters one for one.

It was a forlorn hope. Leigh-Mallory had no new aircraft or ideas to help with Fighter Command's sweeps and so they carried on, as they had in 1941. One of Fighter Command's problems was that the squadrons were still flying the Spitfire Mk VB, while their main opposition in France, JG 26, was now equipped almost completely with Fw 190A-2s, which were some 40 mph faster than this Mark of Spitfire. From March also, the other Jagdgeschwader stationed on the Channel coast in France, JG 2 began re-equipping their staffeln with Fw 190s too. By September, the Jagdwaffe had some 350 serviceable Fw 190s at its disposal on the French coast.

During that year, the RAF lost 492 Spitfires, equivalent to forty-one complete squadrons, most of them together with their pilots, mainly into the English Channel, besides any other aircraft that the Germans claimed as victories.

In *Combat and Command*, Sholto Douglas, still in command of Fighter Command at the beginning of 1942, writes:

> By the spring of 1942 I was preparing for a renewed effort by Fighter Command over the skies of France, but in our planning we found ourselves having to look very carefully at the number of aircraft that we had available in reserve [no mention here of the pilots who flew these aircraft].
>
> The Prime Minister himself expressed his anxiety about this to the Chief of the Air Staff, Charles 'Peter' Portal, pointing out that while the circus operations could pay dividends, we should nevertheless watch our losses.[1]

The total British aircraft losses in 1942 during the Channel offensive came to 574 aircraft of all types. JG 26 lost just ninety-nine Fw 190s to Allied action. JG 2 less. Total German losses from all causes in France in this period were only 272 aircraft, including accidents. Bombers made up most of the extra losses.

During 1941, Fighter Command had lost many experienced pilots, a lot of them veterans of the Battle of Britain. Many of the experienced survivors had by now been posted to places like Malta and the Western Desert. To replace these experienced men were pilots fresh from training schools, who needed yet more training on flying and fighting their Spitfires. Even though by now, an average RAF 'newbie' fighter pilot had some 200 hours flight training, he still needed an extra fifty to a hundred hours on a Spitfire before he could really be expected to survive against the German fighter pilots in France who, even in 1942, were receiving at least 240 hours of flight training before being assigned to a staffel.[2]

Opposing the RAF pilots were the highly experienced pilots, including many 'experten' of the Luftwaffe, in two of their most successful Jagdgeschwaders, JG 2 and JG 26, flying their new, formidable Focke-Wulf Fw 190As.

If insanity is defined as 'doing the same thing over and over again and expecting different results', then Fighter Command's actions over France in 1942 must surely rank as insanity.

In February, the 'Kanaldash' of the 32,000-ton battlecruisers *Scharnhorst* and *Gneisenau*, plus the heavy cruiser *Prinz Eugen*, from Brest, took place through the English Channel to counter a possible British invasion of Norway. With the escort under the planning and command of Adolf Galland, JG 26's legendary leader and ace himself, it was completely successful. Through British ineptitude and sheer luck, particularly with the weather, all three ships completed their mission and the British lost forty-three aircraft, while German fighter losses were just four.[3]

Six Fairey Swordfish torpedo bombers were sent out on an almost suicidal unescorted attack upon the German ships. Leutnant Graf von Eindiedel, who shot down two of them, recounted later:

> We had just overflown the *Scharnhorst* when I sighted torpedo bombers on my port side, which we identified as Swordfish types. They were flying in two formations, a group of four and two together on their own. The crews did not appear particularly experienced; they were making no evasive manoeuvres. I focused on the first formation, ploughing along at no more than 110kph, their fixed undercarriage barely cresting the tops of the waves.[4]

It was also during February that the British base at Singapore was overwhelmed by the Japanese, where Brewster Buffalos and Hawker Hurricanes had tried in vain to stem the Japanese onslaught.

Hugh Dundas, now a squadron leader, had been appointed to lead 56 Squadron on 22 December 1941, the first squadron to be equipped with the new Typhoon fighter. On arrival at Duxford airfield, he recounted, in his book *Flying Start* that his pilots' enthusiasm for the Typhoon 'was lukewarm, to say the least'. Ever since the first Typhoon had been delivered in September, they had been 'nothing but trouble.'

On 1 November there was a fatal accident when a Typhoon had unaccountably dived straight into the ground from some three thousand feet. Carbon monoxide poisoning was the cause, and all pilots were advised to use oxygen at all times from then on.

Dundas recounted:

> While I could stand on the ground beside a Spitfire and lay my hand on the top of the cockpit canopy, the cockpit of a Typhoon towered far above me. Instead of one step onto the wing and a second step into the cockpit of a Spitfire, you had to carry out a minor mountaineering feat to climb up into a Typhoon, eventually entering the cockpit through a door, like that of a motor car.
>
> Dundas first flew a Typhoon on 2 January 1942. He recounted that taxiing out, he felt as though he were about to try and take off in a steam roller. However, once airborne, he was impressed by the Typhoon's speed and power.

Dundas went on to write that although he liked the performance, he thought the rear view was non-existent and that that needed to be fixed and put in an official report to that effect. On 10 February, 'A big conference was held at Duxford to thrash out this and other matters.' Present were Air Vice-Marshal Ralph Sorley, the officer in charge of technical development at the Air Ministry, Sidney Camm, the Typhoon's designer and other representatives from Hawker, Gloster (who were building the Typhoon) and Napier. Despite Camm saying words to the effect that 'the airplane's so fast you don't need to see behind you', Dundas's viewpoint prevailed and 'Camm's staff redesigned the rear end of the cockpit in double quick time'.

Above: Groundcrew
re-arming a 485 Squadron
Spitfire, believed to be
at RAF Station Redhill.
(Air Force Museum of
New Zealand)

Right: The Commanding
Officer of 3 Squadron,
Squadron Leader
R.F. 'Digger' Aitken,
pictured beside a
Hurricane in full flying
clothing. It is believed
the image was taken at
RAF Station Hunsdon.
Squadron Leader Aitken
was 3 Squadron's
CO from April 1941
through to April 1942.
(Air Force Museum of
New Zealand)

Pilots of 3 Squadron RAF debate a combat while standing in front of one of their Hurricanes, almost certainly another image taken at RAF Hunsdon. The squadron's CO, Squadron Leader R.F. 'Digger' Aitken, is in the centre. (Air Force Museum of New Zealand)

Spitfire Mk.Vb W3579 of 485 Squadron, which was coded OU-O and nicknamed *Southland II*, pictured after it crash landed in shallow water on the beach at Dunkirk on 31 October 1941. The pilot was Wing Commander E.N. Ryder. (Air Force Museum of New Zealand)

This 485 Squadron Spitfire was purchased using funds raised in New Zealand. The legend 'W.D.F.U.N.Z. LEVIN' that can be seen painted on the cowling is a reference to the Women's Division Farmers' Union New Zealand. (Air Force Museum of New Zealand)

Hawker Hurricane Z2891 landing at RAF Hunsdon circa 1941. (Air Force Museum of New Zealand)

Five Hurricanes flying above another Hurricane on the ground at Hunsdon circa 1941. *Her Ladyship* is believed to be the aircraft flown by D.J. Scott. (Air Force Museum of New Zealand)

Flying Officer Johnny Pattison in the cockpit of a 485 Squadron Spitfire Mk.Vb, BM239 which was coded OU-N. This aircraft was shot down by anti-aircraft fire near Wassenaar in the Netherlands on the afternoon of 1 September 1942. The pilot at the time, Sergeant R.D. Riley, was taken prisoner. (Air Force Museum of New Zealand)

Ground crew loading ammunition into the port wing of a 485 Squadron Spitfire, that coded OU-A, at RAF Kenley. (Air Force Museum of New Zealand)

W.V. Crawford-Compton, wearing a Mae West, is pictured standing on the wing of his 485 Squadron Spitfire at RAF Kenley. Note the long-range "slipper" fuel tank beneath the fuselage. (Air Force Museum of New Zealand)

Wing Commander John Richard Batten in his Spitfire on his return from a sweep over the Netherlands. Note how the Spitfire has been named *Shangri-La*, but also carries the distinctive 'The Saint' artwork and the name 'Tikkie' – Wing Commander Batten's wife's nickname – beneath. (State Library of Victoria)

The Daimler Benz 601E V12 engine that powered the Messerschmitt Bf 109F-4, note the mechanical fuel injection pump mounted between the cylinder banks. (Daimler-Benz AG)

The Rolls-Royce Merlin 45 V12 engine, which powered the Supermarine Spitfire Mk V. (Author's collection)

An air-to-air shot of a 121 Squadron Supermarine Spitfire Mk.Vb, BM590 and coded AV-R, circa 1941 or early 1942. (Historic Military Press)

Flight Lieutenant J.A.A. Gibson sitting in the cockpit of his 457 Squadron Spitfire, BL384 coded BP-N, in a revetment at either RAF Jurby or RAF Redhill in early 1942. Note the victory markings and Donald Duck nose art. (Air Force Museum of New Zealand)

A three-quarters front view of a 218 Squadron Stirling in 1942. (Air Force Museum of New Zealand)

Wing Commander Douglas Bader between Adolf Galland (left) and another Luftwaffe officer after having been shot down over France on 9 August 1941. (Mark Hillier Collection/Historic Military Press)

A three-quarters view of a Bristol Blenheim, QY-H of 254 Squadron, taken in the summer of 1940. (Historic Military Press)

A Hawker Typhoon 1b of 56 Squadron, possibly pictured whilst the unit was operating from RAF Westhampnett in West Sussex. (Historic Military Press)

Douglas Bader, third from left, pictured at dispersal at Westhampnett in 1941. The other men are, from left to right, Johnnie Johnson, Cocky Dundas and an American pilot. (Mark Hillier Collection/Historic Military Press)

An escorting Supermarine Spitfire Mk.IX of 302 (Polish) Squadron, ML309 coded WX-F, pictured from a USAAF Eighth Air Force Boeing B-17. (Historic Military Press)

Air Chief Marshal Lord Dowding talking with Group Captain Douglas Bader just before a group of veteran fighter pilots took off from North Weald for the Battle of Britain Anniversary fly-past over London on 15 September 1945.

Left: An official portrait of Marshal of the RAF, Sir Charles Portal that was issued in 1944. (Historic Military Press)

Below: A flight of three Short Stirlings Mk.Is of No.1651 Heavy Conversion Unit pictured in the air over the UK circa April 1942. The aircraft nearest the camera aircraft, N6069, failed to return from a raid on Hamburg on 29 July 1942. (Danish National Museum)

Pictured during an inspection of the USAAF airfield at Hardwick, Station 104, in April 1943, Lord Trenchard examines a Consolidated B-24 of the 93rd Bomb Group. He is accompanied by Colonel Edward 'Ted' Timberlake, the Group's Commander. (Historic Military Press)

A Supermarine Spitfire Mk.IX, MH869 of 302 (Polish) Squadron, pictured in the air during a sortie over France. (Historic Military Press)

Air Vice Marshal Sir Keith Park sitting in the cockpit of his Hurricane on 15 September 1941. (Historic Military Press)

A Focke Wulf 190A of the second Staffel of JG26 in France during 1942. (Photo courtesy WorldWarPhotos.com.)

Above: The Messerschmitt Bf 109F of Oberfeldwebel Max Martin of the 8th Staffel of JG26 after landing back in France. He had just returned from taking part in a cross-channel interception in 1941. (Photo courtesy WorldWarPhotos.com)

Right: Air Chief Marshall Sholto Douglas. The Commander of Fighter Command in 1941 and 1942. (Public Domain)

Air Vice Marshall Trafford Leigh-Mallory. The Commander of 11 Group in 1941 up to 1943. (Public Domain)

During February and March, 56 Squadron persevered in the non-operational 'development' role, Dundas particularly mentioning Harold Wareham, the engineer officer. 'He was nearly driven out of his mind by the difficulties he faced, particularly with the Sabre engines, and he felt strongly his responsibility for our safety. His was a notable contribution to the eventual success of the Typhoon aircraft.' No.56 Squadron was finally cleared for operations with the Typhoon on 29 May, but it saw little action until the Dieppe raid later in the year. Typhoons did take part in a few Circus operations in June but saw little action, being more at risk of being shot down by Spitfire pilots, who mistook them for Fw 190s than any actual Fw 190s.[5]

Circus 112 took place on 8 March, Boston bombers in three waves attacked Abbeville, Poissy and Comines. They were escorted by no less than twenty-one squadrons of Spitfires from 11 Group and two by 12 Group. Four Spitfires were lost for two Fw 190s shot down and another lost in a take-off accident.[6]

That March, thirty-two British aircraft were shot down by JG 26 and JG 2, the Germans losing only eleven aircraft. The British claimed they had shot down fifty-three and had 'probably' destroyed another twenty-eight. Of those thirty-two British aircraft, nearly all Spitfires, twenty-seven of their pilots were killed. That was another two-and-a-half squadrons worth of aircraft and over two squadrons of pilots gone. Among those killed was the experienced and much respected Group Captain Victor Beamish DSO, DFC, AFC, Kenley Wing's leader, shot down into the Channel.

Shortly afterwards, Air Chief Marshal Charles Portal wrote to Air Marshal Sholto Douglas:

> In the fighting yesterday, we claimed eight German fighters destroyed plus four probables for the loss of six of our own and I see from today's German communiqué that they claim to have lost nothing. I do not know how they get away with this…. As you well know, I have implicit

faith in the genuineness of the claims put forwards by your pilots…But it would help me if you could obtain a report of the actual evidence of destruction of, say, two or three of the best authenticated casualties.

Sholto Douglas replied with two combat reports from the Wing stationed at Kenley, and another from the Northolt Wing. In them, two pilots claimed to have seen their quarries crash, and the third claimed to have seen the German pilot bale out. None of the three actually happened, it later turned out to be the British pilots' wishful thinking in their claims. Portal replied that those reports satisfied him.

It was at this time that Sholto Douglas, seeing the performance figures for the prototype Spitfire Mk IX, ordered six more Mk Vs to be given back to the Supermarine Company for development purposes. Three were then to be sent to Farnborough for evaluation and 'engine thrashing'. They were desperately needed.[7]

Also in March 1942, 10/JG 2 and 10/JG 26, two new staffeln, had started to use modified Bf 109F-4s, which could carry either one SC500 (1,100-pound bomb) or two SC250 (550-pound bombs). These 'Jagdbombers' (literally – fighter-bombers) would fly across the Channel, keeping so low that the British radar did not pick them up, then climb swiftly over the cliffs and attack 'targets of opportunity' with their bombs and frequently strafe the targets also, before turning back for home, usually with the throttle 'to the wall'. The Bf 109F-4/R1s were replaced by similarly equipped Fw 190s from the summer of that year, which could carry a heavier bomb load faster and the towns of Southern England, from Torquay in the west, to Dover in the east, were raided regularly.

This was a tactic that kept seaside towns in England on their toes for several years during the war. These attacks took place three or four times a week and were much more of a 'nuisance' in their effect than the Germans believed they were. In fact, it was not until the Germans were forced to retreat from their airfields in Northern France after D-Day that the visits to Britain by the Jagdbombers finally ceased.[8]

These attacks caused the British defence great problems, standing patrols of Typhoons and Spitfires Mk IXs being seen as the only fast enough solution but the Spitfire Mk IX did not come into service until later in the year and even then, they had various troubles in actually intercepting the raiders, as with their bombs gone, these were very fast when they ran for home 'on the deck'. The Typhoons were fast enough but were still suffering from various problems, as Squadron Leader Roland 'Bee' Beamont recounted after surviving one very tough patrol in 1942 on 7 March. He later on recounted:

> The spume-streaked North Sea below looked uninviting in the prevailing fierce north-easterly gale, and the yellow and white foaming waters over the Goodwins merged into the rain and sleet ahead when viewed from 2000ft under the lowering cloud base.
>
> It was an uninspiring scene rendered even less attractive by the radiator temperature gauge in the cockpit of my Typhoon, which was oscillating and rising ominously. There was also the insistent R/T Voice of my number two, the Belgian van Lierde saying, 'Crooner leader, bail out, you are streaming smoke!'
>
> The sea state and the temperature on that freezing late winter day did not make the prospect of bailing out or ditching a tad attractive, and the options narrowed of their own accord – I see this so often the case in real crises. My section of 609 Squadron Typhoons had been approaching the French coast on a rhubarb low-level sortie in marginal weather when the radiator gauge had started to rise above normal and now, on the way back, with the Goodwin sands below revealed only by the dense foam of the breaking storm waves, it was a question of

whether the engine would last long enough for a landing to be made on dry land.

A ditching in the violent sea below became a progressively less attractive proposition as the engine ground on, with a subtle change in the view through the rain curtain ahead showed the actual cliffs just as the radiator temperature went past the red and off the clock. With the propeller constant speed lever 'full coarse' to stretch the engine life, and the speed now down to 120 miles an hour the stick was eased back to clear the clifftops, but there was no power left. Amid hot smells and shuddering vibration, the propeller ground to a stop with one blade vertical in front of the windscreen.

Now skimming the ground in heavy sleet, the fields beyond the clifftops were only dimly visible and then, when bracing for a belly landing in the first suitable clear space, a church tower in a small village appeared dead ahead. At less than 90 miles an hour with little margin for manoeuvre above the steeple, a bank to the right and a skating turn with heavy rudder just cleared the buildings and revealed a field ahead up the slope of a hill.

Using all remaining control and finally with the stick hard back, the sloping field came up with the rush and the Typhoon hit tail first with a resounding 'clunk'. I next remember looking through the windscreen at stationary green grass to the accompaniments of sizzling noises, and thinking that I should've switched the fuel and ignition off before now. This proved to be difficult, as did getting rid of the harness straps and climbing out. At this point I noticed that there was blood all over the place and events became blurred until, sometime later, a voice said, 'don't he look a bloody mess!' And kindly hands lifted me away from the wreck, which fortunately had not burned.[9]

By this time, in March 1942, the Germans had developed their radar defence system along the Channel coast to a high degree. Using 'Freya' (the name of the Norse one-eyed goddess) radar stations, the controllers could now see raids developing over the English coasts as the squadrons formed up. Later on in the year, a British commando raid captured one of these radar sets and brought it back to Britain, allowing scientists to understand how well the enemy was doing in detecting incoming raids.

Circus 116 was flown on 24 March. This saw Boston bombers back over Lille and attacking its power station. Another six Bostons attacked the railway yards at Abbeville. Each raid was bounced by a different Gruppe of JG 26, the first and second. Seven Spitfires went down as well as three Fw 190s.[10]

That March also saw JG1, who defended the Dutch and German North Sea coasts right up to Denmark, start to re-equip with Fw 190As.

There were various Ramrods and Rodeos by Fighter Command in the last few days of March and one last Circus operation. RAF losses were twenty-seven pilots and thirty-two Spitfires. JG 2 lost three aircraft; JG 26 four. Churchill's edict to 'Watch your losses' in early 1941 to Sholto Douglas and Leigh-Mallory was not bearing fruit but it did not stop them sending out their Spitfire Mk Vbs, despite the clear superiority of the defending Fw 190s.[11]

Gunther Bloemertz was a pilot in JG 26. In his essay, 'To kill a Man', he wrote:

> That moment there came the order: 'Tommys close off the mouth of the Somme. Take off at once!'
>
> The Englishman would certainly not have spent last night drinking brandy! I ran to my machine. Ulrich too. With puffy eyes and in pyjamas, he was hurrying to his aircraft. As the engine revved up someone threw a lifejacket around me and someone else fastened my parachute harness and belt.

Full throttle! As I left the ground and swept low over the treetops of the forest of Crecy beside Ulrich, I put on my helmet and goggles with my left hand, adjusted the R/T pads around my neck, retracted the undercarriage, raised the flaps, set the trimmer and made the innumerable small manual adjustments which were required.

We were already over the sea, with the visibility of barely a thousand metres. Then, through the grey, damp morning mist, the two Spitfires were all at once rushing towards us. To wrench the stick round, sight, turn, aim and fire was a matter of seconds in which body and brain acted with automatic precision – a mechanical reaction for which I had prepared myself for two years, against a target without conscious volition or regard to the consequences.

The enemy crumpled under my fire. Victory! A transport of happiness and pride possessed me, from which it took me a moment to recover. Finally I turned my aircraft and look around with anxious eyes for Ulrich. Far astern, guns were sparkling in the clear sky over the mainland, the adversaries in a series of steep, tight turns. Before I could help, a small white mushroom unfolded, and slowly sank towards the earth. Ulrich's aircraft spun into a wood, and the Tommy flew on his way.

I circled low over my friend, whose pyjamas were flapping in the breeze. Ulrich waved to me, seemingly unhurt. He had scarcely landed in the small meadow when from all directions gallant infantrymen with rifles at the ready came hurrying to take him prisoner. They had obviously mistaken him for the defeated enemy and me for the victorious German. For the first time since the flights I actually began to laugh – Ulrich, the 'captured Tommy' was standing down there in his pyjamas with his hands above his head![12]

Apart from Malta and the Western Desert, at this time there was also the question of a fighter defence of India. General Wavell, Commander-in-Chief India, telegraphed to Churchill on 14 March 1942, giving his thoughts about the recent fighting in the Far East. He highlighted the astounding range of the Mitsubishi Zero fighter, 'up to 1,500 miles'. As far as the security of India and Burma, he finished his report by writing: 'You have been warned.'

Churchill wrote to Portal immediately: 'This is very grave. You have repeatedly assured me that ranges of this kind were impossible for fighters.'

Portal replied on the same day:

> I suggest you are mistaken in thinking that I have repeatedly assured you that ranges of 1,500 miles are impossible for fighters. We ourselves have for some time possessed the Beaufighter which, as I stated in the attachment to my minute of 3rd March, has a theoretical range still-air range of 1,460 to 1,870 miles according to the armament carried.
>
> I agree that I have repeatedly told you that the long range fighter has little chance when up against the short range fighter, owing to the better performance of the latter. If we had had adequate short range fighter defence in Malaya and Java we should, in General Wavell's words, have 'beaten the Japanese air forces out of the skies' as we did in Burma where it was possible for an exceptionally efficient commander to organise some sort of short range fighter defence.[13]

Of course, Beaufighters by day would have stood very little chance against the Bf 109Fs and Fw 190As of JG 2 and JG 26. Portal probably did not know that the Mitsubishi Zero had no armour plating or self-sealing fuel tanks, which made it very light and gave it its outstanding range. That was all well and good until the Zero was hit. Then, it quickly caught fire or came apart in the air.

April was another bloody month over the Channel. By now the Fw 190A-3 was being supplied to both the Jagdgeschwaders in France and it reigned supreme over the Channel and the French coast. The now fully developed BMW 801D-2 engine, running on 100 octane fuel, instead of the 87 octane used previously, gave some 1,677hp reliably. For armament, this version carried, as before, the two 7.92mm MG17 ahead of the pilot, cowled in behind the engine. It had had the MG FF 20mm cannon moved outboard in the wings and had the new MG 151/20mm cannon in the wing roots. The British lost 107 aircraft and ninety-five pilots this month, including a group captain and two wing leaders. The Germans just twenty-four aircraft. In one engagement alone, that of the interception of Circus 119 on 4 April, no less than fifteen Spitfires were downed for no loss to the Germans.[14]

The Supermarine Spitfire F Mark IX and the Merlin 61

At last measures were being taken by Supermarine and Rolls-Royce to help the situation. On 18 April the Air Ministry ordered Supermarine to take 100 Mk Vc airframes, re-engine them with the Merlin 61, and deliver them to Fighter Command by 31 June, as Mk IXs. In order to get the job done on time, Supermarine converted fifty-two airframes, and the Rolls-Royce flight test centre at Hucknall, under Ray Dorey, managed forty-eight.[15]

July 1942 had seen the Spitfire Mark IX being introduced by the British into squadron service. Its Rolls-Royce Merlin 61 engine, now with a two-speed, two-stage supercharger, complete with intercooling, gave it the power – some 1,560hp in a modified Spitfire Mark V airframe – to take on the Fw 190 on almost equal terms. Its service ceiling was 44,000ft and its maximum speed was 408 mph at 25,000ft. The first 100 Spitfire Mk IXs were hastily re-engined

Mk Vcs. Some of these may originally have been Mk IIs that had been re-engined with Merlin 45s in 1941 as Mk Vbs.

The first squadron to receive the new F Mk IXs was the Hornchurch-based 64 Squadron in June, followed by 611 Squadron in July, and then 401 and the Canadian 402 Squadron also in July. A total of 278 Spitfire Mk Vs were converted to Mk IX specification and deliveries kept going until March 1944 but in the meantime, all-new Mk IXs were being built on Supermarine's production line. Incidentally, Nos. 611 and 341 Squadrons received what was known as the Mark IXb, which had its supercharger set to come in at 21,000ft and this gave it a performance that surpassed the Fw 190A, even more than a 'standard' Mk IX up to 27,000ft. Thus equipped, the Mk IXb was some 30 mph faster and could climb faster than the 190 could, as well. One of the problems that the Luftwaffe fighter pilots now suffered from was the difficulty of telling whether they were fighting a Spitfire Mk V, or a Mk IX. The difference could be deadly.

The Air Ministry had called a halt to engine development at Rolls-Royce after the engine meant for the Spitfire Mk V, the single-stage supercharged Merlin 45, had been developed in 1940/41. Fortunately for RAF fighter pilots, the engineers at Rolls-Royce had thought otherwise to the Air Ministry's optimistic opinion about the Merlin 45 in the Spitfire Mk V and, acting on their own initiative and led by Stanley Hooker, had been working on developing a two-stage, two-speed supercharger for the next Merlin engine in their own time, as a 'private venture'. This was the Merlin 61, which had a much greater power output than the Merlin 45, due to Rolls-Royce's continual development of the Merlin's supercharger, which was now of the two-speed, two-stage variety and which, when installed in a Mk V airframe, now gave that aircraft, the newly named F Mk IX, a maximum speed of 414 mph, enough to fight the formidable Fw 190 on level terms.

Stanley Hooker, later knighted for his work with Rolls-Royce, recounted that:

We had a water-cooled engine, so we would add an extra water-cooled 'Intercooler' after the two superchargers, which would cool the charge to 100 degrees C before it entered the cylinders.

At this point, a happy thought occurred to me. The Rolls-Royce Vulture engine, which had 24 cylinders and was much larger and heavier than the Merlin, gave, by virtue of its size and capacity, 1,000hp at 30,000ft. Since the power of an engine depends approximately on the amount of air and fuel that it consumes, obviously the Vulture supercharge had the right capacity to supply the necessary air as the first stage of the proposed two-stage blower for the Merlin. No design effort on this component was necessary.

[Behind a] Vulture supercharger [we fitted] a Merlin 45 Blower. The result was so good that no further calculation or testing was necessary, and… we were able to go to the main Engine Design Office on the task of combining the two superchargers together as a single compact unit.[16]

Later on, in 1943, the even more powerful Merlin 63 was used in the Mark IX, after production of the Merlin 61 was phased out. The airscrew also changed with the increased power. The Mk IX had the four wooden-blade variable pitch Dowty Rotol propeller.[17]

The Spitfire's pilots claimed that it could turn tighter than the 190, although this claim was later belied in Johnnie Johnson's book *Wing Leader*, when he described an encounter with a Focke-Wulf Fw 190 during the Dieppe raid in August 1942.[18]

One other use of the Merlin engine (one of many) apart from its use in the Hurricane and the P-51 Mustang, was in the de Havilland Mosquito, made mainly of wood, which first flew in 1941 and went into service in 1942. This twin-engine unarmed bomber (which had such excellent performance that later marks were used as night fighters and intruders) could carry a 4,000-pound bombload and, with only two crew, was a far more economical use of both men and materials than the four-engine Avro Lancaster, Handley-Page Halifax and Short Stirling, the 'heavies' of Bomber Command; the Mosquito relied on speed for evasion of enemy fighters, while the 'heavies' carried a ton-and-a-half of defensive guns, turrets, gunners and ammunition.

In terms of value for money and lives, the Mosquito scored over the four-engine 'heavies', by 3:1. The Lancaster, for instance, had a crew more than three times greater. The Lancaster could carry carried three times the bomb load, but for only one-third of the sorties, i.e: an average tour of 20 sorties per crew compared with 60 for the Mosquitoes. What is left out of this picture is the experience of the crews. The Lancaster crews had average experience of 10 trips at any one time and were thus only half-trained. The Mosquito crews had an average experience of about 30+ trips and had a far more satisfactory performance. For an Oboe equipped (Navigational/Bomb aiming radar) Mosquito, carrying a 4,000-pound bomb, the ratio would be almost 50:1.

The defensive armament of the heavy bombers was centred around the .303 calibre machine-gun, which quite often was not potent enough, when it hit a challenging night fighter (which was not often), to cause much damage to it. The 'heavies' would probably have done better had they left the three gunners, their turrets and guns in England as then they would have been able to fly higher and faster, making it more difficult for either flak or fighters to reach them.[19]

Back on the Channel front in April 1942, things were not improving for Fighter Command in its sweeps over Northern France. Shortly afterwards, in May, JG 2 converted from the Bf 109F to the Fw 190, signalling more trouble for the escorting Spitfires that kept up their offensive over the Channel.

One problem that the Jagdwaffe was facing now was a shortage of vital materials from which to build their aircraft. Nickel was now in very short supply and led to many burned valves in the Fw 190 engines. Likewise, 100 octane fuel was becoming scarce as the Allied bombers attacked the oil refineries at Ploesti, in Rumania. The German fighters were forced to fall back on using 87 octane fuel, with a consequent reduction in rpm and power from their engines.[20]

The pressure by the British, in their offensive over the Channel and France was kept up in May with eleven Rodeos, six Circuses and five Ramrods being flown from the UK. In the first nine days of May alone, the British lost thirty-five Spitfires and thirty pilots for just six German aircraft shot down. By the end of the month, Fighter Command were claiming that in the first five months of 1942, 205 German fighters had been shot down, for the loss of 242 British fighters. Reality was somewhat different, the two German Jagdgeschwaders losing only sixty-seven fighters between them.[21]

By 1942, many RAF pilots were being trained in places such as Canada or in America, where the better weather generally allowed more flying time than had they stayed in Britain. By now, the flying time being racked up by trainee pilots had increased from the 150 hours of 1941, to 200 plus. As well, ex-fighter pilots who had had experience of fighting over the Channel and Northern France were able to help new pilots, particularly at the OTUs, by coaching them in the latest tactics that the German Geschwaders were using, and how to combat them. The Luftwaffe was still giving its pupils 240 hours in training. The gap was closing.[22]

Bad weather between 10 and 16 May meant aircraft on both sides were grounded, but when operations began again, on 17 May, The Fw 190s of JG 26 alone shot down nine Spitfires. Three Fw 190s made forced landings. Between 30 May and 4 June, JG 2 claimed fifty victories over their Spitfire opponents, for no loss. Throughout this period the Jagdbomber staffel of JG 26 (10/JG26), still using Bf 109F-4s, was flying hit and run missions over England.

One such was led by Oswald Fischer on 20 May. He later wrote:

I was ordered by Hauptmann Plunser to lead a mission. I worked out a raid on Brighton, since we had not visited the area for some time. I found a feldwebel available who was willing to accompany me as my wingman. I planned to go inland about 20 miles before we hit the harbour, and so we did. All worked out fine, a low flight over the Channel and hedgehopping over the British countryside and right into the harbour at Brighton. I saw a large ship and told my wingman, 'Let's hit that hard!' In we went. The flak sprayed like a fire hose, but we made it, and struck the ship with both bombs.

As we exited I got hit. I heard the impact, but everything seemed to be alright. As soon as we were over the water my temperature gauge shot up to hot, and I could smell the coolant, so I told my wingman to keep going in low flying towards home base. My engine started to smell very bad. I turned around and then belly-landed my airplane in a field. I tried to blow the aircraft up, but the explosive charge would not go off. I became a prisoner of war. I regretted my fate but it was better than drowning in the Channel.[23]

Fischer's Bf 109F-4 was not badly damaged in the belly landing. It was swiftly repaired, and, with a captured DB601E-1 engine fitted, taken to RAF Collyweston, where it was test flown by Flight Lieutenant R.F. Forbes. It was the first time the British had been able to test a DB601E-1 engine.

Circus 178 was flown on 1 June and the Debden Wing was hit hard by JG 26, the wing leader and his wingman being killed, as well as seven other Spitfires being shot down, plus three other severely damaged Spitfires making it back to Britain. Not one of the attacking Fw 190s was even damaged.[24]

A Roadstead and a Rodeo were flown the next day and JG 26 intercepted the British formations again. The Canadians of

403 Squadron, led by Battle of Britain ace Al Deere, took the brunt of the diving Fw 190s and only three of their twelve Spitfires made it back to Rochford, with two more landing at Manston, probably almost out of fuel, with one being damaged so severely it was struck off charge. The Fw 190 equipped staffeln suffered no loss.[25]

During this period, some of the German 'experten' on the Channel front were racking up high scores. 'Pips' Priller had seventy-three victories by June, Johannes Seifert had scored thirty-six victories, 'Wutz' Galland, one of Adolf's brothers, had ten victories and was now the staffelkäpitan (squadron leader) of 5./JG 26. Karl Borris had nineteen victories; Joachim Muncheburg had eighty-three victories. In JG 2, Siegfried Schnell had scored sixty-one victories by 4 June, while Erich Lei claimed forty-eight and Rudolf Pflanz had forty-four. Pflanz was killed on 31 July when his Bf 109G was shot down near Berck-sur-Mer. Other high scorers were Josef Wurmheller, Erich Rudorffer and Egon Meyer.[26]

The highest scoring 'experten' of the war was only just beginning to score in 1942. Erich Hartmann flew a Messerschmitt Bf 109 throughout the war and scored all 352 of his claimed victories in the Messerschmitt fighter on the Eastern Front. About his method of scoring, Hartmann later wrote:

> I've never paid much attention to air combat. I would never fight the Russians in a dogfight. Surprise was my tactic. Climb as much as you can, and if possible, attack by the sun ... ninety per cent of my attacks were surprise attacks. If you succeeded, you'd take time and observe the area again.
>
> Finding the enemy depends only on being where action is happening and in a good visual perception of the area. Earth stations call us on the radio and give enemy position using a coordinate system of our maps. So we can look in the right direction and choose the best altitude

for attack. If the sky is covered, I prefer to attack with full power, underneath and on the side of the sun, because you can glimpse the enemy from far away against the white cloud. Whoever sees the other first has a 50 per cent chance of winning.

The second part of my tactics is the decision making point. That is, you see the enemy and attack immediately, or expect to get a better lead or manoeuvre in an attempt to get a better position or finally decide not to attack. For example, if you have to attack the enemy against the sun, if you have no advantage of altitude, if the enemy is flying outside the clouds, keep it under control far enough, so that you can modify your position relative to the sun or clouds, and dive to exchange altitude for speed. Only then attack. It doesn't matter if it's a lonely aircraft or a group of aircraft in formation. The important thing is to destroy the enemy aircraft. Manoeuvre quickly and aggressively, shoot closely, as close as possible, to ensure that your shells (artillery species) hit the enemy, without wasting ammunition. I speak to my commanders: Only shoot when the enemy aircraft fills all your vision!

Finally, leave the area. If you shoot and leave, think about surviving. Always watch at six o'clock. Get rid of potential attackers, or discover a new point to re-engage in combat, but only do it again if you have an advantage.[27]

A word here about the German 'experten' scores. Research by Dan Case and Nick Hector, two extremely able aviation historians and enthusiasts who used recently published records of the Russian and Allied air forces, which involved checking victory claims against unit diaries and casualty reports, plus any other reliable source data they could use, indicates that the majority of the German top scorers did achieve 80–90 per cent of their claims. Case and Hector's research gives the top scorer in the Second World War as Otto Kittel, with over 235 confirmed kills, just ahead of Günther Rall. Galland scored an actual eighty victories out of the 102 claimed (all in the west) and Erich Hartmann, undoubtedly the darling of the German propaganda machine, who scored nearly all his victories on the Russian front, actually shot down 'only' 151, out of over 350 claimed.

JG 2's first combat against Spitfires in their new Fw 190s came on 3 June 1942, and 7/JG 2 claimed ten Spitfires destroyed, 403 Squadron alone losing seven. On 7 June, they claimed eight Spitfires with no losses. And so, for the RAF, this terrible summer carried on. What must morale in the Spitfire squadrons have been like at this time? This period closely echoed the British losses of 'Bloody April' in 1917, but, just as then, the commanding staff officers refused to call a halt to their ill-judged offensive.

Another Circus was flown on 5 June, one part going to Ostend, the other to Le Havre. The Spitfires that flew on the Ostend raid had no opposition and returned safely, but the Fw 190s of JG 2 fought those going to Le Havre and claimed twenty-three Spitfires, although the British only admitted to losing six. It wasn't only the British who were over claiming.[28]

This raid had seen the RAF try a new tactic, now flying at low level over the Channel, pulling up only when the enemy coast was sighted, and attacking any Fw 190s seen beneath them. As soon as any Fw 190s were seen at the same level, or above them, the Spitfires turned tail and raced back across the Channel. At least this was a tactic which stopped the seemingly ever-present 'Hun in the sun' Fw 190s from diving down from an altitude advantage, 'bouncing' the Spitfires, and then climbing back up to altitude again.

The next day, Fighter Command ordered a Circus to Cherbourg, which was intercepted by JG 2. This time the Focke-Wulf pilots claimed thirteen Spitfires shot down. JG 26 intercepted a Rodeo composed of three wings of Spitfires but when this formation saw the Fw 190s at their height, they dived away back across the Channel.

Circus 191 flew to Bruges on 8 June, with no less than twenty-seven squadrons equipped with Spitfires escorting twelve Boston medium bombers. Four Spitfires were lost, while JG 26 lost one Fw 190.[29]

On 10 June, Air Chief Marshal Charles Portal wrote to Churchill saying that, in view of Fighter Command's losses, it would be 'advisable to moderate our day offensive'. Portal also pointed out that while he had three squadrons of Typhoons now operational, only three Spitfire Mk IXs had been made operational. The new Spitfire was late arriving into service. One hundred had been promised by the end of June, but that number had then slipped back to fifty, and then thirty.

Ever since the Japanese attack on Pearl Harbor and Hitler's declaration of war against America in December 1941, British forces everywhere had been buoyed by the knowledge that, at some time in the future, they would be greatly helped by US forces with their new American equipment. Although little noted at the time, 12 June had seen the first bombing raid by American forces on Occupied Europe, when thirteen B-24 Liberators had flown a round trip of over 2,000 miles from Egypt, to attack the oil refineries at Ploesti in Romania. The group suffered heavy losses.[30]

The very next day, 13 June, Sholto Douglas was forced to call a halt to the Circus operations over France, as the losses, particularly to his Spitfire Mk V equipped squadrons, had been too great for them to continue before re-equipping with Spitfire F Mk IXs. It had finally been the Air Ministry that had told Sholto Douglas to cease operations over Northern France.[31]

If it hadn't been before, it must have now been obvious to Fighter Command, and also to the Air Ministry, that the 'Lean towards France' offensive policy, first proposed by Hugh Trenchard in 1940, had been defeated. The Fw 190s, now being vectored onto their targets by radar and thus nearly always having a height advantage over the incoming raids, could use their favourite tactic, sweeping down to the attack, zoom climb back to altitude and await another opportunity to attack.

The only notable happening in the air war over the Channel after this occurred on the German side on 18 June, when the 'Jabo' staffel, 10./JG 26, swapped its trusty Bf 109F-4/R1s for bomb-carrying Fw 190A2/U3s at Le Bourget. These could carry twice the size of bomb load as the previous Bf 109F-4s had been able to, a 1,100-pound bomb underneath the fuselage and four 110 pounders under the wings.[32]

At this time, there were just 127 serviceable fighters and fighter bombers in JG 26, out of a nominal strength of 154. JG 2's strength was similar, so the two groups were probably still mustering a total of only some 250 aircraft between them to guard the Channel coast.

Sporadic actions across the Channel still carried on, the Fw 190s not always having things their own way against the Spitfires of 11 Group. For instance, although having claimed five Spitfires on 19 June, II./JG 1, recently re-equipped with new Fw 190s, lost two of them in the fight. 1./JG 2 lost two Fw 190s and a Bf 109F-4 on 20 June but claimed five Spitfires. On 22 June, JG 26 lost two Fw 190s in exchange for one damaged Spitfire.

Before operations by 11 Group were actually halted by Leigh-Mallory in mid-July, even after receiving the directive to cease operations on 13 June however, thirty-nine Spitfires had been shot down in exchange for four Fw 190s of JG 26 being lost.[33]

All this year the 'Jabos' of 10/JG 26 and 10/JG 2 had been engaged in 'tip and run' bombing raids on the South Coast of England. In June, Oberleutnant Joachim-Hans Gerburtig was appointed as the staffelführer but he only lasted twelve days before being shot down – fortunately for him, surviving to become a PoW. His British intelligence debriefing said:

> This aircraft [Fw 190] was one of two, which attacked a stationery collier in the Channel, with bombs and machine guns from a height of 140ft. The bombs were near misses and caused slight blast damage while two members of the crew were wounded by machine gun bullets.

The collier returned fire with twin machine guns and claims to have shot this aircraft down. It hit the sea and sank immediately but the pilot managed to struggle to the surface and was picked up by a launch. He maintained that he had not been hit by the ship's fire but that he had failed to pull out of a dive.[34]

Several Fw 190s were captured during the war. There was even a scheme to steal one from a French aerodrome, but this was cancelled after Oberleutnant Arnim Faber mistakenly landed his nearly new example in Wales on 23 June 1942, and one British pilot who flew them extensively was test pilot Eric 'Winkle' Brown. This is what he had to say about this formidable fighter:

From any angle, in the air or on the ground, the Focke-Wulf was an aerodynamic beauty, and it oozed lethality. It sat high on the ground, and in getting into the cockpit it was immediately evident that the ground view left a lot to be desired, for the BMW 801D air-cooled radial engine, although beautifully cowled, could not help but be obtrusive. Nevertheless, it still offered a better view forward than was obtainable from the Bf 109, the Spitfire or the Mustang.

The most impressive feature of the Focke-Wulf was its beautifully light ailerons [they had roller bearing hinges] and high rate of roll. The ailerons maintained their lightness from the stall up to 400 mph, although they became tighter above that speed. At lower speeds the Focke-Wulf tended to tighten up in the turn, and a slight forward pressure on the stick had to be applied. But above that figure, the changeover called for some backward pressure to hold the aircraft in the turn. Rudder control was positive and effective at low speeds and satisfactory at high speeds, when it seldom had to be used for any normal manoeuvre.

It was when one took the three controls together rather than in isolation that one realised that the FW 190's magic as a fighter lay in its superb harmony of control. To be a good dogfighter, and at the same time a good gun platform, required just these very characteristics that the Focke-Wulf possessed in all important matters of stability and control.

Each time that I flew [a FW 190] I was to experience that sense of exhilaration that came from flying an aircraft that one knew to be a top-notcher, yet at the same time demanded handling skills if its high qualities were to be exploited.

Just as the Spitfire Mk IX was probably the most outstanding British fighter aircraft to give service in World War Two, its Teutonic counterpart undoubtedly deserves the same recognition for Germany. Both were supreme in their time and their class. Both were durable and technically superb, and if each had not been there to counter the other, then the balance of air power could have been dramatically altered at a crucial period in the fortunes of both countries.[35]

It was at this time that 10/JG 2, following on from 10/JG 26's example, traded in its Messerschmitt Bf 109F-4s for Focke-Wulf Fw 190A-3/U3s, equipped with bomb racks, to allow that staffel to act as Jagdbombers and to carry on its hit and run raids across the Channel.[36]

Another new variant of the ubiquitous Messerschmitt 109 design was introduced on the Channel front during this period, the Bf 109G, the 'Gustav'. Again, an up-engined fighter, the 109G had the Daimler-Benz 605 engine installed, replacing the Daimler-Benz 601 of the previous 109F variant. Following normal Daimler-Benz practice, this was another inverted V12 engine. This variant of the previous DB601 had a larger capacity than the previous engine, its bore size increase giving it now 35.7 litres, against the DB601's 33.9 litres. Power was increased to 1,455hp and maximum speed of the Bf 109G was now quoted as being 400 mph at 26,669ft.

As far as armament went, several versions of the Bf 109G had the two scuttle-mounted machine-guns of 7.92mm supplanted by the more powerful, and larger MG131 12.7mm guns, which necessitated a bulge in the cowling on each side, to accommodate the larger breeches. These led on to many pilots referring to the Bf 109G as the 'Beule', or bump. Although produced in large numbers (over 12,000 were built) it was obvious that there was more development potential left in the Fw 190, than there was in the now ageing Messerschmitt design.[37]

The Spitfire pilots had always previously believed that despite being out-climbed and out-sped by the Fw 190, they could still escape by using the Spitfire's great manoeuvrability and tighter turning. But during the Dieppe operation, Johnnie Johnson had this to say about one particular combat that he entered into with an Fw 190:

> He snaked towards me, almost head on, and then we both turned hard to the left and whirled around on opposite sides of what appeared to be an ever-decreasing circle.
>
> With wide open throttle I held the Spitfire in the tightest of shuddering vertical turns. I was greying-out, and where was this FW 190, who should, according to my reckoning, be filling my gunsight? I couldn't see him and no wonder, for the brute was gaining on me and another couple of turns would have me in his sights. The over-confidence of but a few seconds before had already given way to irritation at losing my opponent, and this was replaced by a sickening apprehension. I asked the Spitfire for all she'd got in the turn, but the 190 hung on

like a leech and it could only be a matter of time and not much of that!

Stick over and well forward and I plunged into a near vertical dive – a dangerous manoeuvre, for the 190 was faster and more stable than my Spitfire in such a descent but I had decided on a possible method of escape.[38]

Johnson then goes on to describe how he led the Fw 190 at wavetop level over a destroyer lying offshore and the resulting anti-aircraft fire kept the enemy aircraft away. But the point was, the Fw 190 that Johnson encountered on this occasion could out-turn his Spitfire Mk V, thus scotching another favourite belief of the Spitfire pilots that at least they could out-turn it. They couldn't but that was probably very much dependent on the individual pilot's skill.

On the other side of the Channel, 11 (Hohen – High)/JG 2 was re-equipped with the new Bf 109 variant, the G-1, during the last days of July 1942. This staffel had been originally I/JG2 and this new variant of the Bf 109 was intended for high altitude work, having a pressurised cabin. One of its purposes was to act as top cover for the Fw 190s, as they were not as effective as the Bf 109G-1s above 20,000ft.[39]

As a codicil to this striving for high altitude, in August the Germans started sending over to Britain their Junkers Ju 86 high-altitude bombers. Fitted with opposed-piston Jumo diesel engines, they could reach up to 45,000ft. Supermarine stripped two Mk IXs, removing as much weight as possible, including the armour plating. Thus equipped, one of the Spitfires damaged an incoming Ju 86 and the raids ceased.[40]

Even though Sholto Douglas had ordered the Circuses to stop by this time, Leigh-Mallory was still sending Spitfire wings out to try and entice the Germans to come up and fight. On 13 and 15 July, various Allied sweeps along the coast (including twelve Boston medium bombers on the 13th) saw four Spitfires shot down for the loss of one Fw 190.

Twenty unescorted Bostons raided France on 19 July, as Fighter Command's Spitfire Mk Vs were now forbidden even to cross the French coast, due to their inferiority when compared to the Fw 190. Fortunately for the Bostons, they were not intercepted.

It was then time for a quiet period on the Channel front until the 26th, when a nine squadron Rodeo approached St Omer. Both JG 2 and JG 26 intercepted the sweep, which included six Spitfires of the American 31st Fighter Group, flying out of Biggin Hill. This was the US Eighth Air Force's first fighter operation. One of their Spitfires was shot down, but the pilot managed to bale out. On that day, the score was even; two Spitfires had been shot down and two Fw 190s were lost.[41]

Circus 200 took place on 30 July. It escaped interception. That evening several RAF squadrons from Tangmere flew a Ramrod over Cap Gris Nez and were intercepted there, and then again over St Omer. Losses were six Spitfires downed and two Hurricane fighter-bombers. The Hornchurch Wing also lost six Spitfires. During the day's actions, Jagdgeschwader 26 lost four aircraft.[42]

On that same day, a meeting was held in London. Present were the Secretary of State for Air, Sir Archibald Sinclair, Sholto Douglas, Charles Portal and Wilfred Freeman. The Spitfire Mk V was declared obsolete at this meeting, with the arrival of the Mk IX, while the first Merlin-engine Mustang was scheduled to be delivered in September. Sholto Douglas also said that the Typhoon, while making a good ground strafer and 'would be useful in the defensive role', would never make a good fighter.[43]

For once, he was right. Although the Typhoon had achieved some success against the hit and run bomb-carrying Focke-Wulf Fw 190s, which had regularly raided Southern England (and which had been much exaggerated by the British press), it was at first a bomb-carrying fighter-bomber and then a rocket-firing ground-strafer that the Typhoon really came into its own. During the fighting in Normandy after D-Day in particular, the Typhoon-equipped squadrons of the

RAF created havoc among the German panzer divisions, to the extent that most of them could not move about in the open in daylight with impunity. The Typhoon pilots, however, suffered from intense German light flak, as by that time there were not many German fighters around in France to combat the Typhoons.[44]

The last Circus of July, No.201, took place the next day. Twelve Bostons bombed Abbeville-Drucat airfield and JG 26 fought the Spitfires all the way back to Dungeness. It would appear that the Spitfire squadrons lost nine aircraft (twelve were claimed) while two Fw 190s were forced to crash land. Two Bf 109s went down, one being the staffelkäpitan's aircraft, that of Rudi Pflanz, a Knight's Cross holder. He went down in the Channel and was never found. Later on, three more Spitfires were shot down, these being from the new American 'Eagle' wing.[45]

At last, some sort of sense appeared to be getting through to the Air Ministry and Fighter Command as in August, twelve Spitfire squadrons were diverted from the almost futile cross-Channel raids and sent to support the Allied landings in Tunisia, Operation *Torch*. Six more squadrons followed in the first part of 1943.[46]

As an interceptor, the Typhoon really started to show its mettle between October 1942 and June 1943, during which period Typhoons shot down fifty-seven low-flying Fw 190s over the Channel. By late September, the Typhoon squadrons, Nos. 1, 56, 609, 486,257 and 266, were stationed at coastal airfields from the east to the west coasts of southern England. From there, they mounted pairs of aircraft flying low-level patrols along the coast and caught many Fw 190 Jagdbombers over the Channel, or just crossing the South Coast.[47]

James Sheddan (later to be a squadron leader) wrote:

Typhoons were big. At seven tons, they were nearly twice the weight of a Spitfire which, with its Rolls-Royce Merlin engine, had been around for a long time, while the Typhoon, with its Napier Sabre engine, had been rushed into service to help counter the FW 190. These had started tip and run raids on the English south coast and this crash programme left little time to detect and correct developments and construction faults. Now engines and airframes were being plagued with the sort of troubles that would have been found out in the leisurely days of peace.

The main difference between the Spitfire and the Typhoon was normal cruising and maximum speeds, For while a Spitfire cruised well below its top speed, a Typhoon's cruise speed was not much below its maximum, and this high speed made it a difficult aircraft to intercept. This difference in speeds was mainly brought about by the difference in revolutions of the two engines. Whereas a Rolls-Royce Merlin cruised at around 1,800rpm, and had a maximum of 2,800rpm, a Sabre ambled along at a setting of 3,400rpm, which was only 350 below what the engine was capable of producing. As fighter aircraft produced their best efforts at their top speed, the quicker they could attain high revs in emergency such as trying to escape when being bounced by superior numbers, or when pursuing an opponent, the more a Typhoon had a decided advantage over the much slower Spitfire.[48]

Back in the 1980s as part of the same interview with Roland 'Bee' Beamont, who had been seconded to the Hawker company in December 1941 as a production test pilot on Hurricanes, I asked him about the Typhoon. He told me that part of his duties at Hawkers were to flight test and develop the Typhoons coming off the production line. Beamont recalled how impressed he was both by the size of the aircraft compared with the Hurricane that he had previously flown, and also by the sheer power of its Napier Sabre powerplant. According to Beamont, in 1941 a comparison test was carried out at

Hawkers between a Typhoon and a Spitfire Mk V. The Typhoon was faster than the Spitfire by 40 mph above 17,000ft, and even faster below that.

In October 1941, Beamont was posted back on operations, as a flight commander to 56 Squadron, the first to use the Typhoon, and then to command 609 Squadron in January 1943, also equipped with Typhoons. He was instrumental in keeping the Typhoon in squadron service when, in late 1942, the Air Ministry considered concentrating production on the Spitfire Mk IX and cancelling all Typhoon production. Nevertheless, well into 1943 Typhoons were still being lost at the rate of two a month due to structural failure resulting in their tails becoming detached. Twenty-six Typhoons were lost to this fault, later to be cured by a re-sizing of the mass balance weights on the elevator. Only two pilots survived.

Later on in the war, in 1944, British squadrons began to be re-equipped with the Hawker Tempest, a thinner-winged version of the Typhoon which had a very impressive performance. Indeed, in service trim, it may have been the fastest piston-engine aircraft used by the RAF in the war. The tragedy was that the Tempest could have been in service in 1942, just as soon as the Hawker design team had realised the shortcomings of the Typhoon's very thick wing section, which went a long way to keeping the Typhoon from being effective as a fighter above 20,000ft; however, the same could be said about the Fw 190 but that was already in service by late 1941.[49]

The first bombing raid by twelve American B-17s of the US Eighth Air Force, heavily escorted by Spitfires, targeted the railway marshalling yard at Rouen on 17 August 1942. They were commanded by Paul Tibbets, later to be the pilot of *Enola Gay*, the B-29 that dropped the atom bomb on Hiroshima in August 1945. It was the precursor of many more raids to come. Losses to the Fw 190s of JG 26 were three Spitfires, two of them the new Mk IXs.

Jules Meimberg, of 11./JG 2, who was flying a Bf 109G-1, that had a pressurised cockpit, recounted:

We were climbing westwards out over the coast in brilliant sunshine when suddenly out over the glittering sea I saw a sight that left me rubbing my eyes in amazement: a good dozen or so four-engined bombers flying in close and perfect formation heading south. With the sun at our backs the escorts had not spotted us. We threw our kites into a steep dive and closed on the *Viermots* from astern at high speed. I calmly picked out a target.

Suddenly, with an almighty bang! all hell broke loose. My Messerschmitt seemed to have been caught in a web of tracers and every man in that formation seemed to have a heavy machine gun and was unleashing salvo after salvo at one target – myself and my kite. The silhouette of the bombers grew slowly – painfully slowly – ever larger in my gunsight. 'Closer!.... Don't mess this up! Now it's filled the entire gunsight. Open fire!' And then, 'Pull up!' But I had been deceived by the huge wingspan of the behemoth – my rounds fell hopelessly short of the target.[50]

The next day, I./JG 26 scrambled its Fw 190s and made contact with the Biggin Hill Wing over the Channel. In the ensuing fight, two Spitfires were claimed by the German pilots, and one Fw 190 went into the Channel. In the first eighteen days of August, the Germans had lost just five Fw 190s, three of them due to engine problems and only two being shot down by Spitfires.[51]

On 19 August came Operation *Jubilee*, the landing in force at Dieppe by mainly Canadian soldiers, which resulted in a crushing defeat for the Allies and a staggering one day loss of 106 aircraft, mainly Spitfires, of which seventy were shot down. JG 2 alone claimed fifty-nine victories.

The RAF that day flew over 3,000 sorties. In intercepting them, JG 2 and JG 26 combined, under Luftflotte 3, had around a total of

230 battle-ready fighters. JG 26 flew 377 sorties. JG 2 claimed a total of fifty-nine kills and seven 'probables', for the loss of eleven of its Fw 190s, with ten damaged. The two Jagdgeschwaders lost twenty-three aircraft between them.

Sholto Douglas had given command responsibility of the operation to 11 Group's commander, Leigh-Mallory. For the operation, he had over 750 aircraft under his command, including forty-nine fighter squadrons, four of them equipped with the new Spitfire Mk IX. Sholto Douglas:

> What appealed to my imagination about the proposed operation was that it was a splendid opportunity to *gain experience* [author's italics] and, at the same time, to catch the Luftwaffe at a disadvantage and wholly on the defensive. On the day itself the German Air Force accepted the challenge, *and we were not as successful in actual scores as I had hoped for* [author's italics].

Sholto Douglas seems to have overlooked the fact that dead men do not gain experience.[52] After the Dieppe operation, Sholto Douglas wrote:

> Even before the raid on Dieppe, we had come to realise that we were not destroying as many enemy aircraft as we had hoped that we would be able to in our operations out over France and Belgium. ... For the RAF, it was a hard won success, and it provided us with an enormous amount of experience through actual participation in an amphibious operation. We learned in a short time a great deal about methods of giving air support to a seaborne landing on the ground, and it was that experience which was of the greatest value in the gigantic operations of this nature that lay ahead.

Of the results of the Dieppe raid, Sir Arthur Bryant (author of *The Turn of the Tide, 1939–1943*) wrote: 'This bloody affair, though productive of many valuable lessons, ended the summer's attempt to draw off planes from Russia by trailing Fighter Command's coat over Northern France – a gesture that had cost Britain nearly a thousand pilots and aircraft.'

Sholto Douglas wrote, 'That gesture had indeed been a costly one, and while I was not at all happy about having to curtail our activities, we had to ease off with our fighter offensive.' The British had flown over 200 Circuses during 1941 and 1942.[53]

Looking back now, it is difficult to see that any lessons for the Normandy landings on 6 June 1944 were learned from the Dieppe fiasco, except for how not to organise a landing on a hostile shore. As for Sholto Douglas's assertion that, for the RAF, it had been a 'hard won success'…

On 24 August, despite Sholto Douglas's order to Leigh-Mallory to cease operations for the time being, operations were resumed, although now the British fighters were escorting American bombers.

Spitfire Mk IXs escorted Eighth Air Force B-17s to the La Trait shipyards and the Fw 190s of JG 26 caught up to them after they had bombed their target. The B-17s escaped due to the Spitfires holding off the German fighters. In the fighting, JG 26 shot down two Spitfires and three more got back to England damaged. JG 26 suffered no losses.[54]

There were probably not many RAF pilots at this point who realised that a fundamental change for the better was taking place in their day-to-day operations over the Channel, but there was. They would not now be escorting small groups of RAF medium bombers but larger and larger formations of the heavily armed American four-engine B-17 Flying Fortresses and B-24 Liberators, until the American fighter forces took over the job in October 1942.

There were many dogfights over northern France and the Channel on 27 August, when twelve Bostons were sent to bomb Abbeville-

Drucat airfield at low level. The Fw 190s of the 5th Staffel of JG 26 engaged the Spitfire escort right over the airfield and in the ensuing fighting, five Spitfires went down for the loss of two Fw 190s. Later on in the day, Hauptmann Mietusch shot down two Spitfires near Dover.

August ended with Allied raids on the 28th and 29th. The 28th saw B-17s attacking the Potez aircraft factory near to Amiens but the Spitfires again successfully shielded the bombers, and only one Spitfire, a Mk IX, was lost. This was balanced by the loss of one of JG 26's high-flying Bf 109Gs. The 29th saw the B-17s accurately attack JG 26's airfield at Wevelghem in Belgium and some German airmen were killed. The bombers were not intercepted.[55]

But it was not until September 1942 that the tide in the air war over France really started to turn against the Luftwaffe with, as we have seen, a combination of the better training of British fighter pilots, better British fighters, such as the Spitfire Mk IX and the Hawker Typhoon, and, most importantly, with the start of the American daylight bombing offensive in earnest. Although the Fw 190s shot down many B-17s and B-24s during the war, they were seen by the Luftwaffe fighter pilots who opposed them as a much tougher adversary with their multiple defensive turrets and gunners, than the previously used Bristol Blenheims.

The B-17s and B-24s also flew at high altitude, some 25,000ft on average and here the Fw 190's performance was not as good as it was beneath 20,000ft, thus presenting the Luftwaffe's defences with yet one more problem.

During September, the eighth staffel of JG 2 was tasked with defending the U-boats stationed in the submarine pens at Brest from Allied aircraft as they crossed the Bay of Biscay. In the next two months, the staffel shot down ten of these aircraft, mainly Bristol Beaufighters for no loss.[56]

On 5 September, the escorting Spitfire Mk IXs once again fought the Fw 190s of JG 26 as they attempted to get at the raiding B-17s and failed. Five Spitfires were shot down.[57]

During these early Eighth Air Force raids, the RAF, using their Spitfires, escorted the B-17s and B-24s as far as their range would allow, which, even with drop tanks fitted, was not as far into France as the commanders of the Americans and the British would have liked. Consequently, the Germans quickly learned not to attack the bombers until the escort had turned for home.

On 6 September, the Fw 190s finally met the B-17s on their own terms, unescorted, and Hauptmann Meyer shot down one of a force of fifty-one of them. Another went down into the Channel on the way home but JG 2 lost two Fw 190s in return. The B-17s were so big that Meyer had had to adjust his gunsight several times to give a correct range from when to start firing, as he had opened fire first of all when well out of range.[58]

Late September had seen the three 'Eagle' Squadrons of the RAF, which had been composed of Spitfires flown by volunteer American pilots disbanded, so that their pilots could now form part of the 4th Fighter Group of the US Eighth Air Force, based in Britain.

In September, a few weeks after the Dieppe raid, Sholto Douglas was transferred to become Air Officer Commander in Chief of the Desert Air Force. At the end of November, he handed over command of Fighter Command to Trafford Leigh-Mallory, the initial protagonist of the 'Big Wing' argument of 1940. Sholto Douglas had been the Commander of Fighter Command for two years, in a time which had seen the British suffer losses out of all proportion to any victories that they might have achieved.

Trafford Leigh-Mallory, the previous leader of first of all 12 and then 11 Group, kept to the same idea of throwing increasing numbers of fighters over the Channel to fight over France as Sholto Douglas had, but with his Spitfire Mk IXs escorting the increasing raids by the Eighth Air Force's B-17s and B-24s, the result was now different to what had happened over the previous twenty-one months. With the firepower of the American bombers, and the new Spitfire Mk IX escorts, the RAF's fighter losses decreased. The Luftwaffe's JG 2 and JG 26 kept up the same rate of interceptions as before during the remainder of 1942, but life was beginning to get harder for the German fighter pilots.

As the RAF had ceased their Circus operations it continued with various fighter sweeps over Northern France, but rarely tempted the Fw 190s to come up and fight – though they had little need to; the Eighth Air Force was now sending its bombers in increasing numbers on raids, and they were seen as the priority target of the Luftwaffe's fighters.

Although they did not actually shoot down many German fighters, the streams of tracer put up by the multiple gun positions of the B-17s and B-24s acted as a severe deterrent to the Luftwaffe pilots. In fact, when Wing Leader Johnnie Johnson visited the American bomber leaders to discuss the tactics that his Spitfires should use when escorting the US bombers, he was told, to his great relief, not to try and fly close escort to the bombers, as their gunners would simply shoot at any single-engine fighters they saw, believing them to be German.

So, Johnson told his pilots to give the bombers plenty of room, which at the same time meant that his Spitfire pilots had more space and time to intercept the incoming German fighters before they got to the bombers. But the German fighter pilots occasionally scored some severe losses to the American bombers particularly in 1943, and then, later on in 1944.[59]

Adolf Galland, now the general in charge of the Luftwaffe's fighters, had seen the need for increased production of fighters, both the long-established Bf 109 and the newer Fw 190. Galland cooperated with Generalluftzeugmeister Erhard Milch, who was then in charge of aircraft production. Galland and Milch met regularly and, with both of them after the same end, increased fighter production resulted. During July 1942, 470 fighters rolled off the production lines. Galland's ambition was to raise this to 1,000 per month as he could see the danger that the American heavy-bomber raids threatened. But even the ever-prescient Galland could not have foreseen just how quickly the numbers of American bombers would grow, nor that they would be escorted to their targets and back by long-range American fighter escorts by 1944.[60]

On 26 September 1942, 133 (Eagle) Squadron, flying their just acquired, brand new, Spitfire Mk IXs, ran out of fuel over France when attempting to return to Britain against a 100-mph headwind. Eleven new Spitfires were lost to the Germans, thus alerting them to the performance of the new Mk IX. Six of the American pilots became prisoners of war, four were killed and one evaded capture and made his way later on back to the UK.

The first few days of October saw little activity over the French coast, except that several Fw 190s suffered engine failure and had to crash land.

On 9 October, 108 B-17s and B-24s attacked a steel works at Lille. Four bombers were shot down but they took two of the attacking Fw 190s with them. Seeing these raids as a serious threat, Galland wanted a mass attack by German fighters on the American bombers made as quickly as possible, which would cause really big losses and dissuade the Americans from keeping on with their daylight bombing raids. Although the Eighth Air Force took big losses, particularly on their largely unescorted raids to the factories producing ball bearings at Schweinfurt and Regensburg later on, the Americans refused to be deflected.

On 17 October, the Jabo Fw 190s attacked Hastings, strafing buildings on the front. On the way back, they were intercepted by Hawker Typhoons of 486 Squadron, and lost one of their number. In a mirror image of the RAF having no previous knowledge of the Focke-Wulf Fw 190 before it appeared, the German pilots had no previous knowledge of this new British fighter and identified them as Tomahawks (Curtis P-40s).[61]

Adolf Galland visited his old Jagdgeschwader 26 on 18 October. Concerned about the low numbers of American bombers being shot down, he wanted to make sure that Major Schöpfel, the then commander, was taking every possible measure in his attempts to shoot them down.[62]

Circus 232 set out from England and JG 26 was ordered to scramble to intercept it, but due to bad weather it turned back before reaching France and no interceptions took place. The rest of October passed without major incidents in the air war over the Channel.

As winter closed in, RAF Circus operations began to wind down on the Channel front. Adolf Galland's brother, Paul, was killed on the last day of October when a Spitfire caught him unawares. He had been on a raid to Canterbury at low level, escorting some forty-nine bomb-carrying Fw 190s in a 'vengeance' raid, which took the town completely by surprise. Thirty-two civilians were killed in the bombing.[63]

Egon Mayer became the leader of III./JG 2 in early November, when the previous commander, Major Hans 'Assi' Hahn was transferred to take command of II./JG 54 on the Eastern Front. At this time, Hahn had sixty-eight victories.

Mayer believed that the best way of downing the B-17s and B-24s the Germans were now encountering regularly was a frontal attack in an attempt to kill the pilots. This took skill and daring, but was actually less dangerous to the attacking fighter than when striking from the rear, where the relatively slow closing speed gave the American defensive gunners more of a chance to hit the approaching Fw 190s. The tactic was refined so that the ideal position for the German fighters to strike from was with a slight altitude advantage when commencing the head-on attack. 'Fighters at 12 o'clock high' became the famous warning cry among the American bomber crews after this.[64]

In the air war in the West, Spitfires had been the first fighters to escort the American bombing offensive against France's industrial centres in August 1942. The advent of the P-38 Lightning in October 1942 and then the P-47 Thunderbolt in early 1943, both of which had a greater range, meant the American bombers could be escorted further than the RAF Spitfires had been able to.

The twin-engine P-38 Lightning, however, was very cold for its pilot at altitude, having no engine in front of the cockpit to supply at least a little warmth. Cockpit heating was minimal and many pilots had to be helped out of their cockpits at the end of a mission, so numb were they. The complicated systems of cooling and turbocharging the engines in the P-38 did not take kindly to the cooler temperatures of operating in Northern skies either. Add to that the complexity of the throttle, airscrew pitch, radiator openings (eight in all), turbocharger settings and fuel switches to be manipulated and new pilots had little chance when bounced by German fighters of getting their Lightnings into a position to even evade the attacking enemy, or accelerating to combat speed from their cruising speed quickly enough. Used as a low to medium lever photo reconnaissance aircraft, now without the weight of its armament, the F-6 variant of the P-38 was more successful in this role than the fighter version had been over Europe.

The P-38 was more successful in the Pacific; having two engines meant it provided greater security over water if one should fail, plus its greater range helped pilots' morale considerably. In the Pacific theatre the P-38s rarely had to climb to high altitude to escort the medium bombers of the USAAF and that, plus the generally higher ambient temperature, helped pilots' wellbeing.

On 8 November, the Allied armies landed in North Africa. Both II./JG 2 and II./JG 26, the two staffeln equipped with high-altitude Bf 109Gs, were transferred to Tunisia, along with III./JG 2 and its Fw 190s. The German fighter force in France was decreasing.

The B-17s came again on this day, thirty-eight of them, accompanied by no less than fifteen squadrons of Spitfires. The B-17s bombed the Lille locomotive factory, while twelve more bombed the airfields of JG 26. Three bombers were claimed, and five Spitfires were shot down, for no losses to the Germans.

Three more staffeln left the Channel front on 14 November, the German High Command being worried about a possible invasion of Vichy France in the south. These staffeln were 10./JG 26 and 10./JG 2, the Jagdbombers and I./JG 2. Left guarding the Channel coast now were four Jagdgruppen (wings): I./JG 26, II./JG 26, III./JG 26 and III./JG 2. Coincidentally, Adolf Galland was promoted to the rank of generalmajor just five days later, making him the youngest general in the German armed forces.[65]

On 23 November, Mayer was proved right when no less than four B-17Fs were shot down in one pass from head-on attacks by his formation. It was probably this attack which encouraged Boeing's designers to incorporate a chin turret in the next B-17 variant, the 'G' model, which made the frontal attacks by Luftwaffe fighters far riskier.

A new, verbally issued 'Fuhrerbefehl' (order from Adolf Hitler himself) was given to the fighter pilots on 27 November. Now, they were to attack anything they liked over Britain, including civilian targets. The raids were known as 'Störangriff' (harassment raid). Ironically, the very first one went badly for JG 26 when two Fw 190s from 5./JG 26 attacked a train on the English coast. The engine's boiler exploded and parts of it hit one of the Fw 190s, which promptly crashed.

Another of these 'Störangriff' was flown on 30 November by two Fw 190s of 4./JG 26. Both aircraft crashed into the Channel after being hit by anti-aircraft fire. While taking part in a rescue search, another Fw 190 shot down a Hurricane, but then its engine failed and that Fw 190 also finished up in the Channel.[66]

It was back to standard operating procedure on 4 December when all three Gruppen of JG 26 scrambled to intercept twelve Spitfire equipped squadrons conducting a Rodeo. The Fw 190s bounced the formation and in the dogfight that followed the British lost five Spitfires for just one slightly damaged Fw 190.[67]

The next raid by the American bombers was on 6 December and there were two separate ones; the first being by B-24 Liberators on the Abbeville-Drucat airfield. The wing leader of the escorting Spitfires aborted the mission and they all turned for home, as they had not been able to get into their allocated positions in their escort role. Six B-24s pressed on and bombed the airfield but were in turn attacked by II./JG 26. One Liberator went down but so too did two Fw 190s.[68]

Sixty-six B-17s attacked the steel works at Lille an hour later. Their escort consisted of six wings of Spitfires – almost 200 fighters. All three German Gruppen of JG 26 attacked the formation. They shot down a claimed three B-17s, possibly in conjunction with II./JG 1, and three Spitfires. Earlier in the day, the daily reconnaissance Fw 190 of JG 26 to the English coast had surprised and shot down two Spitfires.[69]

Yet another 'Störangriff' flight took place the next day, with the same disastrous result as the first two. One Fw 190 flew into a hill in England and another force-landed back in France after running out of fuel.[70]

There was desultory action over the Channel on 11 December, resulting in one Fw 190 being destroyed. On the 12th, the Eighth Air Force mounted a bombing raid on the aircraft supply park at Romilly-sur-Seine. Cleverly, JG 26's Focke-Wulfs waited until the Spitfire escort turned back and then attacked; two B-17s were downed and several were damaged. Three wings of Spitfires met the returning bombers and the usual dogfight ensued, during which three Spitfires were shot down. JG 26 lost no aircraft nor had any damaged, despite the bombers' gunners claiming to have shot down nineteen of them.[71]

On 17 December, the Typhoons scored one of their first victories. In fact, two Bf 109F-4s were destroyed when Flight Sergeant Frank Murphy and Flight Sergeant Taylor-Cannon of 486 Squadron intercepted them as the pair approached the South Coast of England. The combat record described what happened:

> At first the aircraft did not appear to see Red section, which tuned to port on to 60° course and gave chase. They then turned South East and, closing to about 300 yards clearly recognise them as Bf 109F's and opened fire with several short bursts of cannon fire, closing still further, very rapidly to 100 yards in line abreast. The enemy's speed was estimated as 330 miles an hour.
>
> By this time all four aircraft were right down 'on the deck' and with the enemy aircraft adopting a spiral weave type of evasive action crossing over several times, as Red section attacked with the results of both Red one and two engaging each aircraft, strikes being observed on the fuselage and engine of both aircraft.
>
> They soon abandoned the spiral weave action, straightened out and flew parallel courses, the plane subsequently destroyed by Red two (Taylor-Cannon) jettisoned its hood and with pieces breaking from it, climbed to about 800ft and made a diving turn to starboard and went straight into the sea. The other, destroyed by Red one (Murphy) with smoke pouring from its tanks, lowered its flaps, raised its nose slightly, burst into flames and dived into the water.[72]

Typhoons featured again in a combat with JG 26 on 19 December, shooting down Kurt Müller, the Staffelkommandeur of its 'Jabo' squadron. Once again, the Fw 190 pilots misidentified the Typhoons, calling them Brewster Buffalos.[73]

The following day, 101 B-17s and B-24s, escorted by squadrons of Spitfires, attacked Romilly-sur-Seine again. The German fighter pilots waited once again for the escort to turn back before attacking.

The end result was eight bombers and two Fw 190s destroyed. Six more Fw 190s were written off because of damage incurred when they force landed, out of fuel.[74]

On 30 December, the Eighth Air Force attacked the submarine pens at Lorient. These daylight bombing raids, when effectively escorted by P-47s and P-51s, took over the role of fighting the Jagdwaffe over Europe previously carried out by Fighter Command.

Below is a month-by-month account of the losses of both sides in 1942 and it can be seen from this alone just what defeats the British were suffering in 1942. It was not until the advent of the USAAF bombing raids with their escorting fighters, first of all P-47s and P-38s in 1943 and then P-51 fighters later on in 1943, that the Luftwaffe's fighter capability began to disintegrate under the onslaught.

RAF Losses in 1942:   German losses (JG 2 only):

February
14 Spitfires
4 Blenheims   4 x Bf 109s

March
70 Spitfires   13 x Fw 190s

April
94 Spitfires   23 x Fw 190s

May
48 Spitfires   4 x Fw 190s

June
59 Spitfires   7 x Fw 190s

July
38 Spitfires
1 x P-40
1 x Hurricane
1 x Mosquito   7 x Fw 190s

August
64 x Spitfires
1 x P-39 Airacobra
2 x Hurricanes
1 x Mustang   18 x Fw 190s

September
10 x Spitfires
1 x Boston
3 x B-17s   6 x Fw 190s

October
11 x Spitfires
6 x B-17/24s

November
10 x Spitfires
3 x B-17s   8 x Fw 190s

December
16 x Spitfires
9x B-17s
3 x P-47s   9 x Fw 190s

Chapter 6

1943

There is a tide in the affairs of men, Which taken at the flood, leads on to fortune. Omitted, all the voyage of their life is bound in shallows and in miseries.

William Shakespeare

Undoubtedly, 1943 was the year that saw the turn of the tide on many fronts. The war in the Western Desert had ended in victory for the Allies at the battle of El Alamein in late 1942, and the Germans and Italians there were now in full retreat.

In Russia, the Germans had been defeated by the Red Army at Stalingrad early in the year. Some 110,000 Germans trudged off in the snow to prison camps from which perhaps ten per cent survived to return to Germany after the war ended. The Battle of Kursk in mid-1943 would see the last big offensive by the German army defeated and, from then on, with only a few checks, Hitler's forces were in retreat back to the heart of the Reich.

As noted in the previous chapter, Spitfires were the first fighters to escort the American bombing offensive against France's industrial centres in August 1942, followed in late 1942 by the P-38 Lightning, and then the P-47 Thunderbolt in early 1943. But it was not until 1944 that the North American P-51 Mustang, now with a Rolls-Royce Merlin produced by Packard (known as the V-1650) in place of the previous Allison V12 engine, could escort bombers to Berlin and back again. That aircraft had a total fuel capacity of 348 imperial gallons (419 US gallons) via an extra tank in the fuselage and two drop tanks. With a maximum speed of 422 mph and a service ceiling of 42,500ft, it was a quantum leap over the previous Alison-powered P-51, the P-38 and P-47 in performance.[1]

Although the same multiple cockpit controls were also prevalent in the P-47 Thunderbolt, of which there were 200 in Britain by July 1943, at least their pilots only had one engine to worry about. This was the huge supercharged and turbocharged Pratt and Whitney R2800, a two-row radial producing 2,000 horsepower. The ducting for its turbocharger took up so much space in the P-47's fuselage, that the RAF fighter pilots joked that when attacked, a P-47 pilot could undo his safety straps and dodge around the fuselage. The Thunderbolt's success made many of them change their minds ...

Seventy-five gallon drop tanks became available to them in 1943, which allowed daylight intrusions as escorts into Germany itself.[2]

The Americans did try to incorporate all these cockpit controls into one mechanical computer, as the Germans used in their 'kommandogerat' control in the Fw 190, but it was not as successful as the German variant.[3]

It was during the spring of 1943 that several high-level conferences were held in Germany to discuss engine development. The news was not good. Problems with valves (no nickel was obtainable in Germany by this time) and not enough hydrogenated high octane fuel being available, either in 1943 or in the forthcoming years, made the powers that be realise they had already been beaten by the British in piston aero-engine design and manufacture, particularly with the Napier Sabre developing 2,250bhp and the Merlin 61 giving 1,710bhp. In the circumstances, it was not surprising that the Germans started to devote a lot more development time to the turbojet powered Me 262 twin-engine fighter.[4]

The first mission by P-47 Thunderbolts of the 335th Fighter Squadron into Europe came on 10 March 1943. They penetrated as far as Holland but, apart from the ever-present flak, saw no German fighters but on 15 April, the P-47s had their first combat with Fw 190s.

Despite losing three aircraft, two to the opposition and one through engine trouble, three Fw 190s were shot down.

Major Don Blakeslee, the 335th's operations officer wrote:

I left Felixstowe at 1701 hours on April 15 1943 and that's when I discovered that my Gyro compass was unserviceable. By the fitted compass, I first saw the enemy coast near Knokke, Belgium, about 20 miles north of my intended landfall, flying at twenty-nine thousand feet.

I saw five vapour trails headed west about five miles north of Knokke and 5000ft below us over the water. I made a turn to port and saw three FW 190s below, flying southwest. As soon as they saw us, they turned and started home. Selecting the nearest one, who was in a 15° dive, I started down after him. Two unidentified P 47s took a short burst at him at long-range and were overtaking him rapidly. His only evasive action was to increase his dive. I opened fire at about 700 yards closing to 500 yards, still firing.

I saw traces going over his canopy so I increased the angle of my dive and sawed him through twice. I saw many hits behind, and in front of, his canopy. He lurched sharply and a fraction of a second later crashed into the ground, exploding. My entire attack was made from directly astern and from slightly above. I pulled out of my dive and found myself approaching Ostend. I went over the centre of the city at about 300ft and was not fired at. Proceeding to about mid-Channel on the deck, I climbed to about 3000ft and returned to base, landing at 1820.[5]

German pilots soon learned not to try and out dive the seven-ton Thunderbolt. By July, the P-47s had jettisonable belly tanks fitted to increase their range and now started scoring regularly against the German interceptor force.

During the spring of 1943, the Spitfire Mk IX, previously fitted with the Merlin 61 or 63, started having the Merlin Type 66 fitted on the production line. This engine's supercharger was set to come in at a lower altitude than the Merlin 61/63 did and so powered, the 'new' Mk IXb (an unofficial suffix) became the equal of the Fw 190 at all altitudes.[6]

The Spitfire Mark XIV

While the Rolls-Royce Merlin displaced some 27 litres in Spitfires up to the Mark XIII, the Rolls-Royce Griffon engine which supplemented and replaced it in the later Spitfires, such as the Mk XIV, was introduced in the middle of 1943, displaced 37 litres and was correspondingly more powerful than the Merlin, 2,035hp being available in the more numerous and successful two-stage supercharged Mk XIV.

The first Griffon-powered Spitfire was accepted into RAF service in February 1943, and this was the F Mk XII, the first delivery of which was to 41 Squadron. The Mk XII was the result of a batch of forty-five Mk VBs, which had had the new Griffon engine installed and their airframes strengthened. A further fifty-five Mk VIIIs also received the Griffon VI, to become Mk XIIs. The only squadron to use the Mark XII was number 91, which received their complement in April.

As an aside, it may be possible that one or two of these Mk XIIs, from the Mk VB batch, may have been originally built as Mk IIs. The Mk XII, with its Griffon VI giving 1,815hp, was the equal of the Fw 190 at low level and, later on in 1944, was also used to combat the V1 'Flying Bomb'. One of the problems that the British aircraft industry suffered from continually during the war was a creep-back of delivery dates to the squadrons. For instance, Supermarine had promised the Air Ministry 120 Spitfire Mk XIVs by April 1944, which would have given the RAF an even faster V1 catcher than the then-in-service Mk IX, but by October, only three Spitfire Mk XIVs had been delivered.[7]

Pilots who had flown the Mk V (there were precious few left by 1943) thought that with the Griffon, a larger and heavier engine than the Merlin, the lightness of the Spitfire's handling had deteriorated but the pilots did like the increased performance.[8]

Pilots of 91 Squadron claimed five Fw 190 'Jagdbombers' shot down on 25 May 1943, using F Mk XIIs. Although this primarily low-altitude variant of the Griffon-powered Spitfire scored successes, particularly against the sea- and ground-hugging Jabos, it was the Mark XIV that was by far the most numerous and successful of the later Marks of Spitfire.[9]

During the first half of 1943, as we have seen, the Hawker Typhoon had been instrumental in defeating several sneak 'Jabo' raids on British coastal towns, bringing down both Bf 109s and Fw 190s, mainly due to its superior speed. By now, most of the initial problems of the Typhoon had been cured but some problems, including a nasty habit of shedding their tails, persisted until VE-Day.

There was another problem with operating Typhoons during this time. In his book *The Power to Fly*, L.J.K. Setright wrote the following about the Typhoon and its Sabre engine:

> The pilot's reluctance to fly in Sabre-engined squadrons was increased when the Sabre ran into its second trouble, a mysterious succession of failures while the fighters were patrolling the Channel before D-Day. They were admittedly working very hard, flying virtually all around the clock and being very badly maintained because of the hastiness of the turn around – oil checks were often forgotten – but nevertheless the sudden incidence of engine failures became very disturbing, especially when it reached a level where in one day no fewer than fifteen Sabres conked out over the Channel.

The Air Ministry promptly flew into a tremendous tizzy and virtually put Napiers on the carpet. Sleeve failures were suspected, the sleeve valve commonly being the scapegoat for any Bristol or Napier malfunction in those days, and in fact Napier warned Bristol of what was going on in case the trouble should be traced to a fuel or lubricant condition that might affect them as well. Bristol had had plenty of their own troubles [in developing sleeve valves – Ed] but this particular one, and everybody was at a loss to understand it for a long time, while working furiously to find the explanation.

Eventually, Hall of Napiers concluded that there was absolutely nothing wrong with the engine and that the fault must therefore lie with the men operating it. He therefore arranged for all Sabre-engined aircraft to be fitted with concealed flight recorders, which they did in a couple of Squadrons.

Soon the answer came to light. A bunch of stupid, ignorant and possibly misguided (but by whom?) mechanics had discovered that it was possible to fiddle with the internals of the automatic boost control that integrated the various functions to provide a variable datum governor. This control box should have left the pilots free to control their engine simply by movement of the throttle lever without having to worry about the interrelationships of altitude, boost pressure, airscrew pitch and the like; but the machinations of the ground crews had made possible a condition whereby these fighters were cruising up and down the Channel for long, drawn out patrols with the airscrews in full coarse pitch, the crankshafts turning over at cruising rpm, and the blowers delivering maximum boost! Of course, the engines were hammering themselves to death, and there was practically a riot when the cause was discovered. Thereafter the control boxes were all sealed, and the Sabre gave no more trouble.[10]

August saw Leigh-Mallory, now an Air Marshal, promoted to be the Commander-in-Chief of the Allied Air Expeditionary Force, the 2nd Tactical Air Force, for the forthcoming invasion of France. (The first tactical air force had been formed in the Western Desert in 1942.) He instigated a policy of using his fighters in the ground attack role over France in the run up to the invasion, in order to hinder the movements of the German army during D-Day and its aftermath.

Leigh-Mallory had been unable to restrain himself from sending Circuses and Rodeos across the Channel from time to time after 1942, but by the middle of 1943, the German fighter defences had increasingly been concentrated on trying to combat the ever-increasing American fighter-escorted Eighth Air Force B-17 and B-24 raids into Northern France and, sometimes, into the Reich itself.

It was also in August that documents captured in Sicily by the British were handed over to a Major Bell at General HQ in the Middle East to be translated into English, evaluated and reported upon. He correctly surmised that the Luftwaffe's main supplies of synthetic fuel were being blended at several depots in Germany and that they should be targeted by bombing raids. However, the British Air Ministry thought that Bell's conclusion was incorrect and that, 'The Air Ministry thinks (this conclusion) most unlikely.' The British thus lost an invaluable opportunity to bomb these depots in Germany in 1943 and in the first part of 1944 and basically to strangle the Luftwaffe's fuel supply.[11]

Training time for pilots in the RAF had now increased markedly, up to 335 hours before they were being sent on operations. For the Germans, with their deteriorating fuel supply, training was shortened, from the previous 240 hours to 170. By 1944, that would drop to just 110 hours.[12]

On 17 November 1943, Fighter Command was split into two parts. One was the Air Defence of Great Britain, now commanded until the end of the war by Air Marshal Sir Roderic Hill, and the other was the Second Tactical Air Force, which came under the command, first of all, of Air Marshal Sir John d'Albiac. This was essentially a ground attack force, featuring aircraft such as the bomb-carrying and rocket-firing Hawker Typhoon. Now that the higher flying and faster Hawker Tempest was coming into service, the Typhoon essentially relinquished its previous role as an interceptor fighter and, fitted with eight air to ground rockets, became a ground attack fighter bomber. It performed sterling work in France, particularly during the battle of the Falaise Gap in September 1944, although its losses, primarily to the omnipresent German flak, were high.[13]

It was at this time that, with strenuous denunciations of them by leaders such as Johnnie Johnson, Rhubarbs were finally discontinued. The policy of sending pairs of fighters low over France, to find and shoot up whatever they could, was now recognised as causing more losses to the RAF than damage to the enemy. It's fair to say that they had been disliked by pretty much all the pilots who took part in them. Once again, the German flak defences had been the main cause of the demise of this type of operation.[14] Squadron Leader C.J. Sheddan recalled the following:

> Eventually the top brass had to face the fact that losses far outweighed the results and this type of aerial warfare was largely discontinued. But, obviously, the unfortunate thing was that while this conclusion was filtering through to the higher-ups, a good many pilots were to be lost and at the height these sorties were carried out very few pilots survived the resultant crash.[15]

By 1943, despite being equipped with drop tanks, the limited range of Spitfires meant they were gradually replaced by American bomber escort fighters in fighting the Luftwaffe's fighters over France.

By the Autumn of 1943, German forces in Russia were being forced ever westwards towards the Reich, while the air battles over France and Germany had now substantially sapped the strength of the Jagdwaffe, the force losing a quarter of its strength in the latter-half of 1943. Now, with the introduction of undertrained pilots and the loss of experienced 'Experten' leaders, things were becoming desperate.

The numerical and qualitative superiority of the RAF and the USAAF escort fighters, and also the attacks by the 2nd TAF, were really damaging to the German war effort. In fact, during this time, Field Marshal Manstein and two SS generals, who commanded units on the Eastern Front, met with Hitler privately, and told him that the war was lost and that he needed to negotiate a peace. The trouble was, the Allied leaders had met together in late 1942 in Casablanca and had declared that the war against Germany would be fought until it surrendered unconditionally.[16]

In France in 1943, JG 2 lost almost 200 pilots killed or missing. Compare this with their losses in 1940, in both the battles of France and Britain, where they lost just thirty-six pilots. The war for Germany was going badly.[17]

Chapter 7

1944–1945

After such a long time fighting, the end is a blessed relief in and of itself.

Anon

By the beginning of 1944, the German air defence of Europe was being hard pressed and was crumbling. As well as the Eighth Air Force bombers destroying Germany's factories and sources of fuel by day, the RAF's heavy bombers were persistently bombing and burning the enemy's cities by night, either killing, wounding, or making the German workers and their families homeless.[1]

From its formation in June 1943, the 2nd Tactical Air Force, under Trafford Leigh-Mallory's overall direction, had flown in a mainly ground attack role. Rocket-firing and bomb-carrying Typhoons and bomb-carrying Spitfires attacked targets of opportunity in France, such as locomotives, airstrips, trucks, staff cars – in fact anything that moved on the French roads or tracks. There were complaints about French civilians being killed but Leigh-Mallory brushed these aside.[2]

In January, the commander of the 2nd Tactical Air Force, Air Marshal Sir John d'Albiac, was replaced by Air Marshal Sir Arthur 'Mary' Coningham. ('Mary' was a corruption of 'Maori', as Coningham was a New Zealander.) Coningham had commanded the Desert Air Force in 1943 and was well used to using his air arm to support the British Army in their battles in Libya and Tunisia, instead of taking part in relatively useless fighter sweeps looking for enemy aircraft.

The USAAF also employed P-47 Thunderbolts in the ground attack role, some of them armed with rockets, as well as bombs. The USAAF, besides the heavy bombers of the Eighth Air Force in Europe, also used its medium bombers, such as the B-26 Marauder and the B-25 Mitchell, primarily to attack the German fighter airfields.

During February, the German Jagdwaffe suffered such losses (17.5 per cent of its strength) that it was never again able to mount concerted interceptions against the American bombers. With more and more USAAF P-47, P-38 and P-51 fighters escorting the B-17s and B-24s into Germany itself, the Luftwaffe found itself outnumbered, outgunned and outflown. On some occasions the Eighth Air Force flew over 1,000 bombers on their raids, escorted by ever more P-47s, P-51s and P-38s, in their attempts to sever bridges, bomb airfields and V1 launching sites and supply dumps and to basically make it impossible for the German army to operate in Northern France, prior to the D-Day invasion of Europe.[3]

Concerning the situation over Europe in early 1944, Johnnie Johnson wrote about the fighters escorting the Eighth Air Force's B-17 Flying Fortresses and B-24 Liberators: 'Our Spitfires had the performance but not the range to carry the daylight offensive to Germany, and, unfortunately, our Typhoons had the range but not the ability to live in the air against the Messerschmitts and Focke-Wulfs.'[4]

By May, the Allied commanders belatedly realised that Major Bell, who had correctly surmised from captured German documents in August 1943 that the synthetic fuel supply of Germany was being manufactured at just a few fuel tank depots in Germany itself, ordered them to be bombed. At a stroke, this severely incapacitated the Luftwaffe's attempts at a fighter defence of Germany, against the ever-increasing bomber raids.[5]

By 6 June 1944, when Operation *Overlord*, the Normandy landings, took place, the Allied air forces ruled the skies over Europe. By the end of June, Luftwaffe High Command had given up ordering the German fighters based in France to intercept the American heavy bomber raids on their way to Germany. There were too few of them to make any real difference and those fighters that were still active there now concentrated their efforts on trying to help the Wehrmacht by intercepting Allied fighter bombers and artillery observation aircraft. During June, the Allies had flown some 120,000 to 140,000 sorties, the German Jagdwaffe just 10,061. Now, three German fighter pilots were lost for every one Allied fighter pilot.

Desperately fighting all the way back to the Reich, the Luftwaffe, although introducing new fighters such as the Junkers Jumo-engine powered Focke-Wulf Fw 190D-9, was all but beaten from the skies. This 'new' 190 was a variant of the original Fw 190A series, but now with a liquid-cooled Junkers Jumo 213 V12 engine instead of the air-cooled BMW 801 radial engine previously employed, and it had the performance to match the latest marks of Spitfire – and even the newly introduced Hawker Tempest.[6]

The Hawker Tempest

The Tempest was basically what the Hawker Typhoon should have been in 1942, with a much thinner wing and lengthened fuselage, but still with the same Napier Sabre engine though now well developed. It was fast, certainly well over 420 mph although it probably, in service trim, did not achieve the 450 mph that its makers claimed. The Tempest also should have been in service by 1943 but production difficulties meant that it did not appear in squadron service until 1944.

The Bf 109, in 'G' and 'K' forms fought on but was outclassed against the new generation of American and British fighters. Nevertheless, the 'Experten' often won some significant victories.[7]

In 1944, the Germans had introduced their twin jet-engine fighter, the Me 262, with a performance which could run rings around any Allied fighter. A top speed of 540 mph was claimed and four 30mm cannon were in the nose to give this German fighter a mighty punch.

Luckily for the Allies, it was never produced in great numbers as initial bungling by Hitler, who saw it as a fast bomber, delayed its introduction as a fighter by a year. Even then, it had its problems. The early jet engines were prone to 'flame out' if the throttles were opened too quickly but, as Adolf Galland, the General of Fighters in the Luftwaffe, said when he first flew one, 'It was as if the angels were pushing.'[8]

The problem for the Germans was that, by this time, such was the strain imposed by the terrible losses in aircraft and pilots, both on the Eastern Front against the Russians and in Europe against the massed American heavy bombers, that the Luftwaffe's new pilots had had their training curtailed, which led to a drastic decline in their ability in air-to-air combat. This was also caused by a lack of aviation fuel, again due to the round-the-clock bombing by USAAF B-17s and B-24s by day and the RAF's Lancasters and Halifaxes by night.[9]

This led to a situation where the German 'Experten' were becoming the backbone of the shrinking fighter squadrons until they themselves were killed, presiding over youngsters who, though brave but with little or no experience, were being shot down at an ever-increasing rate, primarily by the American escort fighters such as the P-51D Mustang.

Some of the 'Experten' now had over a hundred victories, some twenty of them had over 200 each and two pilots, Erich Hartmann and Günther Rall, claimed over 300 each during the war.

The Allies, on the whole, 'rested' their fighter pilots after they had completed an allotted number of missions, this usually being anything up to 200 combat mission hours by 1944. No such luck for the German pilots. With rare exceptions, they flew and fought until either death, wounds or the end of the war intervened.

In August 1944, with the Battle for France almost won, Leigh-Mallory was appointed to take command of the RAF in South East Asia. He and his wife took off on their way to Ceylon in an Avro York, a civilian version of the Avro Lancaster bomber, piloted by an experienced RAF pilot. Leigh-Mallory overrode his pilot's objections about the weather that they would encounter. The plane crashed on its way through the Alps, killing all ten people on board. Ironically, Keith Park was appointed to Leigh-Mallory's position.

By September the Allies had won the battle of France and what was left of the Wehrmacht was frantically streaming through what became known as the Falaise Gap, in between the British and Canadian armies, to cross the River Seine back into Germany. Bombarded by artillery on both sides and from the air, with the rocket-firing Typhoons leading the charge, it was a rout. Just as with the British Army at Dunkirk, the German army left most of their heavy equipment behind, on the western side of the river Seine. But by the end of the year, the Allied forces had reached the limit of their supply chains and, over the winter of 1944-45, drew their breath in preparation for the final battle into Germany.[10]

The Battle of the Bulge started in December 1944 when the German army attempted once again, as in 1940, to use the Ardennes Forest as a springboard for a surprise armoured thrust, which would take them to Ostend. To begin with, under cloud and snow-filled skies, their advance went well, until the German armour began running out of fuel. This coincided with the weather improving and the Allies, particularly the American army, who faced the brunt of the fighting regrouped and started pushing the Germans back. With the skies clearing, Allied aircraft took to the air and mercilessly strafed and bombed the retreating Germans until the frontier with Germany was reached.

With the ever-increasing numbers of B-17 and B-24s taking part in the fighter-escorted raids over Germany, the Luftwaffe's fighter force was literally fought out of the sky by the end of 1944.[11]

The Luftwaffe attempted one last throw. On 1 January 1945, Operation *Bodenplatte* took place, which saw almost 1,000 German aircraft, including many fighters, streaking in at dawn at low level across many airfields, shooting and bombing the parked Allied aircraft. Many aircraft were destroyed, but the Allies losses were quickly made good, whereas those of the Luftwaffe, particularly in experienced pilots, were not.

February saw the taking of the Remagen Bridge over the Rhine, which American troops surged across. In front of and accompanying the armies went the fighter-bombers, of both the American and British forces, blowing apart any attempt by the Germans to stop them. March and April saw a steady advance by the armies across a Germany shattered by years of bombing and then the armies of the East and West, the Russians and Americans, met up on the bank of the Elbe River. It was left only for the Russians to take Berlin to bring the war to an end at the beginning of May.

During this latter period, German fighters, mainly Bf 109Gs and Ks, and Fw 190s, both in original BMW 801 radial engine and in 'longnose' V12-engined D-9 form, and the feared Me 262 jet fighter, together with the rocket-powered Me 163, made occasional sorties but were swiftly engaged by Tempests and the latest marks of Spitfire, plus the ever-present USAAF P-51 Mustangs, flying standing patrols over their airfields in an effort to catch the jets landing or taking off.

Far more dangerous than air fighting to the Allied air forces was the German Flakvierlung guns that guarded places like airfields being attacked by Allied fighter bombers. The quadruple barrelled 20mm cannon was particularly effective in this role.

Occasionally, an 'Experte' would show himself in the old flash of flying brilliance, such as when Erich Hartmann defeated a superior number of P-51s, but the usually inadequately trained pilots of the Luftwaffe were destroyed by the superior numbers and performance of the latest Allied fighters.

Although having a last fling with the 540-mph twin-jet engine Me 262, the Luftwaffe was beaten. Ironically, ex-JG 26 leader General Adolf Galland led a Jagdgeschwader (JV44) of Me 262s at the very end of the war, and he was lucky to survive and to surrender to the Allies.[12]

The war in Europe ended on 8 May 1945. Between 3 September 1939 and that final day, RAF Fighter command alone had lost 3,690 men killed, 1,215 wounded and 601 had become prisoners of war.

Chapter 8

Examination 1

Nothing is as hard, as to give wise council before
events; and nothing so easier as, after them,
to make wise reflections.

Sir William Temple

It is difficult now, eighty years after the events described in this book took place, to put ourselves into the minds and psyches of the men in command of Fighter Command in the Second World War. We have the advantage of hindsight. Having said that, the conduct of the men in charge of the strategy and tactics of Fighter Command in 1941 and 1942, bears examination.

As seen in earlier chapters, most of the commanders in the Second World War had previously fought in the First World War. That blood-soaked conflict had seen the British, French and German armies suffer terrible casualties, with their commanders, particularly on the British and French side, seeming to believe that there was an inexhaustible supply of men to be used up, as necessary, in their protracted land battles, even after they had ground to a halt.

It can be argued that the reason that the French army collapsed so fast in 1940 during the Second World War was as a result of the casualties suffered in the First World War. The French army in 1917 had mutinied and refused to advance from their trenches when commanded by General Nivelle after the disastrous Chemin des Dames battle. With the coming of the American army into France in 1917/18, there were enough troops available to the Allies to finally defeat the Great German Offensive of March 1918 and with Germany in retreat and the slow stranglehold of the Royal Navy in the blockade around the German homeland, the country collapsed in starvation and defeat. It should be noted that when Germany sued for an armistice, which was granted on 11 November 1918, ending the war, the German army was still mainly on French soil and marched back to Germany in good order, still with their weapons. This led to Adolf Hitler being able to claim that the German soldiers had been 'stabbed in the back' by war profiteers and Jews. The Treaty of Versailles, which was signed in 1919 and concluded the war, was overbearingly harsh towards Germany. Matters in Europe were not concluded, although the Allies wanted to believe that they were.

Twenty-one years later, the British sent a comparatively small (270,000-strong) British Expeditionary Force to France, in time to be quickly defeated by Hitler's Blitzkrieg that started on 10 May 1940, and most of them were lucky to be extricated from the beaches at Dunkirk in June 1940.

In the chapters preceding this, we have examined the strategy, tactics and aircraft used by the RFC/RAF and the Luftstreitkrafte/Luftwaffe in the two world wars and how development of aircraft, but not the leaders, took place in between these wars. We have also looked at the way that the commanders at the Air Ministry made policy. It is now time to take a look at the results and ask just how effective Fighter Command was in 1941 and 1942, when the RAF went onto the offensive in daylight over France, mainly by using fighter escorted medium bombers.

First of all, we can say that the British can be rightly proud of 'The Few', those fighter pilots who fought the Luftwaffe in the Battle of Britain in 1940. They won a stunning victory during a very hard time in Britain's history. The architect of this victory was Air Marshal Hugh Dowding, ably assisted by Air Vice-Marshal Keith Park, the leader of 11 Group, guarding the South East of England.[1]

Likewise, Britain can be proud of all the pilots (and the ground crews) of both wars. No matter what the situation, they did their best, sometimes against fearful odds, such as over Malta, in the desert, or during the Battle for Singapore. Often overlooked in many books on the subject of air fighting in the two world wars are the casualty rates of both sides, particularly of the ground attack squadrons of the British, such as the rocket-firing Hawker Typhoons in places like Normandy in 1944 and the night-bomber crews from 1939–45, some 55,000 of whom were lost, around 55 per cent of that Command.

What is also mainly overlooked, and what is deeply offensive to the memory of these men, is the way that the high command of the RFC/RAF, both in the First and the Second World War, threw their men's lives away as if they were of little account. This is true of both Fighter Command and Bomber Command.

During the Battle of Britain, today reckoned to have taken place between 10 July and 31 October 1940, some 544 RAF fighter pilots were killed, or died of wounds. Obviously, these losses had to be made up as quickly as possible to bring Fighter Command up to full strength. This required new pilots to man the new aircraft, mainly Spitfires, and there are numerous accounts of how brief and perfunctory their training was.

At the end of 1940, the real problem was in making these new pilots battle ready. Already, several squadrons were beginning to emulate the Jagdwaffe in their fighting tactics, 'Sailor' Malan particularly got rid of the old line astern, 'Vic' of three, line abreast formations and adopted the German 'rotte' and 'schwarm', four-finger type formation. But it was practice that these new pilots needed. Although Operational Training Units were beginning to be formed, to begin with, they were badly organised, the more experienced, battle-proven pilots appointed to them having little to do with the new men. Johnnie Johnson wrote of his time at an OTU at Hawarden:

A further reason for some anxiety was the fact that we V.R.s (Volunteer Reserve) who were replacing casualties were not of the same high quality as the dead and wounded pilots.

Our instructors were a seasoned bunch of fighter pilots, most of whom had fought in France, over Dunkirk or in the preliminary phases of the Battle of Britain. One or two of them wore the mauve-and-silver ribbon of the Distinguished Flying Cross, but they rarely spoke to the pupils of their combats against the Messerschmitts. The unit at Hawarden had only been formed a short time and lectures on combat tactics had not yet been devised. How we longed for this knowledge! What went on when flights of Spitfires and Messerschmitts met? When squadron met squadron and wing met wing? Could the 109s turn inside us? What about the new cannon that fired through the hub of the propeller? What happened when they hurtled down from the sun? Were they aggressive, these pilots who had inherited the traditions of Von Richthofen, the 'Red Knight' of the First World War? And what about their formation leaders who had tested their aircraft and tactics in the Spanish Civil War? What was the most important asset of a fighter pilot – to shoot straight, to keep a good look-out or to be able to stay with his leader at all times?

All these and a hundred other questions remained unanswered, for the handful of instructors hung together and had their work cut out to keep the sausage machine turning.[2]

A lot of new fighter pilots in 1941 particularly went into battle with little knowledge of what they should have been doing.

It is here that it is appropriate to look at what Winston Churchill, then Prime Minister of Britain, did, as regards the air war during 1941 and 1942. First of all he (together with the rest of the War

Cabinet) believed that Hitler would try again, from spring 1941, to invade Britain. For that reason alone, he insisted on keeping his best-equipped fighter squadrons in Britain, to defend the country. He may well have been right in this thinking but his intelligence agencies, due to the cracking of the Enigma codes in May 1940, must have told him that the main forces of the Luftwaffe were being moved to the east by April/May of that year.[3]

Churchill, aided by Sholto Douglas and Trafford Leigh-Mallory could easily, in February/March 1941 have detached a wing of Spitfires to be sent to Malta, to aid the hard-pressed 261 Squadron, equipped with obsolescent Hurricane Mk Is. Production numbers had so increased since the end of the Battle of Britain that, with the increase in fighter pilots, which had also occurred during this time, such a move would have been possible. The squadrons of Spitfires left in Britain would still have been able to cope with a renewed Battle of Britain in 1941. Happily, this did not happen, but the movement of Spitfires to Malta was a missed opportunity.

This time period occupied the first part of 1941 until, to Churchill's welcome surprise, Germany invaded Russia in June 1941. His attitude towards the Circuses that were flown over Northern France during this period appears to have been ambivalent at best, with a careful warning to Sholto Douglas to 'watch your losses'. Sholto Douglas did not.[4]

Following the invasion of Russia on 22 June 1941, Churchill could have ordered his commanders in the RAF to do things that would, in hindsight, have been really useful to the Allied cause, such as re-equipping the defences of Malta, or doing the same with the scanty air defences of Singapore, which then consisted of outdated Brewster Buffalos (Japan's intentions towards Britain's colonies were known at this time), or sending Spitfires to aid the hard pressed P40s of the Desert Air Force in Libya. But he didn't. Not only did he acquiesce to Stalin's demands that the British try to force Germany to divert more of their fighters back to France, he accepted the blandishments and assurances from commanders such as Sholto Douglas and Leigh-Mallory. This was that the Spitfire-equipped squadrons of the RAF were better off flying what turned out to be useless fighter sweeps over Northern France than anything else, until most of 1942 had passed.

Winston Churchill was a great Francophobe. Indeed, in the month after the Germans invaded France in May 1940, he flew to France no less than six times to try and encourage the French government to keep on resisting the German invasion. One of the leaders of the French tank force was a certain General Charles de Gaulle, and after the German victory he commandeered an aircraft and fled to London. There, he set up, with British assistance, an office which commanded the Free French forces that had fled to England after Dunkirk. Churchill, on behalf of the British Government, agreed to pay for the upkeep of this army, the bill to be paid 'when the war was over'.

De Gaulle's relationship with Churchill was not harmonious. At one time, in a *Chicago Herald* interview, he accused Churchill of colluding with the puppet Vichy Government and, in turn, Adolf Hitler. It is possible that he used his influence on Churchill to encourage him with the RAF fighter offensive in 1941/42, to show the French that liberation was coming.

During the Battle of Britain, the Luftwaffe had, by mid-campaign, bombed most of 11 Group's forward airfields almost out of action. It was only Hitler's command to switch targets from RAF airfields to London that saved the defending Fighter Command's airfields, so that they could be repaired and used again, to defeat the Luftwaffe.[5]

Sholto Douglas and Leigh-Mallory knew this. Yet they failed to direct the Circuses of 1941/42 to concentrate on bombing the airfields that JG 2 and JG 26 were using, except occasionally, in 1941/42. Why was this? Once again, these commanders do not seem to have thought deeply enough about the tasks their forces could have carried out.

Another point is that these commanders, with the squadrons that they had to command, felt enormous pressure to do something with them. It is this writer's premise that they failed to think and act in a clear and logical manner.

After the outbreak of war between Japan and the Allies in December 1941, Australia was tested by the Japanese attacking New Guinea and their bombers were within range of Darwin itself. It was not until much later in the war (March 1943) that three Spitfire-equipped squadrons (two of Australian pilots) were transferred from 11 Group to Darwin. This only came about because the Australian government threatened Churchill with the withdrawal of all their fighting men then fighting for Britain, if he did not send some Spitfire equipped squadrons to Australia.[6]

Churchill is worshipped in many parts of the world, particularly in America, for his warnings of Hitler's intent in speeches and in parliament from before the war and then, when he became Prime Minister in May 1940, he urged the British people to hold out against Germany until, to his great relief, Hitler made his attack upon Russia. Only months later, the Japanese bombed Pearl Harbor and Hitler joined his Axis Allies, Japan and Italy, in declaring war against America, according to their treaty obligations. As a man born into an aristocratic family, Winston Churchill believed wholeheartedly in the British Empire of colonies such as India, rather than looking after the people of Britain itself.

There is a common thread running through these commanders' lives. They nearly all came from a class of Englishmen who thought that only they had the right to run the country, in whatever job they found themselves. 'Public Service' it was/is called. There were few exceptions to this and the British upper- and upper-middle-class men who occupied these positions often had been to the same public schools, the same universities and the same clubs and they therefore held very much the same views as one another. Sholto Douglas's book *Combat and Command*, for example, is full of phrases such as: 'One of the chaps in our squadron in 1916 was Freddy ... who I had gone to school with. He would later go on to become Air Vice-Marshal.'

There was something else shared by most of the British officers who would go on to be commanders in the RAF in the Second World War. A seemingly unshakeable belief in the value of the offensive, at all costs and at all times. They never seem to have considered pausing in their offensives, until their losses, being so great, forced them to do so. These commanders, of whom Hugh Trenchard, the general officer in command of the RFC/RAF in the First World War, was the foremost, and Sholto Douglas and Trafford Leigh-Mallory were others in the Second World War, and were typical of their background. It's not difficult to see why Trenchard ordered a non-stop offensive by the RFC in the First World War; his orders killed a lot of his junior officers, their friends and colleagues, but he was just copying the mistakes of his friend, Field Marshal Sir Douglas Haig, who killed off many more English soldiers on the battlefield than he need have done.

Particularly from August 1916, when the new German Albatros fighters arrived on the Western Front until the middle of 1917, when the SE5A and Sopwith Camel started arriving at the front in numbers, the Germans ruled the air over France. 'Bloody April' was not named thus by accident. Why, at this time, there were still numerous British squadrons equipped with the by now obsolete BE2 and they were hopelessly inadequate to defend themselves when faced by the new German fighters. There seemed to have been precious few of the officers in command who could, or did, think 'outside the box'. Certainly, Trenchard was not one of them.

The casualties among pilots and observers of the RFC/RAF during the First World War were markedly greater than the casualties suffered by the men of the opposing German Air Force, the Deutsche Luftstreitkrafte. So contemptuous of the 'ordinary' British citizen was Trenchard that, in 1920, he even advocated using the RAF to bomb strikers/agitators in Britain. Winston Churchill, the then Home Secretary, thankfully ignored this suggestion.

Trenchard's often malign influence persisted right into the Second World War as well. Had it not been for him, the disastrous 'Lean towards

France' policy adopted by the RAF in 1941 may never have gone into force; certainly, the defence of several of Britain's colonies in the Empire could have done with some of those Spitfires and their pilots that were so uselessly thrown into the English Channel in 1941/42.

In *Combat and Command*, Sholto Douglas recounts:

> By the time that I arrived at Fighter Command, in November 1940 [the day fighters] were about to go on the offensive, and to be given a chance to hit back at the Germans over their own territory in occupied France. ... When Air Marshal Charles 'Peter' Portal asked me what I thought about this idea [of Trenchard's, of going on the offensive over France] I had to tell him that I was very doubtful about the value of such a proposal.
>
> I pointed out that our offensive fighter policy on the Western Front in the years between 1914 and 1918 had been very expensive in casualties, although I had to admit that, for the most part, it did enable us to maintain air superiority. But I could not help feeling that the casualties, which we would be likely to suffer in offensive operations across the Channel, would be too severe for the results that we would be likely to achieve. I told Portal that I was not in favour of Trenchard's suggestion.[7]

In reply, Portal told Sholto Douglas to go away and write a paper sustaining his point of view. He recounts:

> But after I had completed my paper and I had had a chance to think more carefully about it, I had to admit to myself that my arguments were pretty feeble. If it proved anything at all it was that, in the circumstances then prevailing, an offensive policy for fighters against the German Air Force in northern France was the right one.

One wonders now (particularly with the value of hindsight) how Sholto Douglas came to change his mind. He must have realised that he would be sending his men and fighter aircraft to face just the same set of problems that the Luftwaffe had faced over Britain in 1940 – short operating range, the escorts flying too close to the bombers – and they had been defeated. There is, of course, the point that, having written a paper examining this proposal and shared it with Portal at the Air Ministry, and then not having implemented it, that paper may, later, have come back to haunt him. Perhaps with other senior staff officers declaiming him for being too hesitant/not courageous enough to use the forces at his disposal? This is, of course, pure conjecture on the author's part.

In other quotes from *Combat and Command*: 'So many times, when I read or listened to the reports of what was happening to my fighters out over France during 1941 and 1942, I was reminded so strongly of my own experiences as a fighter pilot, particularly during the spring of 1917.' Here, it is probable that Sholto Douglas is referring to his memories of what came to be referred to as 'Bloody April' in 1917, when the RFC, then flying mostly obsolete aircraft such as the BE2, lost a large number of men, 211 pilots and observers killed, with a 108 captured by the Germans, who lost just sixty-six aircraft in the same period.

The introduction of the Albatros DI and II, with their top speed of over 100 mph, and two Spandau machine-guns synchronised to fire through the propeller, came as a complete surprise to the RFC, somewhat resembling the shock that the introduction of the Fw 190 into Luftwaffe service in late 1941 on the Channel coast had to the fighter pilots of the RAF.[8]

But if Sholto Douglas was reminded so strongly of his dreadful experience of the First World War, why didn't he have his squadrons stand down and wait for better aircraft, such as the Spitfire Mk IX, which wasn't introduced until July 1942, and better trained pilots later in 1941 and 1942? Although this didn't happen at the time, that was the lesson for the leaders in the Second World War, of 'Bloody April' in 1917, when the inferior aircraft of the RFC suffered devastating casualties due to the new German Albatros biplanes. Trenchard was in charge then and Sholto Douglas was an officer pilot on the Western Front.

Sholto Douglas also ignored the feelings of the French population in 1941/42, who were being bombed and shot at by the aircraft on the British air offensive, which was bound to happen in the confusion of battle.

What might have happened if Sholto Douglas had stuck to his original proposal and written a report, arguing that the 'Lean towards France' idea was a bad one, as he had first thought? He could have written a report to the effect of: 'This policy is going to cost too many of our good pilots their lives, let alone the cost in destroyed aircraft. Why don't we just keep on training, keeping up standing patrols over the Channel against the sneak raids by the German fighter bombers, and sending pilots and aircraft to where else they are needed in the world and work towards when we will one day invade France and drive the Germans out?' We shall never know the answer to that question but quite probably, a lot of British fighter pilots who were to die in the next two years might have survived the war, had a policy such as this been adopted.

The Germans had not yet invaded Russia in December 1940, when the new 'Lean towards France' policy was put into place. But by June 1941, when the raids by Fighter Command had started in earnest, particularly after their first one-sided drubbing by the Luftwaffe, the high command of Fighter Command, in particular Sholto Douglas, could have called the 'Lean towards France' off, but they did not.

Sholto Douglas wrote more in his book about Fighter Command operations in 1941/2, such as:

> All these fighter operations were conceived with far more in mind than just a day's outing for our pilots. [!]

As Commander-in-chief of Fighter Command, it must always be for a purpose ... Fighter and Bomber Commands were the only two forces able to take the war continuously to the Germans, and it became my overriding concern to see that my command was equipped with aircraft and manned with pilots, which would enable us to make the greatest possible use of it.

But for what purpose? If the British had never sent their fighter pilots over the Channel in 1941 and 1942, it wouldn't have made the slightest difference to the outcome of the war, but it would have saved the lives of hundreds of Allied pilots.

Sholto Douglas himself, still in command of Fighter Command at the beginning of 1942 wrote:

Over a period of four months during that spring and early summer we lost three hundred and fourteen fighters and bombers, with the Germans losing only ninety aircraft. The new German fighters [FW 190A and Bf 109F] exacted a serious toll for our intrusion over their air space; *but the pressure had to be maintained.* [Author's italics]

Why?

He goes on to write in his book that 'The Russians ... expected us to help in every way that we could to relieve the pressure on their front in the East.' But the British were strenuously fighting Rommel in Libya on the ground and if anything was going to suck German forces away from Russia, it was this, not fighting in the skies over the English Channel and Northern France.

At one point in 1941, Wing Commander J.A. 'Johnny' Kent DSO DFC, who was at that time leader of the wing based at Northolt aerodrome, attended a conference at Northolt to discuss just how operations were proceeding. The leaders of the other 11 Group fighter wings and the leaders of the bombers were also there. The Air Officer Commanding 11 Group, Leigh-Mallory, presided.

During the conference Kent asked what exactly was the point of these Circuses that were being flown on an almost daily basis, pointing out that if the purpose was for the bombers to severely damage the targets they were aiming at, many more bombers would be needed. If, however, the bombers were merely there to act as bait, to bring the German fighters to battle, then, surely, they should be flying shorter missions, as most of the British fighter pilots were flying and fighting with one eye on their fuel gauge. Apparently, Leigh-Mallory was quite taken aback at this line of questioning and referred the question to Victor Beamish, a very experienced pilot officer and leader, who agreed with Kent.

Searching for an answer which would suit him, Leigh-Mallory then asked one of the other staff officers present, who had fought in the First World War but not in the present conflict what he thought, and this worthy disagreed with Kent, who defended his opinion vociferously. But Leigh-Mallory sided with his staff officer and, as Kent remarked: 'We continued to go to Lille and lose good men, all too little purpose.' That comment really sums up the attitude of Fighter Command's leaders at the Air Ministry during this period of the war.[9]

There is a surviving Pathé News clip featuring Leigh-Mallory reading from a prepared script in 1943, during the third anniversary/celebration of victory during the Battle of Britain. This was probably at the end of November and here is Leigh-Mallory, every inch the upper-class officer, extolling the RAF and how wonderfully they have done in the war. Every now and then Leigh-Mallory looks down at his script and then looks up at the camera. Those are hard eyes looking at you. He looks used to getting his way, a stubborn man.

During the planning of the fiasco that was the raid on Dieppe in August 1942, Leigh-Mallory refused the offered help from 'Bomber' Harris, to use the bombers to 'soften up' the defences, insisting that it should be a Fighter Command operation. Leigh-Mallory expected to lose up to fifty aircraft and pilots. In the event, ninety-seven Allied aircraft and forty-seven pilots were lost in this badly planned and useless operation. One wonders how officers such as Leigh- Mallory kept their jobs. Perhaps it was because so many of the high command at the Air Ministry and above came from the same privileged background and shared the same influential connections.[10]

There was a culture of the offensive and the superiority of the bomber inculcated in the staff at the Air Ministry before and during the Second World War, which is difficult to understand today; it went back to Trenchard's policy in the First World War but carried on through the inter-war years and into the Second World War. 'The bomber will always get through' was virtually the RAF's sole policy, and little was done to change, or even moderate, that line of thought, despite Hugh Dowding's introduction of the new monoplane fighters in the late 1930s. Sadly for their crews, the bombers in the Second World War did not always get through.

There was a lack of hard, dispassionate, logical thinking among the staff officers at the Air Ministry. Witness the events highlighted in this book. We have only to look at the RAF's bomber campaign in both world wars to see how the attitude of the men at the Air Ministry always seems to have been: 'Damn the casualties, we have an Empire with plenty more men where they came from.'

Germany, on the other hand, had commanders who would take to the defensive where necessary, until the time became right to again go on the offensive. Germany was not beaten during the Second World War by tactics, she was beaten by the sheer industrial might of Russia and America. Just witness one remarkable fact: Germany built some 1,400 Tiger tanks from 1941–45. Russia built over 250,000 of their T-34 tanks, which were almost as good, certainly went faster, and the later ones (built from 1943 onwards) mounted an 85mm gun which was on the same level of armour-piercing power as the Tiger's 88mm main gun.

One use Sholto Douglas could have made of his fighter force would have been to use Spitfires to reinforce the defence of places like Malta, already under sustained air attack from Italy (starting in 1940), and then with the Germans from 1941. Malta was an unsinkable aircraft carrier, from which British bombers and torpedo-carrying aircraft could be launched to sink the ships that were bringing supplies to Rommel in North Africa.

The Air Ministry had already blotted its copybook with the Royal Navy in January 1941, when it failed to inform their Headquarters of the move of Fliegerkorps X to Sicily, which it knew about from ULTRA intercepts. This lack of communication allowed the Luftwaffe's Stuka dive-bombers to severely damage HMS *Illustrious*, an aircraft carrier of the Royal Navy. Had the navy known they would be sailing within the range of the Luftwaffe, it's doubtful they would have ordered the operation involving *Illustrious* to take place.[11]

By 12 February 1941, Malta only had a few Hurricanes left defending it. The Germans sent Bf 109E-7s of the 7th Staffel of JG 26 (7./JG 26) from France to assist Fliegerkorps X based in Sicily in the fighting over Malta in late January 1941. Their leader Oberleutnant Joachim Muncheburg, was already an ace and a Knight's Cross holder. In little more than two weeks, the new Bf 109E-7s of Muncheburg's staffel had all but destroyed any meaningful airborne fighter opposition over Malta.

Later on, in June, 7/JG 26 were transferred to Libya until August 1941 and shot down as many of the British aircraft as they found over Malta and the Western Desert, for no loss. By the time this staffel returned to France in late September 1941, its twelve pilots had shot down fifty-two Hurricanes and eighteen other Allied aircraft. Granted that their victories were over inferior fighters, such as tropicalized Hurricanes and later on Curtiss P-40 Tomahawks, but the fact is that 7/JG 26 suffered no losses at all in combat. Had Spitfires been sent out to combat them, the result may have been different.[12]

By 1941, the Hawker Hurricane was obsolete as an interceptor fighter, being too slow and unwieldy against the new Messerschmitt Bf 109F but the Mark IIC version had been introduced by this time, and this version at least carried four 20mm cannon in the wings. In the Mk IID version, two 40mm cannon, one fitted beneath each wing, were used, and these aircraft flew in the desert as tank busters. The Mk II was also used as a fighter-bomber in both France and in the desert, performing much the same task as the Stuka dive bombers of the Luftwaffe did.

No Spitfires were sent to Malta until 7 March 1942, when a paltry fifteen were sent. They didn't last long under the relentless onslaught on the island by the Regia Aeronautica and the Luftwaffe, operating from Sicily. On 27 March another squadron of tropicalized Spitfires was delivered to the besieged island.

There was also the Western Desert, Libya, Cyrenaica, Egypt where, in the spring of 1941, General Erwin Rommel had arrived to head the newly introduced Afrika Korps. The Germans immediately went onto the offensive and pushed the Allies back along the coast to Egypt. While Hurricanes (slowed down even further than in Europe with filters to try to keep sand out of their engines) with a few Gloster Gladiators, and Curtiss P-40 Tomahawks did all they could to stave off the Luftwaffe in Africa, a wing of Spitfires would have been of far more help, particularly if crewed by some of the more experienced British pilots.[13]

Spitfires were not sent out to the Western Desert until August 1942, when the fighting was reaching a crescendo. This left Hurricanes and P-40s to combat the Bf 109s of JG 27, who exacted a fearful toll of them from their very first combat mission over the desert on 19 April 1941. The Curtiss P-40, named the 'Tomahawk' in its early marks, and powered by an Allison V12 giving 1040hp, had been rejected in 1940 by the RAF as unsuitable for home defence, being unsuited for high altitude interception work, and they were sent out to the Western Desert, regarded at that time as a secondary theatre.

When compared with the Bf 109F, the P-40 was a relatively large fighter, its length being 31ft, 8.5in, its wingspan was 37ft, 3.5in and it weighed some 7,000 pounds when ready to fly and fight. Speed was given as 345 mph.

The Tomahawks could hold their own against the Italian Macchis and Fiat fighters of the Regia Aeronautica, but when the Luftwaffe sent Bf 109 equipped JG 27 to Africa, they were decimated. Just about equal in performance terms below 14,500ft, they had to concede the advantage of altitude to the pilots of JG 27, who were able to bounce the mostly South African, Canadian, Australian and Polish aircrew who were the mainstay of the P-40 and Hurricane squadrons in the Western Desert, from out of the blinding sun. It took a while before the P-40 and Hurricane equipped squadrons in the desert worked out tactics to help them when faced with the Bf 109s. The usual tactic was to form a defensive circle, but the German fighter pilots soon learned how to make their way into this circle and shoot down the P-40s. One German pilot, Hans Joachim Marseille claimed 158 victories, over a hundred of them being P-40s, until being killed in an accident in September 1942.[14]

JG 27, with its three Gruppen, claimed to have shot down 1,166 Allied aircraft in the desert war between April 1941 and November 1942, for the loss of 200 aircraft. That is a ratio of over 5:1. Its pilots were not above sometimes strafing downed Allied aircraft in an attempt to kill the pilots who had survived their crash landings.

It is only fair to point out that a lot of over-claiming went on in the desert air battles as well as in Europe; for instance, on 15 September 1942 JG 27 claimed nineteen P-40s destroyed, Marseille himself claiming to have shot down seven in six minutes. Official records show five P-40s being shot down in the encounter, another one being lost to Allied anti-aircraft fire.

On the subject of training, for both the RAF and the Luftwaffe – there does seem to have been an inordinate gap in knowledge of the then current fighting tactics between the new pilots of the RAF, having finished their training and been to an OTU, and then being assigned to a squadron.

What I mean by this is that although the new pilot could fly his Spitfire, it was down to his squadron leader and his new flight mates to teach him the tactics he really needed to adopt once he was in combat. Compared to this somewhat lackadaisical attitude, Adolf Galland, Kommodore of JG 26, rotated one of his staffeln at a time to Audembert airfield, where he was based, where he could fly with and observe the pilots' flying and fighting skills and so help them with advice. This doesn't seem to have happened in the RAF as much.

At this time, the officer in command of Training Command was Air Marshal Lawrence Pattinson, another officer who had fought in the First World War, and it does seem as if the instructions given to training pilots of how to fly and fight in combat – that is, tactics – were seriously neglected.

To be fair to Sholto Douglas, it may have been his fear that Germany would try again to invade Britain in the spring/summer of 1941 that cautioned him to husband his supply of Spitfires then, even though they were coming off the production lines in some numbers by this time. However, once the Germans had invaded Russia on 22 June 1941, it would have been obvious to the Air Ministry, and to Sholto Douglas, that the invasion of Britain was now far from Hitler's mind. After the German invasion of Russia, Operation *Barbarossa*, had taken place in June 1941, Sholto Douglas could easily have dispatched any number of Spitfires to aid Malta, or the Desert Air Force in the Western Desert, instead of wasting them on fruitless sorties over the Channel to Northern France.

During May 1942, another sixty-four Spitfires flew in to Malta from the aircraft carriers HMS *Eagle* and the USS *Wasp*. Despite the Germans and Italians carrying out up to three sorties per day and attempting to catch the defending fighters on the ground, somehow the Spitfires kept on flying and fighting.

Steadily, the tide turned against the Italian and German forces then stationed in North Africa. By the beginning of June, there were more than five squadrons of Spitfires on Malta and the Axis started to suffer severe losses. But how much faster those losses could have occurred had the Air Ministry in Britain not been so tardy in their response to the urgent pleas from Air Vice-Marshal Lloyd, the RAF Commander in Malta, for Spitfires. On 5 March, he had signalled Air Marshal Sir Arthur Tedder, the AOC Middle East: 'Must have more fighters as soon as possible. Delay in Spitfires annoying. Can you hasten dispatch.'[15]

Using the same system of radar and ground control as had been used during the Battle of Britain, the air defence of Malta steadily improved. It was helped further in July 1942 when Air Marshal Sir Keith Park was appointed to replace Air Vice-Marshal Lloyd and head the defence. Arriving there to take command, Park used his extensive knowledge of the tactics that he had employed while commanding 11 Group during the Battle of Britain, and made a great contribution to Malta's defences.

The Spitfires had been used in the defence of Malta over the island itself previously but, with Park's arrival, he ordered them to intercept the Axis bomber raids as they flew across the Mediterranean from Sicily, and not wait for them to arrive over Malta. With radar warning, Park ordered the first of three squadrons airborne to 'bounce' the escorting fighters, using their height advantage, while the second squadron would attack the close escort and the third squadron would carry out head on attacks on the bombers. Within six days the Axis bombers had abandoned daylight raids, only attacking Malta by night.

Much attention was given to Malta's defence by the press and newsreels during the war, the island itself eventually receiving the George Cross from King George VI. However, its primary role as a base for bombers and torpedo-carrying aircraft to attack Axis convoys supplying Rommel in the Western Desert is often overlooked, in favour of highlighting the defences of the island.

Singapore was one of the worst defeats that the British ever suffered; it was to fall relatively easily to the Japanese in February 1942 after being thought virtually impregnable. Its fighter defences were woefully inadequate, consisting mainly of old Brewster Buffalos, which were soon overwhelmed by the Japanese Army 'Oscar' fighters against which they fought. Although ninety-nine Hawker Hurricane Mk IIs were sent to Singapore in January, they were no match for the nimble Japanese army fighters, and many Hurricanes were lost to strafing attacks on their airfields as they were lined up, wingtip to wingtip. No Spitfires were sent to bolster Singapore's defences.

Chapter 9

Examination 2

Sholto Douglas wrote a lengthy memorandum to Air Chief Marshal Sir Wilfred Freeman at the Air Ministry in the autumn of 1941. One part of it read:

> The majority of German fighter pilots that my 'fighter Boys' were meeting three months ago were described by the latter as 'OTU [Operational Training Unit] boys'...
>
> The 'OTU boys' however, have now learnt a good deal in the hard school of experience, while there is no doubt – in fact this is confirmed by intelligence reports – that the enemy has drafted a considerable number of experienced pilots into fighter units in the Pas de Calais area, either from the Russian front, *or more probably, by combing his training schools in Germany* [author's italics].[1]

One wonders where these 'intelligence reports' were coming from. None of the above was true.

Trafford Leigh-Mallory, having received a copy of this letter, as usual proceeded to send a lengthy memorandum about his observations on the situation. He appears to have been adept at writing such memos. Among his comments were these:

> Since it became possible to start regular offensive sweeps over FRANCE on the 14th June 1941, we have averaged two to one aircraft destroyed in our favour...The average was as much as three to one after the first month of the fighting.

And …

> During August, 101 German fighters have been destroyed,
> and 48 probably destroyed for the loss of 74 British fighter
> pilots. Over the period of these 'CIRCUS' operations from
> the 14th June to the 3rd September, 437 German Fighters
> have been destroyed, and 182 probably destroyed, for the
> loss of 194 British fighter pilots.

We now know that these figures were hopelessly inaccurate, actual
German losses being 128 aircraft destroyed, from all causes, and
seventy-six damaged.

Leigh-Mallory does not seem to have reflected upon the fact that
those 194 British fighter pilots lost equalled over sixteen squadrons
worth of men, which, together with their lost aircraft was more than
five wing's worth of men and machines gone. There was more in his
memo in this vein, such as:

> With the assumption of the offensive we have thus gained
> the initiative over the Germans, with the result that
> they are forced to maintain a high state of 'Readiness'
> while we are free to give our Squadrons adequate time
> for meals, recreation and rest. This, coupled with a
> reluctance to come and 'mix it' with British Squadrons,
> even though the Germans are fighting over their own
> territory, must have a very adverse morale effect on their
> Fighter pilots.

And:

> But it will still be necessary to maintain our present air
> superiority and moral ascendancy in Northern France
> and to continue to use this fighting for the training of our
> Squadrons *which have such a high proportion of new pilots*

[author's italics] ... I believe that occasional offensive
operations will be essential during the winter months in
order to maintain the morale of our own squadrons.

But air superiority for what purpose? There were no British troops
on the ground in France to keep superiority over. If Leigh-Mallory
had been considering French citizen's morale, whether the RAF
was overhead or not, they were well and truly under the heel of the
Nazi jackboot and no end of the RAF flying overhead would change
that. Added to which, the propensity of RAF pilots, flying low, to
strafe anything that moved, cannot have endeared them to the French
citizens when, inevitably, mistakes were made. And why was there
'such a high proportion of new pilots'? Because so many of the ones
who had gone before had been shot down, that's why.

Leigh-Mallory concluded his lengthy memorandum with:

Circus Operations ... have enabled us to train Squadrons,
which have been full of *untried pilots* [author's italics]
to fight under difficult circumstances and by so doing to
train Flight Commanders and Wing Leaders of the future.[2]

Leigh-Mallory does not appear to have asked the question: why are
the squadrons full of untrained pilots? And if they were training to
become future leaders, how could they do this when they were being
killed or captured in such numbers?

Later, in the previously mentioned Pathé newsreel celebrating the
third anniversary of the Battle of Britain, Leigh-Mallory is seen reading
from a prepared script and says: 'The scores are still in our favour. We
have established complete air supremacy over the Channel.'

Sholto Douglas did at least write at one point:

It would be most unwise to attach too much importance
to statistics showing the claims made and losses suffered

by our fighters month by month throughout the offensive. The experience of two world wars shows that in large scale offensive operations the claims [as] to the destruction of enemy aircraft made by pilots, however honestly made and carefully scrutinised, are a most inaccurate guide to true situations.[3]

By the end of 1942, the situation in the air war over the Channel being fought between the Luftwaffe and the RAF was this: 1) The Germans had mounted a mighty onslaught on Britain in 1940. They had been beaten by Fighter Command; 2) Fighter Command had mounted an assault over France in 1941 and 1942. They had been beaten by the Jagdwaffe.

Something that Sholto Douglas could have done constructively, when he took over command of Fighter Command late in 1940, would have been to instruct experienced fighter pilots, not being used operationally, to give newly trained pilots extensive training in fighter tactics, including firing practice, while at Operational Training Units (OTUs). He could have specified that these 'new boys' had to stay in air space over the British Isles, and to keep them out of trouble while they practised and honed their skill and tactics. Some of the young British pilots in 1940 had reported to their new squadrons with less than ten hours on Spitfires or Hurricanes.

These training missions could even have been leavened with sorties over France at, say, one-week intervals, to gain experience in actual combat, rather than flying over France operationally straight from OTUs almost every day, which is what took place once the Circus offensive started and which led to such high casualties among the RAF.

Sholto Douglas:

By the spring of 1942 I was preparing for a renewed effort by Fighter Command over the skies of France, but

227

in our planning we found ourselves having to look very carefully at the number of aircraft that we had available in reserve.

Sholto Douglas omits to mention that at the time this happened, he was the overall commander of Fighter Command and could have stood up to Charles Portal and Winston Churchill and declared that he was not prepared to send men out to their almost certain death, flying on operations which were, essentially, pointless.

As well as Sholto Douglas, 'Peter' Portal (as Sholto Douglas refers to him in his book) and the other staff officers at the Air Ministry were complicit in Fighter Command's offensives in 1941 and 1942. Like Sholto Douglas, Portal carried on with it, despite the attrition rate being completely in favour of the Germans. In February 1941, Portal wrote to Air Marshal Sir Richard Peirse, the then head of Bomber Command, mainly about using his Bristol Blenheims as 'bait', with a copy going to Sholto Douglas. In the letter, Portal wrote:

I regard the exercise of the initiative as in itself an extremely important factor in morale, and I would willingly accept equal loss or even more in order to throw the enemy on to the defensive, *and give our own units the moral superiority gained by doing the fighting on the other side* [author's italics].[4]

One wonders how many younger fighter pilots in Fighter Command they spoke with during this period, and asked questions about what they thought of what they were being sent out to do? The staff officers employed to do this in the Air Ministry were, as a whole, not experienced pilots. Yes, some of them may have learned to fly with the RAF and had some experience of flying biplanes in the late 1920s/early 1930s, but very few of them had any experience of air combat in the Second World War and they were the people responsible for allocating targets when the missions were planned. As Johnny Kent later wrote: 'We kept on losing good men over Lille for no practical purpose.'

It now seems probable that very few men of squadron leader, or flight commander, rank would have told either one of their high-ranking commanders that their policy was wrong, as that may have led to them being branded cowards, or 'LMF' (lacking in moral fibre), the term used in describing servicemen in the RAF who could no longer carry on fighting due to mental breakdowns. Such men were usually grounded, stripped of rank and given menial tasks, such as sweeping the hanger floors.

Then there is the amount of time that it took for the high ranking officers at the Air Ministry to realise that their strategy and tactics simply weren't working out as they hoped. The 'Lean towards France' policy had got into its stride in mid-1941, but it wasn't until the end of 1942 that it was finally abandoned, and not until late on in 1943 that the generally hated 'rhubarbs' were also dropped. Here the non-flying group captains and staff officers of Fighter Command must take their share of the blame. They simply did not impress upon Leigh-Mallory or Sholto Douglas the fact that their chosen strategy was wrong. There were some officers, such as Johnny Kent and Victor Beamish, who pointed out to Leigh Mallory that he was ordering the wrong strategy, but they were ignored.

In the Luftwaffe, by contrast, the General der Jagdflieger from the end of 1941 was Adolf Galland. Having recently led JG 26 in France, he was acutely aware of the mistakes that the RAF were making and carried on taking full advantage of them. But, again, just as on the British side, he too had a boss to report to: Hermann Göring, another ex-First World War pilot, who was out of touch with both the situation and the pilots, and who put his political connection with Hitler above the welfare of his aircrews. At least for the Germans, that quarrel did not raise its head in 1941/42.

Sir Charles Portal's role as Commander in Chief at the Air Ministry during the war is interesting. He was equally culpable, if not more so, than Sholto Douglas in adopting Trenchard's 'Lean towards France' policy. He encouraged Trenchard's point of view and, as overall head of the RAF, he retained Sholto Douglas and Trafford Leigh-Mallory, the failures of Fighter Command, the commanders then in power, to carry out this policy. It was they who mostly made the wrong decisions at the wrong time, and with an apparent disregard to the casualties this policy was causing to their own men.

During the war years, intelligence reports from decoded Enigma traffic were sent to the Air Ministry Section A14 from Bletchley Park, rewritten to appear as if this information had come from spies on the ground. As we now know, the German 'Enigma' codes (particularly those used by the Luftwaffe) had been broken by 1940. This was backed up by lower-grade signals from the 'Y' Section and the RAF W/T and radio intercept station at Cheadle.[5]

From the beginning of 1942, the decoded German Enigma signals, from Bletchley Park, were circulated to RAF Fighter, Bomber and Coastal Command, and Nos. 10,11 and 12 Groups. So Sholto Douglas and Leigh-Mallory knew, or should have known, the German fighter losses (or lack thereof) yet they still persisted in sending Circuses over the Channel to raid targets in France, now up against an even better armed opponent. Why?

It's entirely probable that the reports of the German quartermasters in charge of ordering everything, including new aircraft, for the various Geschwaders and Gruppen were included in these reports. If so, that would have told the British high command just how many losses in aircraft the Germans were suffering. For instance, if a Gruppe had lost, say, three Bf 109s during a sortie, the quartermaster, or whoever was responsible for supplies, would have sent a coded signal to his headquarters, asking for three replacement machines very soon afterwards.

So the question has to be asked, how far up the chain of British command did these reports reach in 1941 and 1942? Was it just to the Air Ministry? To William Sholto Douglas while he was employed there? To Trafford Leigh-Mallory at 11 Group? Perhaps these reports were too low level, in the assessment of the intelligence officer at Bletchley Park, to send to anyone really important? We don't know for certain, but it seems now to be obvious that Fighter Command probably knew about the real German losses in 1941 and they certainly did, even down to 11 Group by 1942.

There is yet another possibility. It has become apparent over the years since these wars were fought that many British officers of the First World War, like most career officers of the time, were 'gung ho' on achieving results against the enemy, regardless of their losses in casualties. It was the way to obtain honours and promotion. A lot of them also appear to have been unconcerned at the losses of their own men introduced by this policy of always being on the offensive.

Where the war in the air was concerned, the commanders of the RAF in the Second World War seem to have still been in the thrall of 'Boom' Trenchard.

Having followed Trenchard's offensive policy in the First World War and ignored its high casualty rate immediately afterwards, the commanders of RAF's Fighter Command in 1941 didn't think any further than this and it appears that they were incapable of original thinking. These high in command officers were Trenchard's accomplices, he who was always on the offensive in the First World War, despite the high casualties that this policy caused. Furthermore, he had never forgiven Hugh Dowding for standing up to him during the First World War. He had not changed his thinking about him either, having referred to him then as a 'dismal Jimmy'. So, he was someone to be got rid of, as soon as possible. And as for that confounded 'colonial', Keith Park …

The question is, what would Hugh Dowding and Keith Park have done, had they not been dismissed and had they remained in command positions in Fighter Command in 1941/42? I have to think that Dowding, with his history of conserving his fighters and their pilots during the Battle of Britain, would have carried on with that conservation policy, but we'll never know that for sure.

Keith Park was an energetic and inspiring leader when in command of 11 Group during the Battle of Britain in 1940. He flew, in his white overalls and in his personal Hurricane, to many of the just-bombed airfields of Fighter Command, checking on how things were going and discussing tactics with the local squadron leaders. Having seen for himself, firsthand, what had happened with – and to – the Luftwaffe when they fought over Britain in 1940, it's extremely doubtful whether he would have countenanced a mainly fighter offensive over France in 1941/42. He later on became, as we have seen, the RAF commander in Malta, who defeated the Axis air forces employed there.

Another question is, what would have happened differently in 1941/42 if the 'Lean towards France' policy had not been implemented? Again, we'll never know, but the answer is probably – very little to nothing; with most of the German forces, including their main bomber fleet transferred to the Russian front by May 1941, there were only the two Jagdgeschwaders, 2 and 26, with a few Jagdbombers left in France to carry out the nuisance raids against Britain, which they did anyway, over the following few years. Without the air battles over France, there would have been many more fighters available in Britain to intercept these raids.

First Viscount Hugh Montagu Trenchard died on 10 February 1956, while William Sholto Douglas became the Lord Douglas of Kirtleside and died on 29 October 1969. As we have seen, Air Chief Marshal Sir Trafford Leigh-Mallory was killed in an air crash on his way over the Alps in 1944.

Although on the losing side, the German military commanders mainly seemed to have been one step ahead of the British in their tactics in both world wars. By 1915, for example, German army front-line troops had abandoned using their rifles in trench raids. Bags of hand grenades and entrenching tools and clubs were found to be far more effective than a rifle; leaping from shell hole to shell hole for cover was found to be a much better way of taking a British or French position than climbing out of a trench and walking – yes, walking! – across No-Man's land towards coils of barbed wire with full kit and clutching a rifle, with fixed bayonet, while being cut down by machine-gun bullets and shrapnel from shellfire, as happened to the British at the Battle of the Somme in 1916 and the later battles in France in 1917.

In the Second World War, the Germans used their tanks in their Blitzkrieg offensives in ways which by and large kept their infantry casualties low. In the air, particularly in Russia, their Stuka dive-bombers proved a great weapon to destroy any strongholds opposing the army, which facilitated the advances of their Panzer divisions.

In other words, the Germans appear to have learned lessons that the Allies had not. They appeared to have learned the lessons of their failed assault on Verdun in 1916. In the First World War, they did not try such an offensive again until March 1918 when they mounted one last great offensive, bolstered by divisions freed from the Russian front, which had collapsed with the coming of the revolution there. The German withdrawal across the Somme battlefield from February to March 1917, in order to shorten their line and to retreat to a better prepared defensive Hindenburg line was yet another example of their practicality, in attempting to remain on the defensive in the West and wait for the collapse of Russia in the East, in the way that was most economical with their men's lives.

The German blunders all appear to have been strategic in both wars rather than tactical, whereas the British blunders seem, with few exceptions, to have been tactical. Until Hitler's forces invaded Russia, with the exception of the air battle over Britain in 1940, the Germans had conquered all before them. Add to this the almost minimal training that British fighter pilots received in actual fighter to fighter tactics when learning how to fly and fight in 1940/41, and it can be seen that this, allied to bad command decisions in 1941/42, was the reason that so many Allied pilots died, or were captured in these almost useless sweeps over France.

So, what was the 'Lean towards France' policy of 1941/42 really for? After the Battle of Britain, the German 'Blitz' of British cities by night started. That only stopped in May/June 1941 when the Luftwaffe transferred most of its aircraft to the East in preparation for the invasion of Russia.

The 'Lean towards France' operation had two objectives; before and after June 1941 it was intended to whittle down the strength of the Luftwaffe fighters left in France by attrition. That is, by the RAF shooting down more German fighters over France than they lost. As seen in the previous chapters, that didn't work.

The secondary objective was to try to help the Russians, under immense pressure on the Eastern Front, from 22 June 1941, with the Wehrmacht and the Luftwaffe inflicting tremendous losses upon both. Stalin implored Churchill to help by attempting to draw off some of the Luftwaffe's fighter forces to bolster JG 2 and JG 26. Again, that didn't work. The German High Command never saw the need to bolster the two Jagdgeschwaders left in the West during this period.

But what if they had? Even if they'd sent another Jagdgeschwader from the Eastern Front to help JG 2 and JG 26 on the Channel front, it's doubtful whether the advance of the Wehrmacht in Russia in 1941 would have been slowed down, as the Germans had complete air superiority over the Russian front from their invasion on 22 June 1941, right up to 1943.

Perhaps a third reason was what today we would call 'public relations'; the ability to tell the British people, through the newsreels, the radio and the press, that the RAF was striking back at the Germans, with a non-stop bombing campaign of their own over France, by day and night, to keep the population's spirits up in the middle of a dreadful war.

On the first two counts, the operation of 'Lean towards France' was a failure. On the point of attrition, the British lost far more aircraft and pilots than the Germans did. The fighter staffeln of the Luftwaffe in France established a 4:1 kill ratio over the Spitfires and Hurricanes sent to shoot down the few Bf 109s and the Fw 190s of the two fighter groups stationed there when the rest of the Luftwaffe turned eastward.

On a 'public relations' basis, the jury is still out; it's possible that the average British civilian at the time believed the figures of German fighters shot down being given out daily by the Air Ministry on the radio and in the newspapers, but the RAF fighter pilots certainly didn't. They could see their losses day after day by the empty chairs at the mess tables and they also knew what a deadly foe the Bf 109F was in early 1941, as well as the even more deadly Fw 190, when that aircraft was introduced into front line service later in the year, in August 1941.

There may have been a fourth motive, reaching all the way up to the then Prime Minister, Winston Churchill. With Britain standing alone against Hitler's Germany at the beginning of 1941, he had to hope that America would once again join Britain in fighting Germany, as they had in 1917 during the First World War. Perhaps Churchill felt that he had to show President Roosevelt that Britain was now on the offensive and that America, apart from supplying Britain with arms and food, needed to join the war also.

Luckily for Britain, Germany invaded Russia in June 1941, forestalling a possible invasion of Britain in that year but Churchill probably thought that it was important to keep raiding Northern France by day, in the hope that the Germans would have to send extra fighters to France, to bolster the efforts of JG 2 and JG 26 and show the Americans what a plucky little island Britain was, David attempting to bring Goliath down, as well as taking much-needed Luftwaffe aircraft and pilots away from the Russian front. As we have seen, the German High Command never found this necessary. There's also the fact that, by the beginning of 1942, the Germans were on a temporary retreat in the East, having been beaten in the battle for Moscow. Although many terrible battles lay ahead in the years to follow, it was possible, even then, to discern that the Soviet Union was probably going to beat the Wehrmacht and win.

By that time America had been drawn into the war by the attack on Pearl Harbor by Japan, one of Germany's axis partners. By acting upon their treaty with Japan, Germany declared war upon America. As American aid starting to flow to Britain, Churchill must have seen that the fighter sweeps over France were not achieving a decisive effect, so why did the Air Ministry, in the shape of Sholto Douglas, keep telling Leigh-Mallory to keep sending his pilots to defeat?

To have to go out day after day in inferior aircraft, to face the cream of the Luftwaffe's experienced fighter pilots over the Channel and France must have been a terrifying experience for the many inexperienced Allied fighter pilots. Very few of the British fighter pilots who had survived the Battle of Britain in 1940 survived into 1943. Hence L.J.K. Setright's comment about the really good pilots of the RAF having gone by 1943 turns out to be accurate.

Make no mistake: I am condemning the commanders of Fighter Command for the casualties they caused among their pilots in 1941 and 1942 for no good reason. However, I am also condemning them for their unimaginative use of the forces under their command. Those squadrons of Spitfires, kept in England in 1941 and 1942 would have been far better used in the desert, on Malta, at Singapore – virtually anywhere else where the Allies were fighting, except where they were kept and badly used.

The casualty list of Fighter Command in 1941 and 1942 in the West can be laid squarely on the shoulders of Trenchard, for suggesting the 'Lean towards France' policy, and Sholto Douglas and Leigh-Mallory for implementing it. Sir Charles Portal also deserves blame, as the head of the RAF, for not being decisive with his staff officers, both on the use of fighters and bombers.

If there is one thing this episode of British Military History shows, it is that the commanding officers of the Second World War (and the First) used little original thinking. That fault can be laid squarely with the class system of the British, for it did not reward expertise, it rewarded the 'old boy network'. How many impoverished children might have grown up to be far better leaders of men, if only they had been given the opportunity?

There is an art to war, despite its mayhem, misery and bloodshed. Throwing away your men's lives in a needless fashion and gaining nothing from that action is not a part of it.

To close, I will quote the First World War infantry officer and poet Siegfried Sassoon, and his poem about two British soldiers watching a general passing them by on horseback in 1917:

> 'He's a fine old card,' said Harry to Jack, as they slogged
> up to Arras with rifle and pack.
> But he did for them both in his next attack …

Notes and References

Chapter 1: 1914–1918

1. Sholto, Douglas, *Combat and Command, The Story of an Airman in Two World Wars* (Simon and Schuster, 1963).
2. Mackersey, Ian, *No Empty Chairs* (Orion/Phoenix Books, 2013), p.34.
3. Henshaw, Trevor, *The Sky their Battlefield* (Grub Street, 1995), p.23.
4. ibid, p.32.
5. Mackersey, Ian, op. cit., p.49.
6. ibid, p.104.
7. *Jane's Fighting Aircraft of World War I* (Studio Editions, 1990), p.140.
8. Mackersey, Ian, op. cit., p.36.
9. ibid (p.242) Orion/Phoenix Books, 2013.
10. *Jane's Fighting Aircraft of World War I* (Studio Editions, 1990).
11. Mackersey, Ian, op. cit., p.34.
12. Hart, Peter, *Somme Success* (Pen and Sword, 2013), p.203.
13. Mackersey, Ian, op. cit., p.242.
14. Henshaw, Trevor, *The Sky their Battlefield* (Grub Street, 1995), p.23.
15. *Jane's Fighting Aircraft of World War I* (Studio Editions, 1990).
16. McCudden, James Byford, *Flying Fury* (Casemate Publishers, 2009), p.131.
17. Setright, L.J.K., *The Power to Fly* (George Allen and Unwin, 1971), p.51.

18. McCudden, James Byford, op. cit., p.131.
19. *Jane's Fighting Aircraft of World War I* (Studio Editions, 1990).
20. Douglas, Sholto, *Combat and Command, The Story of an Airman in Two World Wars* (Simon and Schuster, 1963).
21. Guttman, Jon, *Bristol F2 Fighter Aces of World War 1* (Osprey Publishing, 2007).
22. Guttman, Jon, *Reconnaissance and Bomber Aces of World War 1* (Osprey Publishing, 2015).
23. McCudden, James Byford, *Flying Fury*, op. cit., p.131.
24. *Jane's Fighting Aircraft of World War I* (Studio Editions, 1990).
25. Mackersey, Ian, op. cit., p.242.
26. Wilkins, Mark C., *Spad Fighters* (Schiffer Military Publishers, 2019).
27. *Jane's Fighting Aircraft of World War I* (Studio Editions, 1990).
28. ibid.
29. Kilduff, Peter, *Richthofen; Beyond the Legend of the Red Baron* (John Wiley & Sons, 1993).
30. *Jane's Fighting Aircraft of World War I* (Studio Editions, 1990), p.150.
31. ibid, p.152.
32. Mackersey, Ian, op. cit., p.242.
33. *Jane's Fighting Aircraft of World War I* (Studio Editions, 1990).

Chapter 2: 1919–1939

1. Whitmarsh, Andrew, *British Strategic Bombing 1917-1918: The Independent Force and its Predecessors* (Journal of the League of WWI Aviation Historians, 2003).
2. Douhet, Giulio, *The Command of the Air* (Air University Press, Alabama, 2019).
3. Middlemass, Keith and Bates, John, *Baldwin, A Biography* (Weidenfield & Nicolson, 1969), p.722.
4. Setright, L.J.K., *The Power to Fly* (George Allen and Unwin, 1971), p.51.

5. ibid.
6. ibid, p.95.
7. Eves, Edward, *The Schneider Trophy Story* (MBI Publishing, 2001).
8. Setright, L.J.K., op. cit., p.92.
9. Eves, Edward, op. cit.
10. Setright, L.J.K., op. cit., p.83.
11. Eves, Edward, op. cit.
12. Setright, L.J.K., op. cit., p.96.
13. Eves, Edward, op. cit.
14. ibid.
15. ibid.
16. Douglas, Calum E., *The Secret Horsepower Race* (Tempest Books, 2021).
17. Shelton, John K., *From Nighthawk to Spitfire, The Aircraft of R.J. Mitchell* (The History Press, 2015).
18. Gunston, Bill, *The Development of Piston Aero Engines* (Patrick Stephens Ltd, 1999).
19. Rendall, Ivan, *Spitfire, Icon of a Nation* (Metro Books, 2008), p.57.
20. Ibid, p.58.
21. *Jane's Fighting Aircraft of World War 2* (Studio Editions, 1990).
22. McNab, Chris, *The Luftwaffe 1933-45* (Chartwell Books Inc, 2014), p.18.
23. Setright, L.J.K., op. cit., p.148.
24. Weal, John, *Jagdgeschwader 2 Richthofen* (Osprey Publishing, 2000).
25. Birtles, Philip, *Hawker Typhoon and Tempest* (Fonthill Media, 2009), p.9.
26. Shelton, John K., op. cit.
27. Setright, L.J.K., op. cit., p.96.
28. Douglas, Calum E., op. cit.
29. Setright, L.J.K., op. cit., p.149.
30. ibid, p.148.

31. Freudenberg, Matthew, *Negative Gravity* (Charlton Publications, 2003).
32. Douglas, Calum E., op. cit.
33. Setright, L.J.K., op. cit., p.148.
34. Gunston, Bill, *The Development of Piston Aero Engines* (Patrick Stephens Ltd, 1999).
35. Price, Alfred, *The Bomber in World War II* (Charles Scribner's Sons, 1976).
36. McNab, Chris, op. cit., p.18.
37. Johnson, Johnnie, *Wing Leader* (Chatto & Windus, 1956).

Chapter 3: 1940

1. Rendall, Ivan, *Spitfire, Icon of a Nation* (Metro Books, 2008), p.125.
2. ibid, p.126.
3. Hordern, Bert, *Shark Squadron Pilot* (Independent Books, 2002).
4. BBC Interview with Viscount Hugh Dowding 1968.
5. Wilson, Gordon A.A., *The Merlin, The Engine That Won the Second World War* (Amberley Publishing, 2018), p.192.
6. Rendall, Ivan, op. cit.
7. ibid.
8. Wilson, Gordon A.A., op. cit., p.192.
9. Kent, Johnny, *One of the Few* (The History Press Ltd, 2000), p.94.
10. Quill, Jeffrey, *Spitfire – A Test Pilot's Story* (Crecy Books, 1996), p.132.
11. Baker, David, *Adolf Galland, The Authorised Biography* (Windrow and Greene, 1996), p.126.
12. Brown, Eric 'Winkle', *Wings of the Luftwaffe: Flying the Captured German Aircraft of World War II* (Hikoki Publications, 2011), p.152.
13. Rendall, Ivan, op. cit.

14. Obermaaier, Ernest, *Adolf Galland, The Authorised Biography – An Illustrated Biography* (Schiffer Publishing Ltd, 2006), p.98.
15. *Supermarine Spitfire Variants, the Initial Merlin Powered Line*; internet.
16. *HistoryNet's WWII* Magazine, September 1996 edition.
17. Bergström, Christer, *The Battle of Britain: An Epic Conflict Revisited* (Casemate, 2015).
18. Baker, David, op. cit.
19. Dundas, Hugh, *Flying Start* (Thomas Dunne Books, 1989).
20. See www.Jg54greenheart.com/jg54west-40aug12.
21. Donahue, Arthur, *Yankee in a Spitfire!* (Nook, 2016).
22. Dundas, Hugh, op. cit.
23. Hall, Roger, *Clouds of Fear* (www.152hyberadad.co.uk).
24. Baker, David, op. cit.
25. Steinhilper, Ulrich, *Spitfire on my Tail* (Crecy Publishing, 2004).
26. Douglas, Sholto, *Combat and Command, The Story of an Airman in Two World Wars* (Simon & Schuster, 1963).
27. Holmes, Tony, Spitfire II/V versus Bf 109F, Channel front 1940–42, Osprey Publishing 2017.
28. Baker, David, *Adolf Galland, The Authorised Biography,* Windrow and Greene 1996.
29. Brickhill, Paul, *Reach for the Sky,* W.W. Norton (New York) 1954.
30. *Memoirs of a Remarkable Aviator,* Ralph Douglas, Private papers.
31. Douglas, Sholto, *Combat and Command, The Story of an Airman in Two World Wars*, Simon and Schuster 1963.
32. Boyle, Andrew, Trenchard, Man of Vision (p.725) Collins 1962.
33. Douglas, Sholto, *Combat and Command, The Story of an Airman in Two World Wars,* Simon and Schuster 1963.
34. Douglas, Sholto, *Combat and Command, The Story of an Airman in Two World Wars,* Simon and Schuster 1963.
35. Holmes, Tony, *Spitfire II/V versus Bf 109F, Channel front 1940-42,* Osprey Publishing 2017.

Chapter 4: 1941

1. Goss, Chris, Cornwell, Peter, and Rauchbach, Bernd, *Luftwaffe Fighter-Bombers over Britain* (Stackpole Books, 2010.), p.44.
2. Caldwell, Donald, *The JG26 War Diary, Volume One 1939–1942* (Grub Street, London, 1996).
3. ibid.
4. ibid.
5. Hordern, Bert, *Shark Squadron Pilot* (Independent Books, 2002).
6. Tedder, Lord, *With Prejudice* (Little, Brown, 1966).
7. Caldwell, Donald, *The JG26 War Diary, Volume One 1939–1942*.
8. Johnson, J., *Wing Leader* (Ballantine, 1956).
9. Caldwell, Donald, *The JG26 War Diary, Volume One 1939–1942*.
10. Weal, John, *Jagdgeschwader 2 'Richthofen'* (Osprey, 2000).
11. Treadwell, Terry C., and Wood, Alan C., *German Knights of the Air* (Barnes & Noble Inc., 1997), p.138.
12. Holmes, Tony, *Spitfire II/V versus Bf 109F, Channel Front 1940–42* (Osprey Publishing, 2017).
13. Caldwell, Donald, *The JG26 War Diary, Volume One 1939–1942*.
14. Douglas, Sholto, *Combat and Command, The Story of an Airman in Two World Wars* (Simon & Schuster, 1963).
15. Kershaw, Alex, *The Few* (Da Capo, 2006).
16. Kent, Johnny, *One of the Few* (The History Press Ltd, 2000).
17. Holmes, Tony, *Spitfire II/V versus Bf 109F, Channel Front 1940–42*.
18. Galland, Adolf, *The First and the Last* (Methuen 1955).
19. Green, W., *Augsburg Eagle* (Doubleday, 1971).
20. Caidin, Martin, *ME-109, Willy Messerschmitt's Peerless Fighter* (Ballantine Books, 1968).
21. Rendall, Ivan, *Spitfire, Icon of a Nation* (Metro Books, 2008).
22. Holmes, Tony, *Spitfire II/V versus Bf 109F, Channel Front 1940–42*.
23. Johnson, J., *Wing Leader* (Ballantine, 1956).
24. Rendall, Ivan, op. cit.
25. Setright, L.J.K., *The Power to Fly* (George Allen and Unwin, 1971).

26. Rendall, Ivan, op. cit.
27. Caldwell, Donald, *The JG26 War Diary, Volume One 1939–1942*.
28. Kent, Johnny, op. cit.
29. Franks, Norman, *Fighter Command's Air War 1941* (Pen & Sword, 2017), p.9.
30. Caldwell, Donald, *The JG26 War Diary, Volume One 1939–1942*, p.97.
31. ibid.
32. Franks, Norman, *Fighter Command's Air War 1941*, p.21.
33. ibid, p.17.
34. Caldwell, Donald, *The JG26 War Diary, Volume One 1939–1942*, p.147.
35. Franks, Norman, *Fighter Command's Air War 1941*, p.35.
36. Caldwell, Donald, *The JG26 War Diary, Volume One 1939–1942*, p.147.
37. ibid, p.133.
38. ibid, p.136.
39. ibid, p.137.
40. Johnson, J., op. cit.
41. Baker, David, *Adolf Galland, The Authorised Biography* (Windrow and Greene, 1996).
42. Caldwell, Donald, *The JG26 War Diary, Volume One 1939–1942*.
43. ibid.
44. Kent, Johnny, op. cit.
45. Caldwell, Donald, *The JG26 War Diary, Volume One 1939–1942*.
46. *Flight* Magazine, 5 February 1942.
47. Kent, Johnny, op. cit.
48. Dundas, Hugh, *Flying Start* (Thomas Dunne Books, 1989).
49. Holmes, Tony, *Spitfire II/V versus Bf 109F, Channel front 1940–42*.
50. Clayton, Aileen, *The Enemy is Listening* (Ballantyne Books, 1980).
51. Whittel, Giles, *Spitfire Women of World War II* (Harper Press, 2007).

52. Caldwell, Donald, *The JG26 War Diary, Volume One 1939–1942*.

53. ibid.

54. Franks, Norman, *Fighter Command's Air War 1941*, p.35.

55. Kent, Johnny, op. cit.

56. Brown, Eric 'Winkle', *Wings of the Luftwaffe, Flying the captured German Aircraft of World War II* (Hikoki Publications, 2011).

57. Smith, J. Richard, and Creek, Eddie J, *Focke-Wulf Fw 190* (Ian Allan Publishing, 2013).

58. Dibbs, John and Holmes, Tony, *Spitfire, Flying Legend* (Barnes and Noble, 1996).

59. Holmes, Tony, *Spitfire II/V versus Bf 109F, Channel front 1940–42*.

60. Franks, Norman, *Fighter Command's Air War 1941*, p.35.

61. Douglas, Sholto, op. cit.

62. Caldwell, Donald, *The JG26 War Diary, Volume One 1939–1942*.

63. Ibid.

64. Johnson, J., op. cit.

65. Douglas, Sholto, op. cit.

66. Smith, J. Richard, and Creek, Eddie J, op. cit.

67. Douglas, Sholto, op. cit.

68. Johnson, J., *Wing Leader*, Ballantine 1956.

69. Douglas, Sholto, *Combat and Command, The Story of an Airman in Two World Wars*, Simon and Schuster 1963.

70. Smith, J. Richard, and Creek, Eddie J, *Focke-Wulf Fw 190* Ian Allan Publishing, 2013.

71. Douglas, Sholto, *Combat and Command, The Story of an Airman in Two World Wars*, Simon and Schuster 1963.

Chapter 5: 1942

1. Douglas, Sholto, *Combat and Command, The Story of an Airman in Two World Wars* (Simon & Schuster, 1963).

2. Holmes, Tony, *Spitfire II/V versus Bf 109F, Channel Front 1940–42* (Osprey Publishing, 2017).
3. Baker, David, *Adolf Galland, The Authorised Biography* (Windrow and Greene, 1996).
4. Page, Neil, *Day Fighter Aces of the Luftwaffe 1939-45* (Casemate Publishers, 2020).
5. Dundas, Hugh, *Flying Start* (Thomas Dunne Books, 1989).
6. Douglas, Sholto, op. cit.
7. ibid.
8. Goss, Chris, Cornwell, Peter, and Rauchbach, Bernd, *Luftwaffe Fighter-Bombers over Britain* (Stackpole Books, 2010).
9. Reed, Arthur, and Beamont, Roland, *Typhoon and Tempest at War* (Ian Allan Publishing, 1974).
10. Caldwell, Donald, *The JG26 War Diary, Volume One 1939–1942* (Grub Street, London, 1996).
11. Price, Alfred, *Focke Wulf 190 at War* (Ian Allen, 1977).
12. Bloemertz, Gunther, "To kill a man," Essay.
13. Douglas, Sholto, op. cit.
14. Goss, Chris, *Focke-Wulf 190, The Early Years – Operations in the West* (Frontline, 2019).
15. Holmes, Tony, *Spitfire II/V versus Bf 109F, Channel Front 1940–42*.
16. Hooker, Sir Stanley, *Not much of an Engineer* (AirLife Publications, 2004).
17. Dibbs, John, and Holmes, Tony, *Spitfire, Flying Legend* (Barnes and Noble, 1996).
18. Johnson, J., *Wing Leader* (Ballantine, 1956).
19. Bowyer, Chaz, *Mosquito at War* (Ian Allan Ltd, 1973).
20. ?
21. Holmes, Tony, *Spitfire II/V versus Bf 109F, Channel front 1940–42*.
22. ibid
23. Goss, Chris, Cornwell, Peter, and Rauchbach, Bernd, op. cit., p.44.
24. Caldwell, Donald, *The JG26 War Diary, Volume One 1939–1942*.
25. ibid.
26. ibid.

27. Weal, John, *Bf 109 Aces of the Russian Front* (Osprey Publishing, 2001).

28. Weal, John, *Jagdgeschwader 2 'Richthofen'* (Osprey Aviation, 2000).

29. Caldwell, Donald, *The JG26 War Diary, Volume One 1939–1942*.

30. Douglas, Calum E., *The Secret Horsepower Race* (Tempest Books, 2021).

31. Douglas, Sholto, op. cit.

32. Goss, Chris, Cornwell, Peter, and Rauchbach, Bernd, op. cit., p.44.

33. Caldwell, Donald, *The JG26 War Diary, Volume One 1939–1942*.

34. Goss, Chris, Cornwell, Peter, and Rauchbach, Bernd, op. cit., p.44.

35. Dibbs, John and Holmes, Tony, *Spitfire, Flying Legend*, op.cit.

36. Goss, Chris, Cornwell, Peter, and Rauchbach, Bernd, op. cit.

37. Green, William, *Augsburg Eagle* (Doubleday, 1971).

38. Johnson, J., op. cit.

39. Holmes, Tony, *Spitfire II/V versus Bf 109F, Channel front 1940–42*.

40. Rendall, Ivan, *Spitfire, Icon of a Nation* (Metro Books, 2008).

41. Caldwell, Donald, *The JG26 War Diary, Volume One 1939–1942*.

42. ibid.

43. ibid.

44. Golley, John, *The Day of the Typhoon* (Patrick Stephens Ltd, 1986).

45. Caldwell, Donald, *The JG26 War Diary, Volume One 1939–1942*.

46. Dibbs, John, and Holmes, Tony, *Spitfire, Flying Legend* (Barnes and Noble, 1996).

47. Thomas, Chris, *Typhoon and Tempest Aces of World War 2* (Osprey Publishing, 1999).

47. Sheddan, C.J., and Franks, Norman, *Tempest Pilot* (Grub Street, 1993).

49. Birtles, Philip, op. cit.

50. Page, Neil, op. cit.

51. Caldwell, Donald, *The JG26 War Diary, Volume One 1939–1942*.

52. Douglas, Sholto, op. cit.

53. ibid.

54. Caldwell, Donald, *The JG26 War Diary, Volume One 1939–1942*.

55. ibid.

56. Weal, John, *Jagdgeschwader 2 'Richthofen'* (Osprey Aviation, 2000).

57. Caldwell, Donald, *The JG26 War Diary, Volume One 1939–1942*.

58. ibid.

59. Johnson, J., op. cit.

60. Baker, David, op. cit.

61. Goss, Chris, Cornwell, Peter, and Rauchbach, Bernd, op. cit.

62. Weal, John, *Jagdgeschwader 2 'Richthofen'*.

63. Goss, Chris, Cornwell, Peter, and Rauchbach, Bernd, op. cit.

64. Weal, John, *Jagdgeschwader 2 'Richthofen'*.

65. ibid.

66. Goss, Chris, Cornwell, Peter, and Rauchbach, Bernd, op. cit.

67. Caldwell, Donald, *The JG26 War Diary, Volume One 1939–1942*.

68. ibid.

69. ibid.

70. Goss, Chris, Cornwell, Peter, and Rauchbach, Bernd, op. cit.

71. Caldwell, Donald, *The JG26 War Diary, Volume One 1939–1942*.

72. Thomas, Chris, *Typhoon and Tempest Aces of World War 2* (Osprey Publishing, 1999).

73. ibid.

74. Freeman, R., *The Mighty Eighth* (Doubleday, 1970).

Chapter 6: 1943

1. Eden, Paul E., and Moeng, Sophie, *Aircraft Anatomy of Words War II – Technical Drawings of Key Aircraft 1939–1945* (Amber Books Ltd, 2003).

2. ibid.

3. ibid.

4. Douglas, Calum E., *The Secret Horsepower Race* (Tempest Books, 2021).

5. Bernstein, Jonathan, *P-47 Thunderbolt Combat Missions* (Metro, 2015)

6. Dibbs, John & Holmes, Tony, *Spitfire, Flying Legend* (Barnes and Noble, 1996).

7. ibid.

8. ibid.

9. Goss, Chris, Cornwell, Peter, and Rauchbach, Bernd, *Luftwaffe Fighter-Bombers Over Britain* (Stackpole Books, 2010).

10. Setright, L.J.K., *The Power to Fly* (George Allen and Unwin, 1971).

11. Douglas, Calum E., op cit.

12. McNab, Chris, *The Luftwaffe 1933-45, Hitler's Eagles* (Chartwell Books Inc, 2014).

13. Birtles, Philip, *Hawker Typhoon and Tempest, A Formidable Pair* (Fonthill Media Ltd, 2018).

14. Johnson, Johnnie, *Wing Leader* (Ballantine, 1956).

15. Sheddan, C.J., and Norman Franks, *Tempest Pilot* (Grub Street, 1993).

16. Butar, Pritt, *Retribution, The Soviet Reconquest of Central Ukraine, 1943* (Osprey Publishing, 2020).

17. Weal, John, *Jagdgeschwader 2 'Richthofen'* (Osprey Aviation, 2000).

Chapter 7: 1944–1945

1. Primoratz, Igor, *Terror from the Sky* (Berghahn Books, 2014).

2. Shores, Christopher, *2nd Tactical Air Force* (Osprey, 1970).

3. Freeman, R., *The Mighty Eighth* (Doubleday, 1970).

4. Johnson, J., *Wing Leader* (Ballantine, 1956).

5. Douglas, Calum E., *The Secret Horsepower Race* (Tempest Books, 2021).

6. Smith, J. Richard, and Creek, Eddie J, *Focke-Wulf Fw 190* (Ian Allan Publishing, 2013).

7. Caidin, Martin, *ME-109, Willy Messerschmitt's Peerless Fighter* (Ballantine Publishing, 1971).

8. Eden, Paul E., and Moeng, Sophie, *Aircraft Anatomy of Words War II – Technical Drawings of Key Aircraft 1939–1945* (Amber Books Ltd, 2003).

9. Douglas, Calum E., op. cit.

10. Golley, John, *The Day of the Typhoon* (Patrick Stephens Ltd, 1986).

11. Freeman, R., op. cit.

12. Baker, David, *Adolf Galland, The Authorized Biography* (Windrow and Greene, 1996).

Chapter 8: Examination 1

1. Rendall, Ivan, *Spitfire, Icon of a Nation* (Metro Books, 2008).

2. Johnson, J., *Wing Leader* (Ballantine, 1956).

3. Douglas, Sholto, *Combat and Command, The Story of an Airman in Two World Wars* (Simon & Schuster, 1963).

4. Clayton, Aileen, *The Enemy is Listening* (Ballantyne Books, 1980).

5. Bishop, Patrick, *Fighter Boys, Saving Britain, 1940* (Harper Perennial, 2004).

6. www.dfat.gov.au/aboutus/publications/pages/volume-06/12-curtintochurchill

7. Douglas, Sholto, op. cit.

8. Price, Alfred, *Focke Wulf 190 at War* (Ian Allen, 1977).

9. Kent, Johnny, *One of the Few* (The History Press Ltd, 2000).

10. Douglas, Sholto, op. cit.

11. Clayton, Aileen, op. cit.

12. Caldwell, Donald, *The JG26 War Diary, Volume One 1939–1942* (Grub Street, London, 1996).

13. Rendall, Ivan, op. cit.

14. Szlagor, Thomaz, *P40s of the Mediterranean* (Casemate Publishers, 2010).

15. Douglas, Sholto, op. cit.

Chapter 9: Examination 2

1. Douglas, Sholto, *Combat and Command, The Story of an Airman in Two World Wars* (Simon & Schuster, 1963).
2. Franks, Norman, *Fighter Command's Air War 1941* (Pen & Sword, 2017).
3. Douglas, Sholto, op. cit.
4. Franks, Norman, op. cit.
5. Clayton, Aileen, *The Enemy is Listening* (Ballantyne Books, 1980).

Bibliography

Ash, John, and Fone, Stu, *Luftwaffe over Britain*, Key Publishing Ltd, 2018.

Baker, David, *Adolf Galland, the Authorized Biography,* Windrow and Greene, 1996.

Bergström, Christer, *The Battle of Britain: An Epic Conflict Revisited*, Casemate, 2015.

Bernstein, Jonathan, *P-47 Thunderbolt Combat Missions*, Metro, 2015.

Birtles, Philip, *Hawker Typhoon and Tempest, A Formidable Pair*, Fonthill Media, 2018.

Bishop, Patrick, *Fighter Boys*, Harper Perennial, 2003.

Bowyer, Chaz, *Mosquito at War*, Ian Allan Ltd, 1973.

Boyle, Andrew, *Trenchard, Man of* Vision Collins, 1962.

Brickhill, Paul, *Reach for the Sky*, W.W. Norton (New York), 1954.

Brown, Eric 'Winkle', *Wings of the Luftwaffe, Flying the Captured German Aircraft of World War II*, Hikoki Publications, 2011.

Butar, Pritt, *Retribution, The Soviet Reconquest of Central Ukraine, 1943*, Osprey Publishing, 2020.

Caidin, Martin, *ME-109, Willy Messerschmitt's Peerless Fighter,* Ballantine Publishing, 1971.

Caldwell, Donald, *The JG26 War Diary, Volume One, 1939–1942*, Grub Street, London, 1996.

— — *The JG26 War Diary, Volume Two, 1943-1945*, Grub Street, London, 1998.

Clarke, R.M., *Hawker Typhoon Portfolio*, Brooklands Books, 1986.

Clayton, Aileen, *The Enemy is Listening*, Ballantyne Books, 1980.

Clostermann, Pierre, *The Big Show*, Chatto and Windus, Ltd., 1951.

Deere, A.C., *Nine Lives*, Beagle Books, 1959.

Dibbs, John and Holmes, Tony, *Spitfire, Flying Legend*, Barnes and Noble, 1996.

Donahue, Arthur, *Tally-Ho! Yankee in a Spitfire*, Nook, 2016.

Douglas, Calum E., *The Secret Horsepower Race*, Tempest Books, 2021.

Dundas, Hugh, *Flying Start*, Pen & Sword, 2012.

Eden, Paul E. and Soph Moeng, (Eds.), *Aircraft Anatomy of Words War II-Technical Drawings of Key Aircraft 1939–1945*, Amber Books Ltd, 2003.

Eves, Edward, *The Schneider Trophy Story*, MBI Publishing Company, 2001.

Forrester, Larry, *Fly for Your Life*, Bantam (New York), 1956.

Franks, Norman, *Fighter Command's Air War 1941*, Pen & Sword, 2017.

Freeman, R. *The Mighty Eighth*, Doubleday, 1970.

Freudenberg, Matthew, *Negative Gravity, A Life of Beatrice Shilling*, Charlton Publications, 2003.

Galland, Adolf, *The First and the Last*, Methuen, 1955.

Golley, John, *The Day of the Typhoon*, Patrick Stephens Ltd, 1986.

Goodson J., *Tumult in the Clouds*, St Martins, 1983.

Goss, Chris, Cornwell, Peter, and Rauchbach, Bernd, *Luftwaffe Fighter-Bombers over Britain* Stackpole Books, 2010.

Goss, Chris, *Focke-Wulf 190, The Early Years – Operations in the West*, Frontline, 2019.

Gunston, Bill, *The Development of Piston Aero Engines*, Patrick Stephens Ltd, 1999.

Green, William, *Augsburg Eagle*, Doubleday, 1971.

— — *Warplanes of the Third Reich*, W. Doubleday, 1972.

Harvey-Bailey, Alec, *The Merlin in Perspective*, Rolls Royce Heritage Trust, 1983.

Hastings, Max, *Bomber Command*, The Dial Press, 1979.

Held, Werner, and Nauroth, Holger, *The Night Fighters*, Schiffer Military History, 1991.

Holmes, Tony (Ed.), *Dogfight*, Osprey Publishing, 2011.

— — *Spitfire II/V versus Bf 109F, Channel front 1940–42*, Osprey Publishing, 2017.

Hooker, Sir Stanley, *Not much of an Engineer*, AirLife Publications, 2004.

Hordern, Bert, *Shark Squadron Pilot*, Independent Books, 2002.

Jane's Fighting Aircraft of World War I, Studio Editions, 1990.

Jane's Fighting Aircraft of World War II, Studio Editions 1989.

Johnson, Johnnie, *Wing Leader*, Ballantine, 1956.

Kent, Johnny, *One of the Few*, The History Press Ltd, 2000.

Kershaw, Alex, *The Few*, Da Capo, 2006.

Knoke, Heinz, *I Flew for the Führer,* Evans Brothers, 1954.

Lewis, Jon E., *Fighter Pilots*, MJF Books, 2002.

Mackersey, Ian, *No Empty Chairs*, Orion/Phoenix Books, 2013.

McCudden, James, *Flying Fury 1918*, Casemate, 2009.

McKee, A, *Strike from the Sky,* Souvenir Press, 1960.

McNab, Chris, *The Luftwaffe 1933-45, Hitler's Eagles*, Chartwell Books Inc, 2014.

Obermaier, Ernest, *German fighter Ace Werner Molders – An Illustrated Biography*, Schiffer Publishing Ltd, 2006.

O'Leary, Michael, *Lockheed P-38 Lightning*, Osprey Publishing.

Page, Neil, *Day Fighter Aces of the Luftwaffe 1939-45*, Casemate Publishers, 2020.

Price, Alfred, *Focke Wulf 190 at War*, Ian Allen, 1977.

— — *Sky Battles! Dramatic Air Warfare Actions*, Arms and Armour Press, 1993.

Price, Alfred and Spick, Mike, *Great Aircraft of WWII*, Metro Books, 1997.

Primoratz, Igor (Ed.), *Terror from the Sky*, Berghahn Books, 2014.

Quill, Jeffrey, *Spitfire – A Test Pilot's Story*, Crecy, 1996.

Reed, Arthur and Beamont, Roland, *Typhoon and Tempest at War*, Ian Allan, 1974.

BIBLIOGRAPHY

Rendall, Ivan, *Spitfire, Icon of a Nation*, Metro Books, 2008.

Richey, Paul, *Fighter* Pilot, The History Press.

Rubbra, A.A., *Rolls-Royce Piston Aero Engines – A Designer Remembers*, Rolls-Royce Heritage Trust. 2010.

Setright, L.J.K., *The Power to Fly*, George Allen and Unwin, 1971.

Sheddan, C.J., and Franks, Norman, *Tempest Pilot*, Grub Street, 1993.

Sholto Douglas, *Combat and Command, The Story of an Airman in two World Wars*, Simon & Schuster, 1963.

Shores, Christopher, *2nd Tactical Air Force*, Osprey, 1970.

Smith, Herschel, *A History of Aircraft Piston Engines*, Sunflower Press, 1986.

Smith, J. Richard, and Creek, Eddie J., *Focke-Wulf Fw 190*, Ian Allan Publishing, 2013.

Spick, M., *Fighter Pilot Tactics*, Patrick Stephens, 1983.

Steinhilper, Ulrich, *Spitfire on my Tail*, Crecy Publishing, 2004.

Szlagor, Thomaz, *P40s of the Mediterranean*, Casemate Publishers, 2010.

Thomas, Chris and Shores C., *Typhoon and Tempest Story*, Arms and Armour Press, 1988.

Thomas, Chris, *Typhoon and Tempest Aces of World War 2*, Osprey Publishing, 1999.

Tedder, Lord, *With Prejudice*, Little, Brown, 1966.

Treadwell Terry C., and Wood, Alan C., *German Knights of the Air*, Barnes & Noble Inc., 1997.

Weal, John, *Focke-Wulf 190 Aces of the Western Front*, Osprey Publishing, 1996.

— — *Jagdgeschwader 2 'Richthofen'*, Osprey Aviation, 2000

— — *Bf 109 Aces of the Russian Front*, Osprey Publishing, 2001.

— — *Jagdgeschwader 52, The Experten*, Osprey Publishing, 2004.

Whittell, Giles, *Spitfire Women of World War II*, Harper Press, 2007.

Index

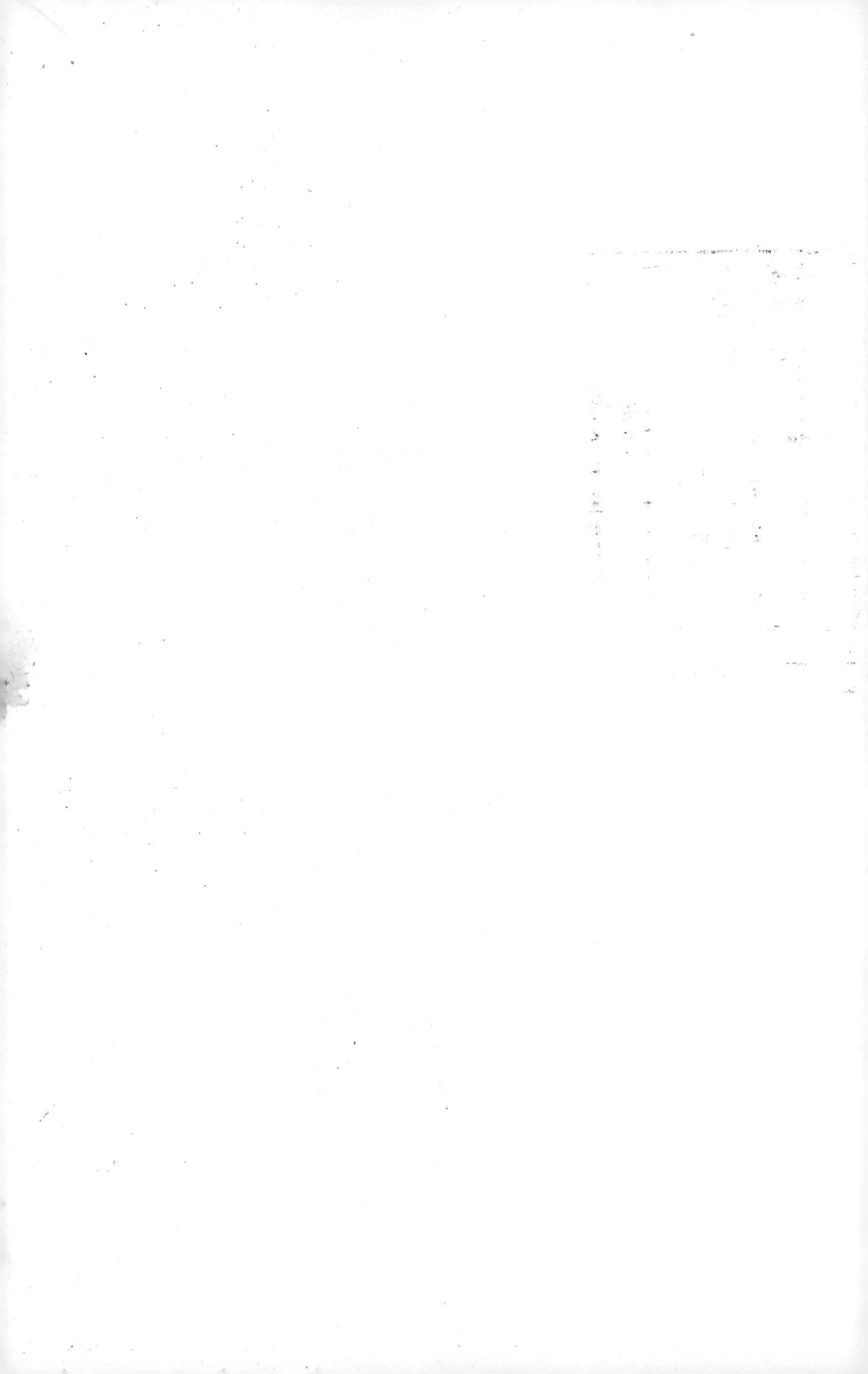